CORPUS LINGUISTICS FOR WRITING DEVELOPMENT

Corpus Linguistics for Writing Development provides a practical introduction to using corpora in the study of first and second language learners' written language over time and across different levels of proficiency. Focusing on development in the use of vocabulary, formulaic language, and grammar, this book

- discusses how corpus research can contribute to our understanding of writing development and to pedagogical practice;
- reviews a range of corpus techniques for studying writing development from the perspectives of vocabulary, grammar, and formulaic language and interrogates the methodological bases of those techniques; and
- guides readers to perform practical analyses of learner writing using the R open-source programming language.

Aimed at the novice researcher, this book will be key reading for advanced undergraduate and postgraduate students in the fields of education, language, and linguistics. It will be of particular interest to those interested in first or second language writing, language assessment, and learner corpus research.

Philip Durrant is Associate Professor in Language Education at the University of Exeter, United Kingdom.

ROUTLEDGE CORPUS LINGUISTICS GUIDES

SERIES CONSULTANT: MICHAEL McCARTHY

Michael McCarthy is Emeritus Professor of Applied Linguistics at the University of Nottingham, UK, Adjunct Professor of Applied Linguistics at the University of Limerick, Ireland and Visiting Professor in Applied Linguistics at Newcastle University, UK. He is co-editor of the Routledge Handbook of Corpus Linguistics, editor of the Routledge Domains of Discourse series and co-editor of the Routledge Applied Corpus Linguistics series.

SERIES CONSULTANT: ANNE O'KEEFFE

Anne O'Keeffe is Senior Lecturer in Applied Linguistics and Director of the Inter-Varietal Applied Corpus Studies (IVACS) Research Centre at Mary Immaculate College, University of Limerick, Ireland. She is co-editor of the Routledge Handbook of Corpus Linguistics and co-editor of the Routledge Applied Corpus Linguistics series.

SERIES CO-FOUNDER: RONALD CARTER

Ronald Carter (1947–2018) was Research Professor of Modern English Language in the School of English at the University of Nottingham, UK. He was also the co-editor of the Routledge Applied Corpus Linguistics series, Routledge Introductions to Applied Linguistics series and Routledge English Language Introductions series.

Routledge Corpus Linguistics Guides provide accessible and practical introductions to using corpus linguistic methods in key sub-fields within linguistics. Corpus linguistics is one of the most dynamic and rapidly developing areas in the field of language studies, and use of corpora is an important part of modern linguistic research. Books in this series provide the ideal guide for students and researchers using corpus data for research and study in a variety of subject areas.

OTHER TITLES IN THIS SERIES

Corpus Linguistics for World Englishes
Claudia Lange and Sven Leuckert

Corpus Linguistics for Education
Pascual Pérez-Paredes

Corpus Linguistics for English for Academic Purposes
Vander Viana and Aisling O'Boyle

Corpus Linguistics for Writing Development
Philip Durrant

More information about this series can be found at www.routledge.com/series/RCLG

CORPUS LINGUISTICS FOR WRITING DEVELOPMENT

A Guide for Research

Philip Durrant

Routledge
Taylor & Francis Group

LONDON AND NEW YORK

Cover image: © Getty Images

First published 2023
by Routledge
4 Park Square, Milton Park, Abingdon, Oxon OX14 4RN

and by Routledge
605 Third Avenue, New York, NY 10158

Routledge is an imprint of the Taylor & Francis Group, an informa business

© 2023 Philip Durrant

British Library Cataloguing-in-Publication Data
A catalogue record for this book is available from the British Library

Library of Congress Cataloging-in-Publication Data
Names: Durrant, Philip, 1976- author.
Title: Corpus linguistics for writing development : a guide for research /
    Philip Durrant.
Description: Abingdon, Oxon ; New York, NY : Routledge, 2022. | Series:
    Routledge corpus linguistics guides | Includes bibliographical
    references and index. | Summary: "Corpus Linguistics for Writing
    Development provides a practical introduction to using corpora in the
    study of first and second language learners' written language over time
    and across different levels of proficiency"-- Provided by publisher.
Identifiers: LCCN 2022026468 (print) | LCCN 2022026469 (ebook) | ISBN
    9780367715793 (hardback) | ISBN 9780367715786 (paperback) | ISBN
    9781003152682 (ebook)
Subjects: LCSH: Written communication--Data processing. | Written
    communication--Research--Methodology. | Language and languages--Study
    and teaching--Research--Methodology. | Corpora (Linguistics)
Classification: LCC P211.4 .D87 2022 (print) | LCC P211.4 (ebook) | DDC
    410.1/88--dc23/eng/20220822
LC record available at https://lccn.loc.gov/2022026468
LC ebook record available at https://lccn.loc.gov/2022026469

ISBN: 978-0-367-71579-3 (hbk)
ISBN: 978-0-367-71578-6 (pbk)
ISBN: 978-1-003-15268-2 (ebk)

DOI: 10.4324/9781003152682

Access the Support Material: www.routledge.com/9780367715786

Typeset in Bembo
by SPi Technologies India Pvt Ltd (Straive)

CONTENTS

ACKNOWLEDGEMENTS

I would like to thank my editors, Mike McCarthy and Anne O'Keefe, both for prompting me to write this book and for helping me through the process. Many thanks also to past and present members of the team at Routledge for their ever-efficient support and guidance, especially Bex Hume, Amy Laurens, Eleni Steck, Nadia Seemungal Owen, and Lizzie Cox. Finally, I owe huge thanks to Ayça Durrant, who read and gave invaluable advice on the whole book (I know there are better ways of spending your spring holiday!).

PART ONE
Foundations

1

STUDYING WRITING DEVELOPMENT WITH A CORPUS

1.1 Introduction

Readers of this book probably need little convincing that writing is an essential social skill. For children learning to navigate the world through their first language, writing will underpin their ability to take part in social, educational, professional, and political life. For second and foreign language learners, writing well in their target language can open doors to international communities that can massively increase their life opportunities. Research into writing development aims to help learners towards these goals by asking, and proposing answers to, practical educational questions. There are many ways of researching writing development, each offering its own distinctive perspective and making its own distinctive contribution to educational theory and practice (volumes by Beard et al., 2009; Hyland, 2019; Polio & Friedman, 2017, offer excellent introductions to many of these). The present book explores in detail one such approach – that of corpus linguistics.

Corpus linguistics is, briefly, a methodology for studying how people use language. The central idea is that a researcher (1) identifies a domain of language use they are interested in (e.g., stories written by primary school children, research reports written by postgraduate students, essays written by second language learners for a language proficiency test), (2) collects a sample of texts which they believe are representative of that domain, (3) stores the sample in an electronic format, and (4) uses computer-aided techniques to investigate how language is used in the sample.

Most of the questions addressed by corpus research into writing development fall under one of two headings: questions about how learners' writing *changes* as their education progresses and questions about what distinguishes more *successful* learner writing from less successful learner writing.

Questions of the first type arise naturally in many educational contexts. For example, teachers, curriculum designers, or language testers might need to decide

DOI: 10.4324/9781003152682-2

at what stage of their education learners should be expected to master particular types of text, use particular grammatical structures, or employ particular types of vocabulary. Educational managers might need to evaluate the outcomes of a programme of learning or a teaching intervention in terms of the changes that have occurred in learners' writing. Or policymakers might want to know whether the writing of particular groups of students (e.g., minority language speakers or students from economically disadvantaged backgrounds) typically develops in different ways or at a different pace from that of other groups, such that they should be offered additional, or different types of, support.

Questions of the second type arise most naturally in the context of testing and assessment. We might want to know, for example, if learners who use particular types of vocabulary tend to get higher scores than those who don't. We might want to know whether our grading rubrics really capture the range of features that are associated with higher scores. Or we might want to devise automatic systems for assigning grades or giving feedback by building on data about the features that graders value.

As in other areas of applied linguistics, practical questions of this sort often lead us to ask broader, more theoretical questions: are there predictable patterns of writing development that hold true across different learners and different educational contexts? How do learners' writing skills in different languages interact? How is writing development linked to a learners' broader cognitive, social, and educational development? What role do particular types of linguistic features play in developing a mature writing style?

This book aims to introduce you to the study of such questions. It will look at writing development from three perspectives: word use, grammar, and formulaic language. In each case, it will introduce the main types of analysis that corpus researchers have developed, discuss the insights into writing development these have offered, and look at some of the theoretical and practical issues that researchers new to the area need to be aware of. The book also includes a series of practical 'hands-on' chapters which illustrate how some of the analyses discussed can be carried out.

In this introductory chapter, we will do some methodological groundwork by discussing both the benefits that corpus methods can bring to writing development research and their limitations. We will see that these methods pose several difficult problems. I believe that thinking about these problems and their implications for research design and interpretation is central to good corpus research, so I will spend substantial time discussing these. I will also reflect briefly on the status of the three main headings around which this book is built – *vocabulary, grammar*, and *formulaic language* – and on how these contribute to our overall picture of writing development.

1.2 Using a corpus to study writing development

Many newcomers to corpus linguistics are struck by its powerful potential as a tool for understanding language. Speaking personally, I first encountered corpus research early in my career as an English language teacher. At the time, I was working at an English-medium university in Turkey, trying to help students deal with the challenges of studying for their degrees in a foreign language. I quickly learned that corpus research was something that I could do from my own kitchen with a minimum of resources (a laptop and some free software) and that it would help me find answers to practical questions about academic language that were both specific and authoritative. Almost overnight, my teaching became 'corpus informed' as I used corpora to study the texts my learners needed to read and write. Later, as a postgraduate student, I learned more about the ways that corpus research had revolutionized our ways of describing and theorizing language. I was impressed by researchers like John Sinclair (2004) and Michael Hoey (2005), who had shown how studying large samples of language with computerized tools could identify emergent patterns of language use that were not visible to the naked eye and that forced me to rethink my naive ideas about how language is structured.

I share this potted professional biography as an example of the immediate appeal that I think corpus research can have for professionals involved in language education. As a researcher, I have remained convinced that such research has a huge amount to offer. One key advantage is that corpus methods help researchers simultaneously study large numbers of texts. An obvious payoff from this is that it enables us to make reliable generalizations. When our data sets are large and include the writing of many different individuals in many different contexts, we can reach general conclusions about the typical development of broad groups of learners, about differences between groups, and about how development differs in different contexts. A less obvious payoff is that some subtle patterns of language use (such as patterns of collocation or semantic prosody) only become evident when we study large samples. Corpus research can, therefore, offer us new and exciting insights into patterns of language use that are difficult to attain by other means.

A second advantage of corpus methods is that they force us to be both specific and explicit about the features we are studying. As later chapters will illustrate, getting a computer to identify linguistic features in a corpus requires us to have explicit definitions of what we are looking for and clear statements about how they can be spotted in a text. This makes for good research in that it promotes transparency and discourages vagueness.

Finally, working with a corpus distances us from texts in potentially helpful ways. As Hunston wrote, studying texts via corpus software "offers us a new perspective on the familiar" (Hunston, 2002, p. 3) that can help us notice patterns that might not fit our usual expectations or presuppositions about how language works.

While these advantages mean that there is much to be gained from a corpus approach, it is important also to be aware of its limitations. Like all research methods, corpus analysis is a lens that brings some things into clearer focus by blurring or obscuring others; it highlights some things by leaving others in the shadow. I will devote substantial space here to these limitations, not because I think they undermine corpus research, but rather because I believe that to design good research, and to interpret findings appropriately, it is important to understand how we might be led astray. To extend the earlier metaphor, we can more effectively use a lens to view and interpret the world around us if we understand the nature of the lens itself.

The first limitation concerns how linguistic features are identified in a corpus. To research a linguistic feature, we need accurate and reliable ways of finding that feature. Many features of interest can only be found once texts have been annotated for the parts of speech and/or syntactic relationship between words. When dealing with large numbers of texts (as is typically the case in corpus research), this means either a huge amount of manual coding or, more typically, some sort of automated process. Because even the best trained and most highly motivated human coders are error-prone, manual coding usually involves teams of multiple coders working to identify features, with each text being checked by more than one coder. This is a hugely expensive and time-consuming process that may be impractical unless you are working on a very well-funded project. For most researchers, therefore, automated identification is the more popular choice. However, this brings its own problems. As we will discuss in more detail in Chapter 6, while computer programmes that can make such annotations are now widely available, they are far from 100% accurate, especially when working with learner texts (Huang et al., 2018; Newman & Cox, 2020). This does not mean that such programmes should not be used, but it does mean that they should be used with caution and careful checks made on their accuracy (Gray, 2019).

Another limitation introduced by automated identification is that researchers may find themselves limited to studying only those features that are easy to identify with existing computer tools. Features that may be developmentally important but that software developers have not included in their annotation schemes, either because they did not think them important or because they are difficult to identify computationally, may be left out of the picture. This may lead corpus researchers to narrow their focus to a routine set of features that are easy to identify. It is important to think carefully about what the most relevant features for a particular study might be, about whether existing tools can identify these, and, if not, about whether alternative methods of identification might be used. If potentially important features can't be studied, researchers need to have a clear awareness of what they are leaving out of the picture.

A further set of limitations can be grouped around the general idea of decontextualization. Three types of decontextualization are particularly relevant. The first is the way that corpus analyses (especially more quantitative types of analysis) remove linguistic features from their textual contexts. A typical analysis might, for example, count how frequently learners modify nouns with a relative clause. While such an analysis can produce very useful results, it is important to remember that it achieves this by leaving out a lot of detail: *which nouns were modified? What verbs were used in the relative clause? What role did the noun-relative clause combinations play in the wider sentence? What sort of meaning relationship was there between the relative clauses and their nouns?*

Constructive simplification – that is, the art of leaving out unnecessary details to enable a broader picture to emerge – is key to effective corpus linguistics.

It is entirely plausible that, for particular groups of learners, the details I have just mentioned are developmentally unimportant and that by leaving them out, our analysis provides a clearer *big picture* that gets to the heart of writing development. But it is also plausible that some of the occluded details may themselves be developmentally important, and that leaving them out distorts our understandings. For this reason, it is important that researchers work at different levels of abstraction to test the relevance of different types of detail and that they are alert to the possibility of important patterning at levels of abstraction they have not yet studied (Durrant, 2022).

The second type of decontextualization is that texts are removed from their original communicative contexts. An email that I send to a colleague about a class we are both teaching this semester, for example, might be written as part of an ongoing conversation between us. The words and phrases that I choose to use might be responses to questions she has asked or jokes she has made in a previous email; they might refer to contents of the class that we are both aware of, or they might be based on long-running jokes that have developed between us over several years of working together. Should that email then be placed in a corpus, this context would be lost, and the significance of those words and phrases lost with it. This issue highlights the importance of getting as much information as possible about the contexts in which texts were produced. Corpora are typically accompanied by *metadata* that record information of this sort for each text (see Chapter 2, Section 4 for further discussion of metadata). While this cannot fully recreate the context in which a text was written, it can go some way towards it. It is, therefore, important to ensure that metadata are as clear and detailed as possible.

The third type of abstraction is the way that corpus analysis focuses on textual products, divorced from the processes by which they were produced. We know *what* language ended up in a text, but we don't know *how* it got there. This is important because writing is a complex and dynamic process, influenced by many factors (Grabe & Kaplan, 1996; Hayes, 2012; Weigle, 2002). As I write this book, the words that make it into the final draft are products of (amongst other things!): my competence in the English language, my knowledge of the topic I'm writing about (and any broader world knowledge that seems relevant to me), my understanding of appropriate genre conventions, my perceptions about my intended readership, the affordances of the computer and word-processing software I'm using (which help me to write and revise each sentence and phrase multiple times, and give me a polite nudge if my spelling, grammar, or style seem to be going awry), my access to resources such as a good library or dictionaries, my fluctuating levels of enthusiasm and energy (themselves related to my access to a comfortable and quiet place to work, to sources of sugar and caffeine, to a good night's sleep, to the occasional elusive appearance of English sunshine, and so on), the pressures of impending deadlines, and the interventions and recommendations of reviewers and editors.

From one perspective, it is a great strength of corpus linguistics that it captures the outcomes of this complex, contextualized process. Other methods of studying writing – by, for example, eliciting texts under controlled conditions or by capturing writing in action through eye-tracking or think-aloud protocols – are apt to interfere with one or more aspects of its natural performance and so sacrifice authenticity. The associated limitation of corpus linguistics is that it is difficult to make claims that go beyond the texts themselves. Writing development researchers rarely want to draw conclusions only about the contents of texts. Rather, they want to make claims about writers' developing linguistic proficiencies, their understandings of genre conventions, their appreciation of audience, etc. Such claims are problematic because it is difficult to unpack the influence on our data of the proficiencies, understandings, appreciations, etc., in which we are interested from the other things that may have influenced our texts' contents.

When dealing with writing done in schools or other educational settings, a particularly strong influence will be class content and teacher guidance. In my own study of children's writing at schools in England, for example, I found a strong peak in the use of the cohesive markers *firstly*, *secondly*, and *thirdly* in the writing of Year 2 students. On closer examination, this turned out to be attributable to a fixed template for creating argument texts that had been provided by a teacher and that was repeated both by many different students and by individual students across many different tasks, as illustrated by Texts 1–3 (Durrant, 2022). I have highlighted the forms that were found across texts, and so that would have seen unusually high counts in this part of the corpus.

Text 1
Should the Spangebob liv ande de si? **We have been discussting whetheer** Spongbob should live under the sea.
Many people believe that Spongbok should live ander the see, **bicase firstly** he soaks up water. **Secenly** hi wash the rocs in the see. **On the adh meni pepo beliv** he shut not liv in the see **bicoss** hi is not e fihs.
In conclusion there are many great reasons for and against for spong bov should liv andr the see bicos deris hi hous.
Wat do uia finc?

Text 2
Should Jhingerbred man be eaten?
We have been discasing wether Jhingrbred man should be eaten or not.
Many people belive that the Jinjerbred man should be eaten **because firstly** he is quit mean and he runs away from the cow and the silly old horse. **Secondly** the cow and the silly old horse are hungry.
On the ather hand people disagry they think Jinjer bread man shouldn't be eaten.
In conclusion there are many great reasons why Gingrbread man shouldn't be eaten because he woudnt fill the animalls up. But I belive he shouldn't be eaten because he is tiny.
I think he should be eaten because he myte feell angry and chase the animals **what do you think?**

Text 3
Should Sleeping Beaty stay asleep? **We have been discussing wheather** Sleeping Beaty <u>should stay</u> asleep.
Many people belive that Sleeping Beauty should stay because fistly, she has been sleeping for one hundread years. **Secondly**, she wants to be lazy. **Lastly** she doesn't want to work!
On the other hand some people dissagre that's because she has been sleeping nearly forever.
In conclusion, there are many great reasons for and against for sleeping Beauty to <u>stay</u> asleep but I think that Sleeping Beauty should have made the corect choice
She has to wacke up because she is a princess. **What do you think?**

One common response to this problem is to compile a corpus under controlled conditions. Thus, if researchers are primarily interested in the development of language proficiency, they often attempt to neutralize the influence of factors such as topic knowledge and teacher input by eliciting texts in a setting where these things can be controlled. Of course, this sacrifices authenticity – the texts collected are not the same texts that might have been produced as part of learners' regular work – but for many research purposes, this may be a sacrifice worth making.

A second approach is to rely on statistical techniques to understand what variables in the writing process most influenced the features we are studying. A traditional, idealized, statistical approach would be to build our corpus as a stratified random sample. If we are interested in the influence of language proficiency, for example, we might randomly sample large numbers of texts from writers at each proficiency level. We could then assume that variation in other variables (topic knowledge, motivation, teacher input, etc.) will be averaged out across the sample and so not impact significantly on our findings. This approach has two major drawbacks, however.

One is that the practical limitations of data collection do not usually allow us to create true stratified random samples. Even with a relatively restricted and well-defined target population (e.g., international students of engineering at UK universities), we are unlikely to be able to sample randomly from the population. The texts we collect are likely to depend on personal or institutional contacts (such as universities that are willing to help us contact their students) and on finding learners who are willing to volunteer their writing. Most real-world corpus samples are, therefore, likely to include *clusters* of texts from the same educational institution (many of which are likely to have been taught by the same teacher and/or written on the same topic), or from the same learner. Sampling of this sort invalidates traditional statistical methods, which are based on the assumption that each data point (i.e., each text) is unrelated to (independent from) each of the other data points.

The second drawback is that, should a randomized sample successfully neutralize the impacts of all but the variable of central interest, we may lose sight of developmentally important effects. As we saw previously, writing (and so also writing development) is a complex process. The impact of teacher input, school context, text topic or genre, the learners' first language, etc., are not simply annoying 'noise' that needs to be eliminated (Larsen-Freeman & Cameron, 2008); they are important aspects of the developmental process. Attempting to narrow our focus to a single aspect of that process may, therefore, present us with a distorted or misleading picture of that process.

In response to issues like these, many corpus researchers now base their statistical analyses around mixed-effects models (Gries, 2015; Winter, 2019, provide excellent introductions). These allow us to take account of the ways that texts in a corpus tend to both cluster (e.g., multiple texts elicited from the same class) and nest within each other (e.g., multiple texts from the same class and multiple classes from the same school), to estimate the extent to which our findings can be ascribed to *random variables* (i.e., variables that are not systematically sampled, such as individual learners, teachers and schools, text topics), and to determine how much of our findings can be ascribed to *fixed variables* (those we have systematically sampled, such as learner level or text genre) once random variables have been parcelled out.

A further type of response – often used in conjunction with mixed-effects models – is that of following up initial quantitative analyses with more detailed analyses to understand the reasons underlying any patterns found. This has much in common with the sequential-explanatory model of mixed-methods research often employed in social sciences, where quantitative findings (e.g., from a questionnaire) are followed up by qualitative research that attempts to explain those findings (Teddie & Tashakkori, 2009). The key difference from this model is that the follow-up need not be exclusively qualitative (or quantitative), but rather can blend both fine-grained quantitative analysis and qualitative analysis in whatever way best enables the researcher to understand their findings.

I draw three main methodological conclusions from these considerations. The first is that corpus research is an ongoing, interpretive process. Patterns that emerge from our analyses need to be constantly interrogated, from a variety of angles, to understand what they might mean for writing development. The second is that we need to take a broad view of how findings should be interpreted. Differences in language use between learners at different levels are unlikely to be pure reflections of linguistic development, for example. While such development well may be part of the mix, it is likely to be accompanied by influences such as shifts in topic or in learners' knowledge about that topic, shifts in text or assignment types, shifts in learners' affective attitudes towards their task, or shifts in the classroom context or the range of resources that writers are able to draw on. Researchers, therefore, need to be alert to a panoply of factors which may be influencing the patterns found in their data.

My third conclusion is that we should expect many developmental patterns to be *local*. While some patterns of development may hold true across different learners and different learning contexts, many will not. Indeed, the research literature to date confirms this expectation. In a systematic review of almost 250 first and second language studies into writing development, my colleagues and I (Durrant et al., 2021) found only a small number of linguistic variables (especially mean length of T-unit; mean length of noun phrase; vocabulary diversity) that consistently correlated with development across multiple studies.

The reasons for this diversity become clear when we consider the ways that research contexts can differ. We would not expect development across the length of a ten-week intensive second language programme, for example, to be the same as development across ten weeks of a regular school term. Development across time is dependent on both the nature of the students involved (e.g., first vs. second language; older vs. younger; higher vs. lower starting level) and on what those students are doing over the period of time studied (e.g., the type of language instruction they receive, if any, or the context of their daily lives). Development in quality is dependent on both the type of text that is being written (the properties of a good academic report, for example, are not always similar to the properties of a good poem) and on the way it is assessed. While we would hope that textual beauty is not completely in the eye of the beholder (which would undermine the whole endeavour of language assessment), there will clearly be differences between different assessment schemes and between the individual raters tasked with evaluating student work.

I hope this section has shown that using a corpus to research learner writing development both brings substantial benefits and raises some difficult problems. I have devoted extensive space to the latter because doing research that makes a genuine contribution to our understandings of writing development requires us to grapple seriously with these problems and to have a clear understanding of what our data are, and are not, telling us. These are ideas that researchers need to keep in mind at all stages of their work.

1.3 How does writing development relate to vocabulary, grammar, formulaic language?

This book is organized around three main headings: *understanding vocabulary, understanding grammar*, and *understanding formulaic language*.[1] Categories such as these are often referred to by researchers as components of language proficiency. Bachman and Palmer (1996, 2010), for example, describe *knowledge of syntax, knowledge of vocabulary*, and *knowledge of phonology/graphology* as subcomponents of the construct of *grammatical knowledge*. Grammatical knowledge, in turn, is a component of the broader construct of *language competence*, which is, itself, a component of *communicative language ability*. This model, therefore, assigns knowledge of grammar and vocabulary rather minor positions as sub-sub-sub-categories of language proficiency, hiding away in a dusty corner of the construct. Given this, it might be wondered why I have chosen to give them such prominence in this book.

Understanding this requires a slight shift in focus. In this book, I think of the three categories not as *components* of writing proficiency, but rather as *lenses* through which writing proficiency can be studied. Vocabulary, grammar, and formulaic language are, on this view, analytical constructs that we analysts apply to our data, rather than independent things in the world. There are two main reasons for thinking this is a useful approach.

First, it reduces the temptation to think of *vocabulary, formulaic language*, and *grammar* as distinct entities. As linguists of many theoretical stripes have emphasized for several decades, sharp distinctions between these categories are artificial (Römer, 2009). This is seen, for example, in the way that particular words tend to occur in particular grammatical structures and particular structures tend to be realized in particular words; in the way that idiomatic phrases exhibit local semantic, syntactic, and pragmatic properties that could not be predicted based on a knowledge of more generally applicable rules; and in the way that so much of language is comprised of formulaic expressions which combine lexical, syntactic, and pragmatic choices in a single holistic structure (e.g., Sinclair, 1991; Wray, 2002).

Second, the component view gives a misleadingly narrow impression of what we learn from a study of these areas. Such models depict vocabulary, formulaic language, and grammar as occupying a particular corner of the broader proficiency construct and as interacting with other elements of that construct (e.g., topical/word knowledge, processing skills) and with aspects of the context to generate language performance. However, this neglects the fact that by studying the vocabulary, grammar, and formulaic language of texts, we can learn about the whole writing proficiency construct. As I argued in the previous section, corpus research can tell us about many different aspects of writing development. It can tell us about language development per se, about the genres and topics that writers are addressing, about the types of tasks they are set, about the types of classroom input they are drawing on, about the motivations and predilections of particular writers or groups of writers, and more. Vocabulary, grammar, and formulaic language are three lenses which can give us distinctive viewpoints on all these phenomena.

1.4 Outline of the book

This book is organized around four main parts: the current, introductory, part is followed by parts on vocabulary, grammar, and formulaic language. Each part comprises two chapters. In each case, the first introduces the area of study, discussing the main types of analysis that are found in the literature, the insights they yield, and the theoretical and practical issues that face researchers. The second chapter in each part is more 'hands-on'. These will illustrate how some of the types of analysis discussed in the first chapter can be carried out. For reasons I will discuss in the next chapter, the main tool I will use in these chapters is the open-source programming language, R. I will not assume any previous experience of programming on the part of the reader, but the chapters do build on each other, so I would advise working through them in order. I hope these will both give an insight into the processes of corpus research into writing development and provide researchers with the confidence to undertake work of their own.

Note

1 For anyone new to the idea, *formulaic language* refers to sequences of words that can be usefully treated as single units. Prominent types include polywords, such as *for the most part*; collocations, such as *catch cold*; and lexical bundles, such as *on the other hand*. For a fuller discussion of the nature and types of formulaic language, see Chapter 7.

References

Bachman, L., & Palmer, A. (1996). *Language testing in practice*. Oxford University Press.

Bachman, L., & Palmer, A. (2010). *Language assessment in practice*. Oxford University Press.

Beard, R., Myhill, D., Riley, J., & Nystrand, M. (Eds.). (2009). *The SAGE handbook of writing development*. SAGE Publications.

Durrant, P. (2022). Studying children's writing development with a corpus. *Applied Corpus Linguistics*.

Durrant, P., Brenchley, M., & McCallum, L. (2021). *Understanding development and proficiency in writing: Quantitative corpus linguistic approaches*. Cambridge University Press. https://doi.org/10.1017/9781108770101

Grabe, W., & Kaplan, R. B. (1996). *Theory and practice of writing: An applied linguistic perspective*. Longman.

Gray, B. (2019). Tagging and counting linguistic features for multi-dimensional analysis. In T. Berber Sardinha & M. V. Pinto (Eds.), *Multi-dimensional analysis: Research methods and current issues* (pp. 43–66). Bloomsbury Academic. https://doi.org/10.5040/9781350023857.0011

Gries, S. T. (2015). The most under-used statistical method in corpus linguistics: Multilevel (and mixed-effects) models. *Corpora, 10*(1), 95–125. https://doi.org/10.3366/cor.2015.0068

Hayes, J. R. (2012). Modelling and remodeling writing. *Written Communication, 29*(3), 369–88. https://doi.org/10.1177/0741088312451260

Hoey, M. (2005). *Lexical priming: A new theory of words and language*. Routledge.

Huang, Y., Murakami, A., Alexopoulou, T., & Korhonen, A. (2018). Dependency parsing of learner English. *International Journal of Corpus Linguistics, 23*(1), 28–54. https://doi.org/10.1075/ijcl.16080.hua

Hunston, S. (2002). *Corpora in applied linguistics*. Cambridge University Press. https://doi.org/10.1017/CBO9781139524773

Hyland, K. (2019). *Second language writing* (2nd ed.). Cambridge University Press. https://doi.org/10.1017/9781108635547

Larsen-Freeman, D., & Cameron, L. (2008). *Complex systems and applied linguistics*. Oxford University Press.

Newman, J., & Cox, C. (2020). Corpus annotation. In M. Paquot & S. T. Gries (Eds.), *A practical handbook of corpus linguistics* (pp. 25–48). Springer Nature. https://doi.org/10.1007/978-3-030-46216-1_2

Polio, C., & Friedman, D. A. (2017). *Understanding, evaluating, and conducting second language writing research*. Routledge. https://doi.org/10.4324/9781315747293

Römer, U. (2009). The inseparability of lexis and grammar: Corpus linguistic perspectives. *Annual Review of Applied Linguistics, 7*, 140–62. https://doi.org/10.1075/arcl.7.06rom

Sinclair, J. M. (1991). *Corpus, concordance, collocation*. Oxford University Press.

Sinclair, J. M. (2004). *Trust the text: Language, corpus and discourse*. Routledge. https://doi.org/10.4324/9780203594070

Teddie, C., & Tashakkori, A. (2009). *Foundations of mixed methods research: Integrating quantitative and qualitative approaches in the social and behavioural sciences*. SAGE Publications.

Weigle, S. C. (2002). *Assessing writing*. Cambridge University Press. https://doi.org/10.1017/CBO9780511732997

Winter, B. (2019). *Statistics for linguists: An introduction using R*: Routledge. https://doi.org/10.4324/9781315165547

Wray, A. (2002). *Formulaic language and the lexicon*. Cambridge University Press. https://doi.org/10.1017/CBO9780511519772

2
LEARNER CORPUS ANALYSIS IN PRACTICE

Some basics

2.1 Introduction

The even-numbered chapters of this book aim to illustrate how the ideas found in the other chapters can be put into practice. In Chapters 4, 6, and 8, I demonstrate how particular analyses can be carried out and their results interpreted. I would recommend following along with these chapters by conducting the same analyses yourself. To do this, you will need to use the open-source programming language, R. Sections 2.2 and 2.3 of this chapter will discuss how to set this up on your computer and give a brief grounding in its use. If you are new to R, these sections will be an essential foundation for work in subsequent chapters.

To follow along with the hands-on chapters, you will also need access to a corpus of learner writing and a suitable reference corpus. I have chosen to use two corpora with which I am familiar: the *Growth in Grammar* (GiG) corpus of children's writing and the *British Academic Written English* corpus of university student writing. These will be introduced further in Section 2.5, where I will also give information about how you can access these resources.

It is also possible to follow along using corpora of your own choice. If you decide to go down this route, it will be important to ensure that they are suitably prepared, formatted, and parsed. For anyone taking this option, Sections 2.4, 2.5, and 2.6 will be essential reading. Section 2.4 introduces ideas about encoding, markup, and annotation; Section 2.5, points to resources for corpus preparation; and Section 2.6 describes how a corpus can be parsed using the Stanford CoreNLP programme.

DOI: 10.4324/9781003152682-3

2.2 Some housekeeping: getting your computer ready

To try out the examples in the even-numbered chapters of this book, you will need to download and install *R*. The most recent version can be found on *The R Project for Statistical Computing* website (https://www.r-project.org). Follow the link to *download R* and select a mirror site near you. Then choose to download the version of R that matches your operating system (Linux, MacOS, or Windows).

A very useful way of interacting with R is through *RStudio Desktop* version, which I also recommend downloading and installing. All the R screenshots that I share will be from *RStudio*. This can be downloaded from the *RStudio* website (https://www.rstudio.com). RStudio comes in several versions. The free *RStudio Desktop* version is fine for our purposes.

Following examples will be easier if you have a set of folders on your computer that mirrors those I have used on my own. Within the home directory on my computer (which has a Mac operating system, so the home directory is called 'Users/ philipdurrant'), I have created a folder called 'CLWD' (my abbreviation for the title of this book), within which I have stored all the material used in this book. CLWD contains four subfolders:

- 'corpora': where the various corpora used in the examples are stored, along with their accompanying metadata;
- 'output': where the outputs of the various analyses will be stored. These will include spreadsheets of quantitative results, graphs, and lists of collocations;
- 'R_code': where I save the R_scripts that are described in the chapters; and
- 'reference': two of the examples in following chapters rely on bringing external data into our analysis. The files for these are stored here.

2.3 Getting to know R and RStudio

2.3.1 Introduction: why learn R?

Thanks to the skill, hard work, and generosity of members of the corpus linguistics community, many very good computer packages for analysing corpora are now freely available. Perhaps most prominent amongst these are the excellent suits of tools created by Laurence Anthony[1] (including *AntConc*, which is frequently used to teach corpus linguistics) and Kristopher Kyle[2] (including *TAALES* and *TAASC*) and the *Lancsbox* toolbox, created by Vaclaz Brezina and his colleagues at the University of Lancaster.[3] Given the ready availability of such tools, and their relative ease of use, some may wonder why I have gone for the apparently 'harder' option of asking readers to programme their own analyses with *R*.

Chief amongst my reasons is that programming your own analyses enables a versatility that is not possible with the ready-made tools. When we use an existing package to research a corpus, we are restricted to performing the types of analysis that the programmer has decided to include. These may enable us to do what we need. But then again, they may not. As Laurence Anthony has himself observed, this can lead to the unfortunate outcome of "letting the tool dictate what we search for" (Anthony, as cited in Larsson, 2020). This is clearly not ideal; our analyses should be based on our research questions, rather than on the affordances of our software. In my own practice as a researcher, I have found that most of the analyses I want to perform are either impossible or impractical with existing programmes.

Gries (2020) notes that it is often asked whether learning to programme is a good use of researchers' valuable time, given the availability of existing software. One answer to this is the point made in the previous paragraph that suitable analyses may not be possible with that software. Another is that, far from wasting time, learning to programme can actually be very time efficient. Speaking from my own experience, I came to applied linguistic research from a thoroughly non-computational background (an undergraduate degree in philosophy followed by a career as an English teacher). When embarking on my PhD, programming was an entirely closed book to me, and unfortunately, it remained so until the later stages of my doctorate. However, I found that much of the corpus research I was conducting with corpus packages involved a huge amount of tediously repetitive work (such as carrying out the same analysis separately for each text in a corpus). Noticing that some researchers seemed to find better ways of working, and wondering if I could speed things up, I dug out some simple introductions to the *Python* language and tried to figure out ways of automating my work. Within a week or so, I came up with a script that could perform in a matter of minutes an analysis that might have taken me months of drudgery. Thus, a relatively small investment turned out to save me a huge amount of time and indeed made it possible to perform analyses that I would not even have considered doing by hand. I also found that I had learned some skills that stood me in good stead for future work of the same kind. Further, as Gries (2020) points out, once you have created a programme to do a job, you will find that it can be re-used in many situations. Building up a small library of programmes that perform the tasks you most frequently need can again save huge amounts of time in the long run.

Another advantage of using R, rather than off-the-shelf corpus programmes, is the transparency it provides. This is true in two ways. First, it makes your analysis transparent to yourself. As we will see in later chapters, conducting a corpus analysis entails a range of important operational decisions, such as *How should texts be divided into lexical units? How should symbols, non-Latin letters, pictures, etc. be handled? Which words should be classified as* lexical words *and which words as* function words? In ready-made corpus packages, such decisions are typically set to a default by the programmer. It is sometimes (though not always) possible to learn what these defaults are by digging through the manual, and it is sometimes (though not always) possible to change those defaults. By writing your own programme, however, you have control over such matters from the start.

The second type of transparency is transparency to other researchers. By creating a programme that performs an analysis for us, we simultaneously create a detailed record of what we have done. And this is a record in which all the fiddly operational decisions mentioned in the previous paragraph are set out in full. Analyzing a corpus in this way, therefore, promotes the kind of openness that is essential to the development of a healthy research field (Winter, 2019).

Finally, R has the great benefit of incorporating not only functions that are useful to corpus research but also functions for visualizing and statistically analyzing data. It, therefore, offers a coherent environment in which researchers can interrogate their corpus, visualize the results, and perform statistical analyses.

Before going any further, I should acknowledge that, as I have already hinted, I am far from being a professional computer programmer. I am an applied linguist who has benefitted greatly from picking up a smattering of skills in R. I have no doubt that a proficient programmer would find the scripts I describe in this book laughably naïve (indeed, in some cases, they are intentionally naïve for the purpose of making the presentation more accessible). But this is part of the point. One does not need to be a highly proficient programmer to make use of R. Even an elementary user like me can get a lot out of it.

I should also note that this book is not intended to be a general introduction to doing corpus linguistics with R. There are several excellent books on the market, written by people far better qualified for the task than me, that already serve this function (see Section 2.8 for ideas on further reading). Likewise, the book does not demonstrate how to conduct statistical analyses with R (again, many excellent books already serve this function). Rather, it aims to illustrate how some analyses I take to be central to writing development research can be carried out in R. I hope that this will give you both a practical sense of how relevant R scripts can be created and a small repertoire of code that you can use and adapt in your own research. To make an analogy, the book is more akin to a phrasebook than to a grammar. It aims to give readers a set of tools for getting started in this field and the confidence to tackle the 'grammar' books should they want to take things further.

2.3.2 Entering commands: the Console and Scripts

Once you have installed R and RStudio, you can get started by simply opening the RStudio application (you won't need to open R itself). This will present you with a window like that in Figure 2.1. There are two main ways of entering code into RStudio. One is to type commands into the *Console* window, which you will see on the left-hand side of your screen on opening RStudio.

If you click on the Console, the curser should start to flash next to the '>' symbol. If you type a command into this window and hit the Return key on your computer (I'd suggest trying this now!), R will execute the command and (where appropriate) provide an answer in the same Console window, as Figure 2.2 illustrates:

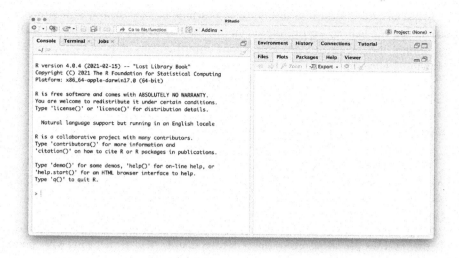

FIGURE 2.1 RStudio interface, with new R Script open

```
> 1+1
[1] 2
```

FIGURE 2.2 Entering a command in the Console

The second way is to open a Script. To do this, go to the 'New file' button in the top left of the RStudio window and select 'R Script' from the dropdown menu. This will open a new window, directly above the Console with the heading 'Untitled1'.

If you type a command into this window and press Return, R will not execute the command. Rather, the cursor will move down to the next line, much as it would do in a word processor. To execute the command, you need to press the *Run* button at the top of the window. Once you have pressed this, both the command and any output will appear in the Console as before (alternatively, you could use the keyboard shortcut **Control+Enter)**. To run multiple lines of script, select everything you want to run using the curser before pressing 'Run'. To run the whole script, you can use the keyboard shortcut **Control+Alt+R** (for Windows) or **Option+Command+R** (for Mac).

Using a script, therefore, takes slightly longer than entering commands directly into the Console. However, it also has some important advantages. First, by using a script, we can enter multiple lines of code simultaneously. Second, unlike commands entered directly, scripts can be edited after they have been executed. They can also be saved for use on another occasion. When we are building up longer chains of commands, these features are essential, so most of the work we do in subsequent chapters will be through the Script window.

Many script screenshots in this book will include not only commands but also comments that help to explain those commands. These are preceded by the hash (#) symbol and appear in a different colour from the main body of the Script, as shown in Figure 2.3.

```
# add 1 to 1
1 + 1
```

FIGURE 2.3 Adding comments to a Script

The hash symbol lets R know that the contents of that line should not be interpreted as an instruction it needs to follow. Comments like this are useful to remind yourself (or inform others) about the aims of each section of your Script or your reasons for doing things in a particular way.

Scripts can be saved and re-opened in a way that will be familiar to anyone who has used a word processor: go to the 'File' menu and select 'Save'. This will open a dialogue box that allows you to save your Script to the place of your choosing. Similarly, the 'Open File' option in the same menu will allow you to open a previously saved Script.

2.3.3 Functions

Everything we do with R in subsequent chapters will involve *functions*. Functions are instructions that tell R to perform a specified task. The function shown in Figure 2.4, for example, will apply the function 'sqrt' (i.e., square root) to the argument '9', and so return the square root of 9 (i.e., 3). The part of this command that comes before the brackets (in this case *sqrt*) is the name of the function. The part inside the brackets (in this case *9*) is known as the *argument*.

```
> sqrt(9)
[1] 3
```

FIGURE 2.4 The *sqrt()* function

R has an extensive and ever-growing library of functions, which are stored in a number of *packages*. Each package contains a suit of functions. Some packages are installed by default with R, others need to be downloaded. You can see which packages have been installed in your version of R by looking in the Packages tab in the bottom-right window of RStudio. We will learn how to download and install a package when we come to creating graphs in Chapter 4.

Alongside the object to which they are applied (e.g., *9*), R functions can also take additional arguments in their brackets, giving more detail about how the function should be applied. For example, the function *log()*, which returns the logarithm of a number, can take a second argument showing the base to which the logarithm should be calculated. Figure 2.5, for example, gives us the logarithm of 100 to base 10.

```
> log(100, 10)
[1] 2
```

FIGURE 2.5 *log()* function with *base* argument

It is possible to spell out the meaning of each argument by referring to them by name. Thus, the command in Figure 2.6 has exactly the same meaning as that in Figure 2.5.

```
> log(x = 100, base = 10)
[1] 2
```

FIGURE 2.6 Specifying argument names

If the names ('x' and 'base') are not used, R will assume that the arguments come in a specified order and will interpret arguments based on that order. In the current example, the first argument is assumed to be the object to which it should be applied and the second argument the base. Most arguments (other than 'x', the object to which the function should be applied) have default values, so if the argument is not entered in the command, R will assume you want to use the default value. The default value of 'base', for example, is e = exp1, so the command in Figure 2.7 returns the logarithm of 100 to that base.

```
> log(x = 100)
[1] 4.60517
```

FIGURE 2.7 *log()* function with default base

2.3.4 Vectors

So far, we have used commands that write their output directly to the Console window. Much of the time, however, we do not want to see the output of a command immediately; rather, we want to store it for use at a later stage. Vectors are a useful way of doing this. For example, revisiting our *sqrt()* example (see p. 20), we could embellish our command as shown in Figure 2.8.

```
> a <- sqrt(9)
```

FIGURE 2.8 Storing the output of a function

This creates a new vector (called *a*), which stores the output of our calculation. The assignment operator (<−) is a 'less than' symbol followed by a minus symbol, and it instructs R to store the output of the function to the vector *a*. Since no such vector yet exists, R will automatically create it.

To view the contents of a vector, we can simply enter its name into the Console and press Enter, as shown in Figure 2.9.

```
> a
[1] 3
```

FIGURE 2.9 Recalling an output using its vector name

We can also now include *a* in our further calculations, as in Figure 2.10.

```
> a*10
[1] 30
```

FIGURE 2.10 Including a stored output in a calculation

Vectors are not restricted to storing numbers and are not restricted to containing a single element. For example, the function *rep()*, which outputs a set number of repetitions of a given argument, could be used to create a longer vector, as shown in Figure 2.11.

```
> b <- rep('word', 5)
```

FIGURE 2.11 Creating a longer vector

This would give us the vector shown in Figure 2.12.

```
> b
[1] "word" "word" "word" "word" "word"
```

FIGURE 2.12 A longer vector

The *length()* function shows us how many elements there are in each of our vectors (see Figure 2.13).

```
> length(a)
[1] 1
> length(b)
[1] 5
```

FIGURE 2.13 Using *length()* to count the elements in a vector

Vectors containing both numbers and strings of text will play vital roles in the scripts we create in later chapters.

2.3.5 Getting help

Working with a language like *R* can require perseverance, especially in the early days. An important general message to keep in mind is that making mistakes is a normal part of the learning curve. Indeed, it is a part of the learning curve that you can expect never to fully leave behind. Winter (2019, p. 22) cites the experienced programmers Wickham and Grolemund, who note "I have been writing R code for years, and every day I still write code that doesn't work!" The lesson to keep in mind here is that the inevitable error messages (which I continue to receive almost every time I use R) should be accepted in the spirit of helpful feedback.

Two very useful sources of help exist when things are going wrong, or when you need more guidance. One is the help files within R itself. To learn more about a particular function you want to use, you can type a question mark in front of the function's name in the Console and press Enter, as shown in Figure 2.14.

```
> ?rep
```

FIGURE 2.14 Opening a help file in R

This will open a Help window in the bottom-right corner of R Studio detailing the use of the function.

A second source of help – one which is often more accessible for novices than the help files – is the vibrant online R community. A simple internet search for the thing you want to do (e.g., *generating tables in r*) or asking for an explanation of an error message you have received (e.g., *r error message unused argument*) will yield numerous helpful explanations and demonstrations. It's likely that pretty much any problem you face has been faced by others before, so you will find most topics are covered.

If you have difficulty recreating the scripts described in this book, complete versions are available for download. See the supplementary information at www. routledge.com/9780367715786 for information on accessing these.

2.4 Some fundamentals of corpus research: encoding, markup, annotation, and metadata

Novice researchers often create their first corpus by downloading texts from websites and analyzing them through software such as *AntConc* or *LancsBox*, only to find that their wordlists and concordance lines feature strange symbols or uninterpretable strings of letters/numbers which don't appear to be in the original texts. Issues of this sort are a result of how text is encoded by our computers.

Most of us are used to electronically creating, viewing, and editing texts without giving much thought to how our computers make sense of them. The word processor I am using to write this book, for example, responds to my keystrokes by displaying characters on the screen and storing the resulting documents in its hard drive. Of course, my computer does not understand the characters I type in the same way that I do. Rather, like everything in computers, characters are represented by strings of '1's and '0's. These strings are associated with the characters we write and read by a set of conventions, known as *character encoding standards*.

For most everyday purposes, we do not need to give much thought to character encoding. However, difficulties can arise due to the fact that different computer programmes, and different computer manufacturers, often use their own unique standards unless you specifically ask them not to. For the core characters used in

English (the letters a–z/A–Z and the numbers 0–9), this is not usually a problem because most standards encode these in the same way. However, this is not always the case for non-alphanumeric characters, such as the various symbols which are common in scientific texts or for alphabetical characters used in other languages. For characters of this sort, a text prepared in one programme may be misinterpreted by another. Microsoft, for example, notes that character number 201 in its Cyrillic encoding standard corresponds to the letter Й, while the same number in its Western European standard corresponds to É.[4]

It is this mismatch between encoding standards that causes the problems noted at the start of this section. Encoding is important because we want to make sure our corpora can be viewed and used in the same way by anybody, regardless of their software or brand of computer. Since creating a corpus is a substantial undertaking, we also want to make sure that it can be used in 30 years' time, when our word processor and computers capable of using it may be obsolete.

Issues such as these have led to the development of international encoding standards which can be used for all languages, across different computer types and programmes. Most prominent amongst these is the Unicode standard, which has been widely adopted by corpus linguists, specifically in its UTF-8 format (McEnery & Xiao, 2005, give an accessible overview of the history of these standards' development and of the reasons for adopting UTF-8).

In practical terms, this means that when creating a corpus, you should save documents in the UTF-8 format. Because not all word processors allow you to do this, it is advisable to create and edit corpus documents in plain text editors, such as Microsoft's *Notepad* or Apple's *TextEdit*, both of which allow you easily to choose your encoding standard. The method for doing this can change as operating systems are updated, so you should consult the online helpfiles for your own system for instructions. With UTF-8 encoding selected, corpus files are usually then saved as '.txt' files, a simple file type which allows them to be opened by a wide range of applications.

Thus far, we have looked at how the basic characters of a text are represented in a corpus. However, authentic texts include more than just plain text. Characters may be formatted in particular ways, such as in **bold**, *italics*, or superscript. Text may be divided into sections or paragraphs, it may include headings and sub-headings, or be organized into tables. Texts may also include material such as images, horizontal lines dividing sections, hyperlinks, and so on.

Depending on the aims of our project, we may not need to preserve all these features. But some may be important for us. And if we are creating a corpus that we want others to use later, we may also want to preserve features that could be of interest to subsequent users. The method for recording information of this sort is known as *markup*.

Corpus linguists also often need to record information beyond mere formatting. For example, we might want to note that a particular word or grammatical construction used by a language learner in their writing is erroneous. For many applications in vocabulary research, we might want to record both the original spelling and the corrected version. We might want to note the part of speech of words, of their grammatical relationship to each other. Or we might want to record the discourse function of a stretch of text. Information of this more interpretive, analytical, sort, is known as *annotation*.

As with character encoding, it is important to have a standard set of conventions for markup and annotation that can be interpreted in the same way by everyone, regardless of their computer setup. Such a standard exists in the *Text Encoding Initiative* (TEI), a set of guidelines created and maintained by the *Text Encoding Consortium*.[5] These conventions are expressed in terms of a widely used markup language called the *Extensible Markup Language* (XML), so when you encounter corpus texts that follow TEI conventions, you will notice that their filenames have the extension '.xml', rather than '.txt'. Most common-used corpus programmes, such as *AntConc*, can handle both of these file types.

The XML language employs a series of *tags* in angular brackets to represent features of a text. To show that a word is in bold font, for example, XML uses the notation "word", where indicates the beginning and the end of a sequence of bolded characters. For the interested reader, an excellent introduction to the conventions of XML can be found at https://www.tei-c.org/release/doc/tei-p5-doc/en/html/SG.html.

The full set of TEI guidelines is designed to meet the needs of a wide range of researchers with an interest in electronic texts. Because not all these conventions are usually relevant to corpus linguists, most of us do not need to use the full set. And the guidelines are designed with this in mind: individual researchers can select the parts of the conventions which are useful to them and ignore the rest. Despite this flexibility though, it can be easy for researchers without a specialist interest in text encoding to get lost in the extensive forest of guidelines, and some have, therefore, argued that corpus linguists should aim to work with a slimmed-down version of TEI. Hardie's (2014) guidelines are an influential suggestion along these lines and will give most corpus linguists a sufficiently powerful set of markup/annotation tools for their purposes.

While markup and annotation give us information about individual features appearing within a text, for most research purposes, it is also important to record information about properties of whole texts that will be important for users of the corpus. For written texts, key examples include information about the writer (e.g., their age, first language, level of proficiency in the language in which they are writing), about the text type (e.g., whether it was a work of fiction, a newspaper article, a school assignment), and about the context in which the text was written (e.g., if it was an assignment, what task was it responding to, what resources were available to the writer, was it written by hand or on a computer).

Information of this sort is known as *metadata* and is invaluable when trying to understand authentic texts. Metadata is commonly captured in a separate document (usually a spreadsheet), which serves as an index showing the properties of each text. It can also be recorded within an XML-encoded *header* at the top of each text (key conventions concerning headers can be found in the TEI guidelines: https://tei-c.org/release/doc/tei-p5-doc/en/html/HD.html).

A portion of the metadata that accompanies the *GiG* corpus of children's writing, which I will be using extensively in this book (see Section 2.5[6]), can be seen in Figure 2.15. This includes information about the school (*batch_id*) that each text

	A	B	C	D	E	F	G	H	I
1	batch_id	text_id	date_of_birt	production_	year_group	attainment_	gender	ses	eal
2	2	6a	04-Jun-09	Nov-15	2	B1	m	no_fsm	n
3	2	6b	04-Jun-09	Dec-15	2	B1	m	no_fsm	n
4	2	6c	04-Jun-09	NA	2	B1	m	no_fsm	n
5	2	6d	04-Jun-09	Jan-16	2	B1	m	no_fsm	n
6	2	7a	19-Oct-08	Jan-16	2	A1	f	no_fsm	n
7	2	8a	17-Jul-09	Nov-15	2	B1	f	no_fsm	n
8	2	8b	17-Jul-09	Dec-15	2	B1	f	no_fsm	n
9	2	8c	17-Jul-09	NA	2	B1	f	no_fsm	n
10	2	8d	17-Jul-09	Jan-16	2	B1	f	no_fsm	n
11	2	9a	03-Feb-09	Dec-15	2	A0	m	no_fsm	n

FIGURE 2.15 Metadata excerpt from the *GiG* corpus

came from. It includes a unique *text_id*, where each number represents an individual student and each letter represents different texts submitted by that student (so student 6, for example, submitted four texts, labelled a–d). It also includes information about the student's date of birth, the date when the text was produced, the year group of the student, and so on. The full list of variables included in the metadata is shown in Table 2.1. A rich array of information such as this allows researchers to

TABLE 2.1 Variables in the GiG metadata

Variable	Gloss
batch_id	the school from which a text was collected
text_id	unique identifier for each text. Numerals indicate the writer. Letters indicate different texts written by a single writer
date_of_birth	DOB of the writer
production_date	date the text was written
year_group	school year group of the writer
attainment_level	attainment level of the writer, as assigned by class teacher. Different systems of attainment grading are used in different schools. Attainment usually refers to the work of the student as a whole rather than to a particular text
gender	gender of the writer
ses	whether the writer is eligible for pupil premium/free school means
eal	whether the writer is classified as speaking English as an additional language
ethnicity	ethnicity of the writer
discipline	the academic discipline within which the text was produced. This was assigned retrospectively by the project team
medium	whether the text was handwritten or produced on a computer
genre	genre of the text. Assigned retrospectively by the project team
learning_objective	stated learning objective of the task to which the writer is responding
grammar_specific_ learning_objective	any specific grammatical learning objective of the task to which the writer is responding
GiG_title	text title, assigned retrospectively by the project team
context	relevant background information on the task
supplementary_notes	any additional relevant information

take account of a wide range of variables that might be influencing language use and are essential for the sorts of mixed effects analyses and explanatory follow-up work discussed in Chapter 1 (Section 2.3).

2.5 Corpora used in this book

In the examples throughout the book, I will be using two freely available corpora: the *GiG* corpus and the *British Academic Written English* (BAWE) corpus (Nesi et al., 2008). The former is a corpus of texts written by children at schools in England, which I collected with my colleagues Mark Brenchley and Debra Myhill. The latter is a corpus of assignments written by students at four British universities and was developed by Hilary Nesi, Sheena Gardner, Paul Thompson, and Paul Wickens. Further information about these corpora, and details of how to download them, can be found at www.routledge.com/9780367715786.

Though I will be using the aforementioned corpora, it should be possible to apply the techniques described in this book to any suitably formatted corpus. If you are using your own corpus and are unsure about how to prepare this for analysis, the CIABATTA tool kit (https://writecrow.org/ciabatta/) offers excellent advice on this (note especially the Corpus Text Processor, which can be used to get texts into an appropriate format). You will also need to create a parsed version of your corpus. This will be the topic of the next section.

2.6 Automatically annotating your corpus for part of speech and syntactic relationships

2.6.1 Introduction

As we saw in Section 2.4, we often need to supplement the basic textual information in our texts with grammatical information about the parts of speech (POS) of individual words and about the syntactic relationships that those words have to each other.

While it is possible to add grammatical information by hand, this can be a time-consuming and error-prone process. For many purposes, it is, therefore, advisable to use an automated POS tagger and syntactic parser. Several programmes that can do this job are now available. Good examples include CLAWS (Garside & Smith, 1997) and the koRpus R package (Michalke, 2021). Through the course of this book, I will be using the Stanford CoreNLP programme (Manning et al., 2014). This has the advantages of being free to use, relatively simple to operate, and providing information on both POS and syntactic relationships.

The following sections will review the key steps of annotating a corpus using CoreNLP. If you plan to follow the practical sections of this book using the corpora described in Section 2.5, you will be able to download pre-parsed versions of these corpora, so you will not need to complete the processes described in this section. If you want to apply the analyses to your own corpus, however, you will need to parse the corpus yourself, so the following processes will be essential.

It is important to remember that, within the space of this book, I can only offer a brief introduction to using the parsing software, and one that will no doubt go out of date before too long. For further (and updated) guidance, you should refer to the CoreNLP website (https://stanfordnlp.github.io/CoreNLP/). A helpful tutorial for using the parser can also be found at linguisticsweb.org (https://tinyurl.com/3wehrasx). Perhaps most accessible of all is Larissa Goulart's excellent video tutorial, which covers all the key steps in detail (https://youtu.be/MpCerrRxwBc).

Before embarking on this adventure, you should be aware that processing a large corpus can take a considerable amount of time. While small corpora can be done relatively quickly, if you are dealing with a corpus that runs into the millions of words, you should be ready to leave the process running for several hours (depending on the speed of your computer). Moreover, parsing a corpus can be a resource-heavy job, so if your computer has limited memory capacity, you may find other applications slowing down while CoreNLP is working. See Section 2.6.4 for a tip on breaking this job down into smaller chunks if this becomes a problem.

2.6.2 Make sure you have the required software

CoreNLP can be downloaded from https://stanfordnlp.github.io/CoreNLP/. Once you have downloaded the files, you will need to decompress/extract them (your computer should do this automatically when you click on the download) and store them in an easy-to-find place on your computer.

To use the programme, you will also need to have Java 8 installed (later versions of Java are not recommended, as these require changes to the commands described later in this section). This can be downloaded from https://tinyurl.com/2p8553ca.

2.6.3 Prepare the corpus for parsing

Installing CoreNLP will create a new folder (called 'coreNLP') on your computer, which I would recommend placing in your home directory for ease of access. You should also create two new subfolders within coreNLP to store the original version of your corpus and to receive the parsed version. I would suggest calling the former 'input' and the latter 'output'. You can then copy your corpus files into the 'input' folder. These should be plain .txt files, with no markup or annotation. As I mentioned in Section 2.5, the CIABATTA toolkit[7] offers excellent guidance and tools to facilitate this.

2.6.4 Make a list of the files you want to process

If you are tagging a corpus consisting of multiple files (which is true of the GiG and BAWE corpora), it is useful to start by making a list of the files you want to tag. Once you have deposited the file in the 'input' folder (see Section 2.6.3), you can create a list of these files using R. The script shown in Figure 2.16 will perform this task for you. Don't worry about understanding how this works for now – the functions that are used here will be explained in detail later in the book. You should open a 'New R Script' in RStudio, type in the script as shown, and save the script to your 'R_code' folder (see Section 2.2). To save, you can either click on the disk image at the top of the script (see Figure 2.16) or use menus File > Save As…

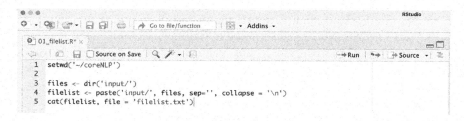

FIGURE 2.16 Creating a list of corpus files for parsing

Running this will create a new.txt file within the coreNLP folder called 'filelist.txt'. This will list the names of the files in your corpus, as illustrated in Figure 2.17.

```
input/1_1.txt
input/1_2.txt
input/1_3.txt
input/1_4.txt
input/1_5.txt
input/10_526.txt
input/10_527.txt
input/10_528.txt
input/10_529.txt
input/10_530.txt
input/10_531.txt
input/10_532.txt
input/10_533.txt
input/10_534.txt
input/10_535.txt
```

FIGURE 2.17 List of corpus files for parsing

2.6.5 Run the CoreNLP pipeline

To run the annotator, you need to open your computer's *command line*. On Windows systems, this means opening *Windows PowerShell ISE*; on Mac, the programme is called *Terminal*. Using this interface, you first need to tell your computer where the coreNLP folder is located, and then tell it to run the annotator.

To locate the coreNLP folder, use the *cd* command.

For example, on my machine, coreNLP is located within the folder structure:

- Macintosh HD > Users > philipdurrant > coreNLP
  By default, the Terminal window starts automatically within the 'Macintosh HD > Users > philipdurrant' folder, so I don't need to tell it about this part. I can go to the coreNLP folder with the command:
- cd coreNLP
  To instruct the computer to apply the annotator, enter the command:
- java -cp "*" -Xmx2g edu.stanford.nlp.pipeline.StanfordCoreNLP -annotators tokenize, ssplit, pos, lemma, ner, parse, dcoref -parse.flags " -makeCopulaHead" -filelist filelist.txt -outputFormat conll -outputDirectory output

This will start the annotator. You will be able to follow its progress through the PowerShell/Terminal. Once a few initial start-up processes have been completed, it will move through the texts in your corpus one by one. As each text is completed, the parsed version should appear in the 'output' folder. Note that annotating a complete corpus may take several hours, especially if the corpus is large. If you do not want to leave your computer running continuously, one method of breaking it into smaller parts is to stop the programme (by closing the *PowerShell* or *Terminal* window), and then, in your filelist.txt, deleting the path/filenames of all of the files that have already been processed (you can check which files have been processed by looking in the 'output' folder). When you restart the parser using the aforementioned command line, it will start from the file which is now first on your list.

2.7 Conclusion

This chapter has laid the groundwork for the hands-on chapters you will encounter later in this book. Key points with which you should now be familiar are

- how to organize a set of folders on your computer to store the work you will do later in the book;
- how to download R and RStudio;
- some basic points about using R, including how to enter and execute commands either in the Console or in a Script, saving your work, using some basic functions (sqrt(); log(); rep(); length()), using vectors, and getting further help;
- encoding, markup, annotation, and metadata;
- accessing the corpora used in this book; and
- automatically annotating a corpus using the Stanford CoreNLP programme.

2.8 Taking it further

Stefan Gries has been responsible for much of the popularity of R in corpus linguistics. In particular, the pair of books from which I gained my own grounding in R, now in their second and third editions, respectively, are essential reading:

Gries, S. T. (2020). *Quantitative corpus linguistics with R: A practical introduction*. Routledge.
Gries, S. T. (2021). *Statistics for linguistics with R: A practical introduction*. Mouton de Gruyter.

Another very good addition to the literature, with a focus on statistical issues that are not covered in the current book, is Winter's recent book.

Winter, B. (2019). *Statistics for linguists: An introduction using R*. Routledge.

Notes

1 http://www.laurenceanthony.net
2 https://www.linguisticanalysistools.org.
3 http://corpora.lancs.ac.uk/lancsbox/.
4 https://support.microsoft.com/en-us/office/choose-text-encoding-when-you-open-and-save-files-60d59c21-88b5-4006-831c-d536d42fd861 (this and all other URLs cited in this chapter were last accessed 23 March 2022).
5 The full set of guidelines can be viewed at TEI: https://tei-c.org/guidelines/.
6 Note that, for ease of presentation in the current book, a simplified version of the GiG metadata will be used in Chapters 4, 6, and 8.
7 https://writecrow.org/ciabatta/.

References

Garside, R., & Smith, N. (1997). A hybrid grammatical tagger: CLAWS4. In R. Garside, G. Leech, & A. McEnery (Eds.), *Corpus Annotation: Linguistic Information for Computer Text Corpora* (pp. 102–21). Longman. https://doi.org/10.4324/9781315841366
Gries, S. T. (2020). *Quantitative corpus linguistics with R: A practical introduction*. Routledge.
Hardie, A. (2014). Modest XML for corpora: Not a standard, but a suggestion. *ICAME Journal, 38*(1), 73–103. https://doi.org/10.2478/icame-2014-0004
Larsson, T. (2020, November 4). Corpus tools, programming, and linguistically informative research questions. *Linguistics with a Corpus.* https://linguisticswithacorpus.wordpress.com/2020/11/04/corpus-tools-programming-and-linguistically-informative-research-questions/
Manning, C. D., Surdeanu, M., Bauer, J., Finkel, J., Bethard, S. J., & McClosky, D. (2014). The Stanford CoreNLP natural language processing toolkit. *Proceedings of the 52nd Annual Meeting of the Association for Computational Linguistics: System Demonstrations*, 55–60. https://doi.org/10.3115/v1/P14-5010
McEnery, A., & Xiao, Z. (2005). Character encoding in corpus construction. In *Developing linguistic corpora: A guide to good practice*. AHDS. https://eprints.lancs.ac.uk/id/eprint/60/

Michalke, M. (2021). *koRpus: Text analysis with emphasis on POS tagging, readability, and lexical diversity.* In (Version Version 0.13-8) https://reaktanz.de/?c=hacking&s=koRpus

Nesi, H., Gardner, S., Thompson, P. et al. (2008). *British academic written English corpus.* Oxford Text Archive.

Winter, B. (2019). *Statistics for Linguists: An introduction using R.* Routledge. https://doi.org/10.4324/9781315165547

PART TWO
Studying vocabulary in writing development

3

UNDERSTANDING VOCABULARY IN LEARNER WRITING

3.1 Introduction

In this chapter and the next, we will look at writing development from the perspective of vocabulary. The methods we will look at focus on two main types of questions: how many different words are used? And what sorts of words are used? The former is usually described as indicating vocabulary *diversity* and the latter vocabulary *sophistication*. The umbrella term *lexical richness* is commonly used to refer to both types of measure (Kyle, 2021). In this chapter, I will first (Section 3.2) briefly discuss the theory of vocabulary development, focusing particularly on ways of thinking about the concept of vocabulary knowledge. I will then describe some of the key measures of vocabulary richness found in the research literature (Section 3.3) before going on to discuss important issues that researchers need to take account of when researching vocabulary development in writing.

3.2 Theorizing development in vocabulary

3.2.1 Introduction

There is a rich literature, going back several decades, on the nature of vocabulary knowledge (for recent reviews, see Durrant et al., 2022; Leńko-Szymańska, 2020). This literature provides many concepts and distinctions that can help us to think more clearly about vocabulary development. Particularly important are the notions of *breadth*, *depth*, and *fluency* of vocabulary knowledge and of the different types of knowledge that we can have about a word.

DOI: 10.4324/9781003152682-5

3.2.2 Breadth, depth, and fluency

The distinction between breadth and depth of vocabulary knowledge is one of the most long-standing ideas in vocabulary research (Schmitt, 2014 is an excellent general introduction to these terms). Breadth refers to the size of a learner's vocabulary – the number of words they know. But, of course, we know more about some words than others. There are some words that I can use accurately, with a clear knowledge of their connotative, as well as their denotative, meanings, with confidence about their most appropriate collocates and grammatical patterns, and with a feeling for the social contexts in which it would be appropriate or inappropriate to use them. There are other words that I have a much more tentative grasp of. While I can recognize that *parabloid*, for example, has something to do with geometry, I'm not at all clear on its precise meaning and would not attempt to use it in a sentence. Depth of vocabulary knowledge refers to this distinction between words that learners know more or less well.

Some researchers have also distinguished a third axis of vocabulary knowledge, often referred to as *fluency* (H. Daller et al., 2007) or *automaticity* (Segalowitz & Hulstijn, 2005). This describes how quickly and efficiently a learner is able to recall information about a word when they need it (Godfroid, 2020, is an excellent recent discussion of this concept). Because fluency relates to the *process* of word use, rather than to the textual *products* that corpus linguists study, most corpus studies do not address this aspect of vocabulary knowledge, though some have argued for an indirect link between the number of words in a text and vocabulary fluency (e.g., Leńko-Szymańska, 2020). An exciting recent development has been the integration of keystroke logging into corpora (Deane & Quinlan, 2010; Gilquin, 2022), which may enable us to study vocabulary fluency more directly in the future, but to date, this possibility has been little explored.

3.2.3 Aspects of word knowledge

Another way of thinking about vocabulary knowledge is in terms of the specific types of knowledge we can have about each word. This can be seen as a way of unpacking the notion of vocabulary depth. That is, it is a way of describing what we can know about each word. Several frameworks have been proposed to capture this (Chapelle, 1994; Nation, 2013; Perfetti & Hart, 2002; J. C. Richards, 1976). While these differ in some of their details, their main thrust has remained fairly constant. Durrant et al. (2022) summarize them as follows:

- Features of *phonology* and *orthography*: how words are pronounced or spelled.
- *Morphemic* features: the morphemic elements that make up words, including their roots and any inflectional or derivation affixes.
- *Syntactic* features: the grammatical patterns in which a word can be used, or is most typically used.
- *Semantic* features: the range of meanings a word can have and how a word is related to other words.

- *Collocational* features: the words with which a word is typically combined.
- *Register* features: the contexts in which a word is typically used.

When evaluating learner vocabulary, it is important to think about which of these aspects you need to evaluate and about what methods are best suited to assessing knowledge of that type. As we will see in Section 3.3, corpus methods have, so far, tended to be rather narrow in the types of knowledge they assess.

3.3 Measures of vocabulary development

3.3.1 Introduction

As noted at the start of this chapter, most research on written vocabulary development has focused either on the number of different words that writers use (*lexical diversity*) or on the nature of those words (*lexical sophistication*). This section will be organized around these two types of analysis, which are discussed in Sections 3.3.2 and 3.3.3, respectively. I will then move on (Section 3.3.3) to discuss some complicating issues that researchers need to consider when working in this area.

3.3.2 Lexical diversity

The term *lexical diversity* usually refers to the range of different words used in a text. A text which uses many different word types, with little repetition, has high lexical diversity. Researchers have been interested in diversity on the assumptions that (a) a diverse text indicates that a writer has a large vocabulary (Kyle, 2021) and (b) diverse texts will be perceived as higher quality than more repetitive texts (e.g., Treffers-Daller et al., 2018).

Broadly speaking, research has shown these assumptions to be true (Durrant et al., 2021). As with most measures discussed in this book, however, it is important to remember that differences in lexical diversity do not only reflect differences in the proficiency of the writer or the quality of the text. Different text genres can also differ widely in their typical levels of diversity. Narrative texts, for example, tend to be more diverse that informative/persuasive texts (Durrant & Brenchley, 2019; Olinghouse & Wilson, 2013). We also know that repetition can be used deliberately to create cohesion within a text (Halliday & Hasan, 1976) or for playful/creative purposes (Carter, 2004; Cook, 2000). As Jarvis (2013a) has pointed out, repetition (using the same word multiple times) is, therefore, not the same thing as redundancy (using the same word more times than the reader needs to see it). This implies that the equation of *more diverse = better/more proficient* must be treated with caution and due consideration given to other variables that may be influencing the measure.

The simplest way to quantify a text's lexical diversity is to count how many distinct words (known by researchers as *word types*) it contains. An obvious problem with this approach is that longer texts will, other things being equal, include more types than shorter texts. This is problematic because researchers commonly want to compare texts of different lengths, especially when making comparisons across children of different ages or learners at different levels of proficiency. Designing a measure that can be used across different length texts, however, has turned out to be surprisingly difficult (Jarvis, 2013b includes an interesting history of developments).

One possibility is simply to divide the number of types in a text by the total number of words (researchers refer to the total number of words in a text as the number of *word tokens*). This gives the *type-token ratio* (TTR), perhaps the best-known measure of diversity. While TTR is intuitive and easy to calculate, it is unfortunately not very effective. Because the range of so-far-unused words available to a writer decreases as a text continues, TTR systematically decreases as texts get longer (Malvern & Richards, 1997). This has led some researchers to suggest tweaks to the TTR formula which aim to correct for this tendency by reducing the 'downward pull' exerted by high token counts in longer texts. The most prominent of these are Guiraud's index (e.g., Bulté & Housen, 2014; Treffers-Daller et al., 2018), which divides the number of types by the square root of the number of tokens, and the corrected type-token ratio (CTTR), which divides the type count by the square root of *twice* the token count (e.g., Lorenzo & Rodríguez, 2014; Olinghouse & Leaird, 2009).

A second type of solution to the problem of comparing variety across texts of different lengths has been to standardize text length in some way. For some researchers, this has meant extracting samples of equal lengths from each text and counting the types in each (e.g., Hou et al., 2016; Koutsoftas & Gray, 2012; Lorenzo & Rodríguez, 2014). While this allows fair comparisons, it has the disadvantage of restricting all samples to the length of the shortest texts in the corpus, meaning that lots of potentially valuable data are discarded and that short complete texts might be compared with incomplete portions of much longer texts, which may make for an unfair comparison. A more satisfying alternative is to divide each text into a number of equal samples, retrieve type counts for each sample, and average these counts to arrive at a diversity score (e.g., Clendon & Erikson, 2008). Perhaps the best-developed technique of this sort has been suggested by Covington and McFall (2010). Their *moving-average type-token ratio* (MATTR) involves setting a text window (e.g., 500 words), then calculating the TTR for, e.g., words 1–500, then for words 2–502, and 3–503 until the end of the window coincides with the end of the text. Overall text diversity is then taken as the average TTR for all windows.

While all of the measures discussed so far are mathematically simple, some researchers have taken a more complex approach. Two measures in particular – *D* and the *Measure of Textual Lexical Diversity* (MTLD) – have been popular in studies of writing development. D, which was proposed by Malvern and Richards (1997), calculates TTR for progressively longer segments of a text. These TTRs can then be plotted on a curve showing the way that TTR decreases with increasing text length. The shape of this curve is summarized by the value D, whereby higher values indicate greater diversity. MTLD, which was suggested by McCarthy and Jarvis

(2010), also exploits the fact that TTR decreases as length increases. In this case, the researcher specifies in advance a particular threshold value of TTR. TTR is then calculated for increasingly longer stretches of text until it drops to the prespecified value, at which point counts reset and the process starts again. MTLD is the mean number of words that need to be counted for TTR to drop to the specified value. The more tokens need to be counted for TTR to drop below the specified value, the higher the MTLD score, and the more diverse the vocabulary.

3.3.3 Lexical sophistication

The term *lexical sophistication* is widely used in vocabulary research, but different researchers have used it in rather different ways. Some define sophistication in terms of "the relative difficulty of learning and/or using a lexical item" (Kyle, 2020, p. 461). That is, words that are *difficult* are sophisticated. In research taking this approach, a word might be considered difficult if, for example, it is infrequent in the language, it expresses an abstract concept, or it is only used in a narrow range of contexts (Kyle, 2020). A different version of sophistication is expressed by Bulté et al. (2008, p. 279), who define it as "the perception of a L2 user's lexical proficiency formed by, among other things, his [*sic*] use of semantically more specific and/or pragmatically more appropriate different words from among a set of related words". The emphasis of this definition is importantly different from Kyle's in that it focuses, not on how difficult words are for the writer, but rather on the impression they create on the reader. As any teacher will know, if a learner packs their text with difficult words, this does not necessarily create a perception of proficiency (indeed, it may achieve exactly the opposite!). Thus, Bulté et al. (2008) cite semantically specific/pragmatically appropriate words, rather than low-frequency or abstract ones, as key examples of sophisticated vocabulary.

In practice, research into lexical sophistication has focused almost entirely on the use of words that are thought to be difficult for learners. The variable of appropriateness, which was highlighted by Bulté et al.'s definition, has been left almost entirely unstudied (Leńko-Szymańska, 2020). Indeed, even Bulté et al. (2008) end up operationalizing lexical sophistication in terms of the simpler notion of low frequency. The only attempt to measure appropriateness that I am aware of is my own measure of register appropriateness (Durrant & Brenchley, 2019; Durrant & Durrant, 2022) described in Section 3.3.3.3.

3.3.3.1 Word length

One long-standing approach that researchers have taken to quantifying lexical sophistication is to measure the average lengths of words in a text. The assumption here is that words that contain more letters or more syllables (both options have been used) are more sophisticated. The logic of this assumption is perhaps that longer words are typically harder to remember or to spell correctly. Though intuitive, however, evidence on the length–difficulty relationship is mixed, with some studies even finding that longer words can be easier to acquire than shorter words in some learning situations (see Peters, 2020 for a review of the evidence). Durrant et al.'s (2021) systematic literature review suggested that there is no general association between use of long words and development over time or quality, suggesting that it is not a reliable indicator of sophistication.

3.3.3.2 Word frequency

A more promising group of measures is based around the idea of word frequency. It is commonly assumed that low-frequency words are difficult to learn, and so are markers of sophistication. This makes intuitive sense: if a word is frequent, learners are likely to meet it more often, and so learn it earlier. Many researchers have studied writing development in terms of word frequency by calculating the percentage of words in a text that comes from a list of high-frequency vocabulary. Perhaps the most widely used measure is the *Lexical Frequency Profile* (LFP), first developed by Laufer and Nation (1995) and later built into tools such as Range, VocabProfile, and, more recently, AntWordProfiler. LFP calculates the percentage of words taken from each of several word lists which represent broad frequency bands – e.g., the most frequent 1,000 words in English, the second most frequent 1,000 words. Texts are considered more lexically sophisticated if they take a lower percentage of their vocabulary from the highest frequency band lists. A variation on this approach is Meara and Bell's *lambda* measure (implemented in their *P_Lex* tool), which summarizes with a single number the density of high- vs. low-frequency words across different text segments (Meara & Bell, 2001).

A problem with these list-based measures is that they rely on a rather blunt binary distinction between each word either being on a list or not being on the list. This can disguise a huge amount of variation: a text that, for instance, takes 80% of its vocabulary from the 2,000 most frequent words and the remainder of its vocabulary from the 2–3,000 most frequent words is very different from a text that takes 80% of its vocabulary from the 2,000 most frequent words and the remainder from the 2–10,000 most frequent words.

One solution to this is to use measures based on a larger number of banded word lists. This has been implemented in measures such as *S* (Kojima & Yamashita, 2014) and *lexical stretch* (Douglas, 2015). A more widespread method has been to list all the words in a text and check the frequency of each in a reference corpus. An overall frequency value is then calculated as the mean frequency of all words in the text. This approach is found in Kyle and Crossley's (2015) Tool for the Automatic Analysis of Lexical Sophistication (TAALES), which enables researchers to find mean frequencies based on several different reference corpora.

An issue with the mean frequency approach is that word frequencies tend to be highly skewed, in the sense that a small number of words have extremely high frequencies, while the vast majority of words are very infrequent. To illustrate this problem, consider Sentences 1–3 below, where each word is shown together with its frequency per million words, as attested in the Corpus of Contemporary American

(COCA; Davies, 2008-). Although Sentences 1 and 2 look quite different, in that Sentence 2 uses much less frequent alternatives to their corresponding words in Sentence 1, the mean frequencies of the two sentences are very similar (Sentence 1 = 15,429; Sentence 2 = 15,399), because both means are strongly influenced by the very frequent word *the*. When *the* is replaced with *a*, as in Sentence 3, the mean frequency drops dramatically to 7,321. However, I take it that most readers will agree that, in terms of lexical sophistication, Sentence 3 should be considered more similar to Sentence 1 and less sophisticated overall than Sentence 2.

1.	*The*	*fat*	*cat*	*sat*	*on*	*the*	*mat*
	(50,420)	(77)	(42)	(92)	(6,949)	(50,420)	(6)
2.	*The*	*obese*	*feline*	*reclined*	*on*	*the*	*chaise longue*
	(50,420)	(5)	(1)	(0.4)	(6,949)	(50,420)	(0.2)
3.	*A*	*fat*	*cat*	*sat*	*on*	*a*	*mat*
	(22,042)	(77)	(42)	(92)	(6,949)	(22,042)	(6)

One solution to this problem is to treat lexical words and grammatical words separately. This is helpful, firstly, because lexical words probably have a greater influence on our impression of lexical sophistication than grammatical words and, secondly, because it is grammatical words that have the highest frequencies, and so exercise the greatest distorting influence on mean values. In our examples, a measure based on lexical words only would give Sentences 1 and 3 an identical mean frequency of 54.25 and Sentence 2 the much lower mean frequency of 1.65.

Another possibility is to apply a log transformation to frequency values. In the examples, if each word's frequency is transformed to its base ten logarithm, the mean frequencies become: Sentence 1 = 2.79; Sentence 2 = 1.84; Sentence 3 = 2.68. This is intuitively satisfying, with Sentences 1 and 3 now quite similar to each other and Sentence 2 much lower than both. It also keeps the mean values within a relatively small range that allows easy comparison. Of course, these two approaches can also be combined. That is, we can look at the log frequencies of lexical words only. TAALES offers researchers all these solutions, providing separate mean frequency values for all words, lexical words only, and function words only, and providing means based on both raw and log frequencies in each case.

3.3.3.3 Register-based measures

An important, but often neglected, aspect of vocabulary sophistication is the fact that words that would be considered sophisticated in one context (e.g., a book about corpus linguistics) might be jarringly out of place in another (e.g., a text message to a friend). This is an issue of *register*, i.e., the ways in which the communicative demands and social conventions of specific situations give rise to distinctive ways of speaking or writing (Biber & Conrad, 2009). The key implication for measures of vocabulary sophistication is that it may be misleading to see particular words as sophisticated in their own right. Rather, a word may be more or less sophisticated depending on the context in which it is used.

Much research on register has focused on Greco-Latin vocabulary (e.g., Berman & Nir-Sagiv, 2007; Corson, 1984) or the closely related category of *academic vocabulary* (e.g., H. Daller et al., 2013; Olinghouse & Wilson, 2013; Roessingh et al., 2016; Verspoor et al., 2017). Academic vocabulary is typically identified with reference to an existing list of academic words, especially Coxhead's (2000) *Academic Word List*, which was based on an analysis of a corpus of academic writing and is built into many lexical analysis tools, including *Range, AntWordProfiler*, and *TAALES*.

A limitation of these measures is that they focus only on words that are typical of a single register (academic prose). In an attempt to give a more rounded picture, Durrant and Brenchley (2019) have suggested a measure of *register appropriateness* (an idea further developed in Durrant & Durrant, 2022). This assigns each lexical word in a learner text a set of values representing how closely associated that word is with each of a group of chosen registers. The associations between a word and each register are calculated based on the relative frequencies of that word across different registers in a reference corpus. As with the previously discussed frequency measures, an average is then taken from across the words in the text to provide an overall score for how typical that text's words are of each of the registers studied. Validation of this method has shown that first language child writing demonstrates significant development across year groups with respect to use of academic, fiction, news, and magazine words. For non-fiction writing, the academic and fiction registers were especially important, with strong increases in the former and strong decreases in the latter as children matured (Durrant & Durrant, 2022).

3.3.3.4 Contextual distinctiveness

Contextual distinctiveness (a category described by Kyle, 2020) refers to the tendency for a word to be used in a narrower vs. wider range of contexts. It, therefore, bears some resemblance to the measures of register appropriateness discussed in the previous section. However, whereas those measures focus on words associated with a defined register (asking questions like *how academic is this text's vocabulary?*), measures of distinctiveness focus on the degree to which words are context restricted (asking the question *how specialized is this text's vocabulary?*). The rationale for these measures is that words used in a narrow range of contexts will be encountered less frequently and so be more difficult to learn. Key measures of contextual distinctiveness are *range* (the percentage of texts in which a word is found in a reference corpus), *semantic distinctiveness* (also known as *SemD*, which uses latent semantic analysis to identify words that appear in a narrow range of contexts), *word associates* (the number of other types a word typically brings to mind in a word association task), and *entropy* (a measure of how evenly distributed a word is across sections of a corpus (Gries & Ellis, 2015).

3.3.3.5 Semantic measures

Semantic measures are indices based on aspects of a word's meaning. These are of two main types: measures based on subjective perceptions of word meaning and measures based on a word's relationship to other words in a language's overall system of meanings.

Of the first type, the most widely studied measures relate to the concept of *abstractness*. In some studies, abstractness has been defined using a rating scale, like that reproduced in Table 3.1, which shows the scale of nominal abstractness used by Berman and Nir-Sagiv (2007). Referring to this, researchers can read through the nouns in a text and code each for abstractness. While this approach has the great advantage of allowing for a clear and customizable definition of abstraction, the requirement for hand-coding obviously restricts the number of texts that can be studied.

An alternative to hand-coding is to use scores from pre-existing lists of words linked with abstractness scores (or to their inverse: *concreteness* scores). The Coh-Metrix and TAALES tools, for example, use the MRC psycholinguistic database (Coltheart, 1981; Wilson, 1988), which provides a concreteness rating for just over 8,000 words. Much as with the frequency-based methods discussed in the previous section, these tools assign a value from the list to each word in the corpus and calculate a mean to represent the concreteness of vocabulary in each text as a whole. Using the same approach, these tools also provide values for the other subjectively defined semantic measures of *imageability* – defined as "how easy it is to create an image of a word" (Kyle & Crossley, 2015, p. 762) – and *meaningfulness* – somewhat less clearly defined as "how a word is related to other words" (Kyle & Crossley, 2015, p. 762).

The second main type of semantic measure is based on how a word's meaning relates to that of other words. These are the measures of *polysemy* and *hypernymy*. Polysemy is defined as the "number of different (but related) senses (i.e., meanings) a word form has" (Kyle & Crossley, 2016, p. 15). Hypernymy "refers to the number of subordinate terms a word has" (Kyle & Crossley, 2016, p. 15), where *subordinate*

TABLE 3.1 Nominal abstractness scale (Berman & Nir-Sagiv, 2007)

Rating	Definition	Examples
1 (least abstract)	concrete objects and specific people	*John; a ball; flowers*
2	categorical nouns, roles and locations, and generic nouns	*a teacher; every teacher; the city; people*
3	a) nonabstract, high-register, or rare nouns	a) *rival; cult*
	b) abstract but common terms	b) *fight; war*
	c) metaphorical extensions of concrete terms	c) *path to success*
4 (most abstract)	nouns that are nonimageable, abstract, and low frequency	*relationship; lack; existence*

refers to the relationship between a category and its types: e.g., *spaniel* is a hypernym of *dog*; *dog* is a hypernym of *animal*. *Dog* has fewer hypernyms than *animal* and is, therefore, more specific. As with the measures described in the previous paragraph, Coh-Metrix and TAALES implement these measures using an existing database – in this case, *Wordnet* (Fellbaum, 1998) – to assign scores to each word in the corpus.

Semantics can also be studied using the SemD measure mentioned in Section 2.2.4. As previously described, this indicates the range of different contexts in which a word is used (hence its appearance under the "Contextual Distinctiveness" heading of Section 3.3.3.4). Its creators, however, see SemD's primary function as that of measuring ambiguity (Hoffman, Lambon-Ralph, & Rogers, 2013). This is based on the idea that words appearing in a narrower range of contexts are likely to be less ambiguous.

3.3.3.6 Psycholinguistic measures

Psycholinguistic measures are based on data about language users. We have already discussed one example of information about how users perceive words in the case of abstractness ratings. We saw there that Coh-Metrix and TAALES base their abstractness measurements on databases of how abstract (or rather, how concrete) users perceive a word to be. Similar ratings are also provided for users' perceptions of the familiarity, imageability, and meaningfulness of words.[1]

Other psycholinguistic measures, similarly based on existing databases, concern the age at which children typically learn a word in their first language and the speed with which users recognize a word under experimental conditions, and the number of associates a word typically brings to mind in a word association test (Kyle et al., 2018). Each of these is assumed to correlate with the difficulty of a word, and so with one version of lexical sophistication.

3.4 Complicating factors

3.4.1 Introduction

Researchers studying development in terms of lexical richness face several issues that I have glossed over in the discussion so far for ease of presentation. This section will look at those issues and, where possible, try to offer some guidance.

3.4.2 What is a 'word'?

3.4.2.1 Defining words

Although this part of the book is about analyzing writing development in terms of words, I have not yet said exactly what I mean by *word*. It may surprise readers new to vocabulary studies that defining *word* is not at all a straightforward task and that it continues to lead to disagreement amongst researchers. Doing vocabulary research requires us to be very clear about our position on this debate.

The key issues boil down to two main questions: how can the stream of language be divided up into separate word units (the issue of defining word tokens)? And how should these units be grouped together as examples of the *same* word (the issue of defining word types)? I will discuss each of these in turn.

3.4.2.2 Defining word tokens

The task of dividing written language into its component words looks, at first glance, straightforward. Because, in modern English orthography (unlike ancient Greek or modern Thai), each word is conveniently surrounded by white space and/ or punctuation marks, we simply need to split the text at these points to divide it into words. For example:

There	*are*	*seven*	*words*	*in*	*this*	*sentence*
1	2	3	4	5	6	7

However, things are not always this easy. One issue is whether we should treat strings of letters that are separated by punctuation marks, but not by spaces, as one word or two. In some cases, we might want to think of these as single words:

He works **part-time** in a local supermarket.

In others, we might want to think of them as separate words:

I've been waiting for you all morning.

Such cases present researchers with both conceptual and practical challenges. The conceptual challenge is that we need to consider the range of possible forms with intervening punctuation marks and decide, for the purposes of our own research, which ones we want to count separately. From the previous examples, for instance, we might want to say that compounds like *part-time* are counted as single words but that pronoun + auxiliary verb combinations like *I've* are not.

The practical challenge is that a single punctuation mark can serve multiple functions. Nation (2016, p. 65) summarizes the functions of the hyphen, for example, as follows:

- syllabification in justified texts (i.e., the hyphen that conjoins words that are split over two lines);
- linking affixes to their base word to avoid awkwardness when adjacent vowels are pronounced separately (e.g., *co-operate*, rather than *cooperate*) or when we need to avoid ambiguity (e.g., *re-store* with the meaning of 'store again');
- linking elements in a complex attributive adjective (e.g., *a long-term relationship*);
- linking elements in a compound word (e.g., *north-east*);
- linking duplicated words (e.g., *a softly-softly approach*);
- replacing letters in a censored word (e.g., *This tastes like sh-t!*).

Because researchers may want to split some of these types, but not others, into separate words, a uniform decision to combine or separate character strings containing a hyphen may not be sufficient. In an ideal world, this may lead researchers to deal with different uses of a punctuation mark in different ways. Of course, this could potentially be a very large job, which researchers may be unwilling or unable to undertake. In such cases, it is essential at least to be conscious of the types of errors that treating all cases in the same way may introduce.

Another set of challenges concerns sequences that we might want to think of as single words but that have white space *within* them. A clear example is the phrase *by and large*. Many researchers would want to treat this as a word in its own right. The three components surrounded by white space in this sequence do not have any obvious relationship to the meaning of the overall expression and do not follow the usual grammatical rules associated with them (it would usually be ungrammatical to join a preposition and an adjective with a coordinating conjunction – compare *on and small*). This suggests that it is misleading to treat the phrase as a combination of three separate words and that it is better to see this as a single extended item. A similar case could be made for phrasal verbs (e.g., *shut up*, with the meaning of *be quiet*, or *carry out*, with the meaning of *do*), for compound nouns (*prime minister*) and for idioms (*under the weather*). Stretching the point further, some researchers might want to treat binomials (*alive and well*), pragmatic formulas (*bless you*), or collocations (*catch cold*) as independent words.

There is no single correct answer to the question of how such sequences should be treated, and huge amounts of research have gone into defining, classifying, and understanding them. Because they raise such complex issues, and because distinctive corpus methods have been developed for their study, I have devoted a separate part of the book to these, under the heading of *formulaic language* (see Chapters 7 and 8).

3.4.2.3 Defining word types

Once we have defined the tokens in a corpus, we next need to decide which tokens should be grouped together as examples of *the same* word. Consider the sentence:

I'm not rude; you're rude!

Most of this sentence is straightforward. We have two instances of the type *rude*, and one each of *I*, *you*, and *not*. But what about *'m'* and *'re'*? These are both forms of the verb *to be*, so should perhaps be counted as a single type. On the other hand, they are spelled differently from each other, have different grammatical constraints on them, and need to be acquired separately by language learners. These reasons might make us consider treating them as separate words.

Dilemmas of this sort come under the heading of *type definition*. The simplest approach to type definition is to treat identically spelled tokens as the same, and differently spelled tokens as different. This is known as defining types at the level of the *word form*. While this is easy to implement, there are reasons to think that it is not always the best option. One set of concerns surrounds examples like the verb *to be*, as in the previous example. That is, we might, for some purposes, want to treat differently spelled forms as representing the same type. Relationships between differently spelled forms of a word come in different varieties. At the simplest level, we have forms that differ only in terms of a regular inflectional suffix. This can be seen in cases like *I play-he plays* and *one house-two houses*. More complex are cases like the verb *to be*, or *to run*, where inflected forms are not linked via regular affixes and so must be learned separately. We also need to think about forms that are related by derivation, such as *like-likeable* and *vain-vanity*, where a wide range of affixes can be used with greater or lesser degree of productivity and regularity to create 'new' words.

A second issue with the word form approach is the converse of the first. That is, there may be items that are identically spelled but that we wish to treat as different types. This is seen most clearly in homographs such as **tap** *water* vs. **tap** *dancer*. For some purposes, we might also want to separate polysemes (e.g., *he is* **playing** *the guitar* vs. *the radio was* **playing**) or words with different parts of speech (e.g., *he* **records** *all of his meetings* vs. *he keeps* **records** *all of his meetings*).

Four main ways of defining types are currently common in vocabulary research. The first is the *word form* approach where any tokens with the same spelling are classified as being the same type. The second is the *lemma* approach. This combines tokens that are related by inflection (so *play-plays* and *am-are-is-was-were-be-been-being* would be grouped together) but separates words with different parts of speech (so the verb and noun versions of *record* would be different types). Third is the *flemma* approach. This is a slight variation on the lemma approach. Inflected words are again grouped together, but no distinction is made between words with different parts of speech (so the verb and noun forms of *record* would be the same type). Fourth is the *word family* approach, which groups together both inflectionally and derivationally related words. Thus, not only would the forms in *I* **like** *John* and *he* **likes** *John* be combined, but so too would *John is* **likeable** and *John's* **likeability** *won him many friends*. Bauer and Nation (1993) have influentially argued that word families can be defined at different levels, varying according to the difficulty of the derivations involved (e.g., derivation using *-ly* or *un-* is rated as relatively easy, whereas *-ee* or *re-* is rated as more difficult). However, these suggested levels have been criticized for lacking an empirical basis, failing to consider the interaction between affixes and stems, and being difficult to apply due to the same affixes appearing at multiple levels (Brown et al., 2020; Gardner, 2008).

While there has been a great deal of discussion about how types should be defined (good examples are Brown et al., 2020; Gardner, 2008; Nation, 2016; Treffers-Daller et al., 2018), it is important to remember that different research purposes and different types of analysis often require different choices. When reading the advice from such studies, it is, therefore, important to think carefully about how that advice suits your own research and how the choices you make will affect your findings.

When analyzing lexical diversity, for example, the key consideration is that grouping more tokens together will lead to lower scores. To take the two extremes, an analysis which treats each word form as its own type, regardless of inflectional/ derivational similarities to other forms, will end up with far more types than an analysis which treats all inflectionally and derivationally linked tokens as examples of the same type. At a theoretical level, the question researchers need to consider is whether writers who use two related words should be credited with one word or two. If we believe, for example, that using *he argues*, as well as *I argue*, should increase the lexical diversity of a text, we probably want to define types at the word form level. If not, we should probably move to the lemma level. If we think that using *argumentative* as well as *argue* should increase diversity, the lemma level might be appropriate. If we believe that the derived form does not add to the diversity of the text, the word family level would be a better choice. There has been little empirical study of the effects of different type definitions on the outcomes of diversity studies, but in one of the few systematic attempts to study this, Treffers-Daller et al. (2018) found that diversity measures based on lemma types predicted scores on an L2 proficiency test better than those based on word forms or families.

When analyzing lexical sophistication in terms of mean reference corpus frequencies (as described in Section 3.3.2), the chief effect of grouping more tokens together will be to reduce the level of sophistication ascribed to tokens that are part of a large family. For example, while the word *argument* has a frequency (in the current version of COCA[2]) of 69/million words, the family of which it is a part (which includes the forms *argue, arguable, arguably, argued, argues, arguing, argument, argumentation, argumentative, argumentatively, argumentativeness, arguments, unarguable*, and *unarguably*) has a frequency of 225/million words. Thus, the sophistication of *argument* will be substantially downgraded in an analysis that uses word families.

Importantly, this downgrading can be very different for different words, with words in small families affected much less than words in large families. The form *crisis*, for example, is similar in frequency to *argument* but is part of a much smaller family (*crises* and the unconventional *crisises*), so its frequency would shift only slightly (from 67 to 74/million words). The shift will also be much greater for the least frequent members of a family. Whereas the frequency awarded to *argument* would increase by a factor of approximately 3, the frequency of the least frequent form in its family (*argumentativeness*, which has a frequency of 0.01/million words) would increase by a factor of over 20,000.

The theoretical decision to be made here is whether we think the sophistication of a word should be evaluated based on the frequency of the individual form or on that of its family. Does the fact that *argument* is part of a large and cumulatively frequent family mean that it is less sophisticated than *crisis*? Similarly, does the fact that *argumentativeness* is part of this large family mean that this form is less sophisticated than its individual frequency would suggest? Your answer to these questions is likely to differ depending on your research aims and your theoretical beliefs about language learning. Let's suppose, for example, that like many researchers in this area (see Section 3.3), you think of sophistication as an indicator of *difficulty* and that you believe difficulty is correlated with frequency. The question then becomes that of which frequency is most relevant to determining a word's difficulty: the frequency of its form, its lemma, or its family.

While the evidence is not yet sufficiently strong to give a firm answer to this question, there is reason to think that lemmas may be the most relevant level. A growing body of studies suggests that learners who recognize one member of a lemma are usually able to recognize other members but that the same is not true of word families; knowing one form within a family does not usually imply knowing the others (Brown et al., 2020 provide an excellent recent review of the evidence). This suggests that the frequency of different members of a lemma may work cumulatively to increase its familiarity to learners but that the frequency of different members of a word family does not.

So far, we have discussed the choice between different definitions of word type in theoretical terms. However, it is also important to consider the practicalities of the different definitions. For all their potential shortcomings, word forms have the practical advantage of being easy to identify. Word families and flemmas require a little more sophistication as researchers will need to do the work of grouping forms under headwords (some applications, such as AntConc and AntWordProfiler now make this a relatively straightforward task). Lemmatization is slightly more complex as it requires our corpus to be tagged for part of speech. More problematic are homographs and polysemes of the same part of speech. To distinguish these, we need to distinguish different senses of a word, something that cannot yet be reliably done computationally. This places practical limits on the ways in which types can currently be operationalized.

3.4.3 Choosing a suitable reference corpus

Reference corpora play an important role in measures of vocabulary sophistication. We saw in Section 3.3 how measures of word frequency and register appropriateness assign values to words based on their frequency distributions in a reference corpus. This raises the question of how such a corpus should be chosen.

Two main types of reference corpus can be distinguished: *input corpora* and *target corpora*. An input corpus aims to represent language to which learners are likely to have been exposed. For example, a study of L1 English children's writing might take as its reference corpus the reading section of the *Oxford Corpus*,[3] which contains books aimed specifically at children.

Many researchers use an input corpus on the grounds that the frequency of words in a learner's input will correlate with the likelihood of their knowing that word, and hence with difficulty (cf., Section 3.3.2). Some researchers are also interested in tracing how more complex features of input, such as the tendency of particular words to appear in particular grammatical constructions or particular collocations, impact upon learning (research of this latter sort will be discussed in more detail in Chapters 5 and 7).

A difficulty with this approach is that it is often difficult to find representative corpora of learner input. Many researchers, therefore, end up using large national corpora, such as the British National Corpus (BNC) or COCA, as proxy input corpora. This is problematic as there are likely to be substantial differences between such corpora and learner input (Egbert, 2017). National corpora are typically designed as balanced samples from across a language variety and so differ radically from most individuals' experiences of that language. For example, whereas most people who read newspapers are likely to concentrate on a few particular titles, and perhaps particular sections within those titles, national corpora deliberately include a wide range of different titles and sections. Similarly, whereas most university students get most of their academic language input from a few disciplinary areas in which they are interested, national corpora deliberately sample from across the widest possible range of areas.

Such differences are likely to have important impacts on the distribution of vocabulary items in a national corpus vs. a genuine input corpus. Because real learner input is much narrower than a national corpus, it is likely to feature a less diverse set of vocabulary, and particular items will be repeated much more frequently (e.g., a reader of the current book will encounter the word *language* far more frequently than it would appear in a multi-discipline academic corpus). This point is especially important for studies drawing on usage-based models of language learning as such models highlight exactly this type of skewed learner input as crucial to the learning process (e.g., Goldberg, 2006).

Whereas input corpora attempt to represent language to which learners have been exposed, *target corpora* attempt to represent language which learners are aiming to produce. We can distinguish two importantly different types of target corpus. A *peer target corpus* represents successful writing by learners at the same educational level as those being studied. For example, if we were studying the writing of university-level writers, a good peer target corpus might be the BAWE corpus, which represents university writing that has been awarded a high grade by tutors on the relevant academic programme.

The second type of target corpus is a *prospective target corpus*. This represents writing that learners might realistically hope to produce at some point in the future. For example, though we would not expect most undergraduate students to publish research articles or academic monographs, a corpus of research articles and/or monographs might be used to represent the writing for which their university education might ultimately prepare them.

The two types of target corpus have distinctive strengths and limitations. A key advantage of a peer corpus is that it will be closely matched to the types of writing that learners produce. Undergraduate assignments, for example, are in many ways a unique genre of writing, which differs in important ways from other types of academic writing, such as textbooks, research articles, or published monographs (Hyland, 2008). It may, therefore, be misleading to use other types of academic writing as a reference point for student essays. It is possible, for example, that particular words or phrases that are well-suited to a research article are not well-suited to undergraduate assignments. Using a peer target corpus overcomes this problem. They are, therefore, an excellent way of evaluating learners' writing against good examples of exactly the types of writing they are being asked to produce.

Peer target corpora have two key problems, however. One is the practical issue that, for many types of learners, there may not be a high-quality reference corpus of peer writing available. The second is the more fundamental issue that, in many cases, peer target corpora do now allow us to trace development across learner levels. Consider a learner corpus of child writing spanning several years of schooling. Because the types of text that these children write will change across year groups, several different peer reference corpora will be required, resulting in different standards of measurement being applied to each level. This is akin to measuring a child's height as they grow older while changing the definition of 'cm' each year. To trace development across year groups, a prospective target corpus which represents the sorts of writing we might expect learners to do at the end of their education would allow for a constant reference point that could be applied across levels. In this case, therefore, a prospective target corpus would be a more appropriate choice.

3.4.4 Relationships between measures of diversity and sophistication

An important unresolved issue with the types of analysis outlined in Section 3.3 is that of how different measures, and the theoretical constructs they are intended to access, relate to each other. At one level, this issue is illustrated in the fact that individual measures can appear under different theoretical headings. SemD, for example, can be seen as a measure of contextual distinctiveness or of semantic ambiguity; concreteness can be theorized as a psycholinguistic measure or as a semantic measure. At another level, it is seen in the fact that many measures of sophistication correlate with each other. Word frequency, for example, is known to correlate with (to name just a few!): word length (more frequent words tend to be shorter), range (more frequent words tend to occur in more texts), semantic distinctiveness (more frequent words appear in a wider range of contexts), and reaction times (more frequent words are recognized more rapidly). It can even be difficult to disentangle the broad constructs of diversity and sophistication. This is most clearly seen in the fact that scores for diversity and frequency tend to correlate with each other. This is because, once the most frequent words have been used, the only way of adding to a text's diversity score is by using lower-frequency words. Thus, as diversity increases, so does the use of lower-frequency words (B. Richards & Malvern, 2010). These considerations raise the questions of whether the various types of measure discussed in Section 3.3 are genuinely measuring different things and of how they each relate to each other and to the broader construct of vocabulary richness. Research on these issues is, to date, limited. However, some empirical and theoretical work does exist to guide future studies.

One relevant strand is Jarvis's work on the concept of lexical diversity (2013a, 2013b, 2017). He argues that we should move away from the traditional notion of diversity as lack of repetition towards a broader, more perceptually based definition, which sees lack of repetition as just one aspect of diversity. Jarvis argues that, although the traditional view puts diversity on an objective (*etic*) scale, it should instead be seen as a subjective (*emic*) phenomenon. As we noted earlier, texts often require a certain degree of repetition to maintain grammaticality and coherence. On Jarvis's view, a text lacks diversity if its reader finds repetitions to be more than is needed (*redundant*). He, therefore, distinguishes between an objective axis of repetition-variability and a subjective axis of redundancy-diversity. Two texts which have equivalent amounts of repetition may differ in their perceived diversity, depending on several other factors.

Jarvis fleshes out some of these factors by describing diversity as being associated with seven characteristics of texts (2013a, 2013b, 2017)[4]: volume (the number of tokens in a text), abundance (the number of types in a text), variety (the degree of repetition – i.e., the traditional notion of diversity), evenness (the skew of frequencies between words; texts in which most words are repeated with similar levels of frequency are *even*), dispersion (the length of intervals between repetitions), specialness (the use of infrequent words/words with high information content), and disparity. Jarvis argues that a measure that can capture our perceptions of diversity must ultimately incorporate all these factors.

Readers will have noted that Jarvis's notion of *specialness* (the use of infrequent words) is equivalent to one of the key operationalizations of sophistication discussed previously. We have already seen that measures of diversity and frequency tend to be strongly correlated. Jarvis's work goes further by seeing frequency as one aspect of diversity. Research I have conducted with my colleagues also suggests that vocabulary sophistication should not be seen as independent of vocabulary diversity, at least in the context of school children's L1 writing. Studies of both the frequency (Durrant & Brenchley, 2019) and the register appropriateness (Durrant & Durrant, 2022) of children's vocabulary indicate that the word types young children use are not individually more frequent or more closely associated with their target registers than those used by older children. From primary school onwards, children use both infrequent (e.g., *caldron, earworm, hideout, wisp*) and appropriately academic (e.g., *organism, importantly, interval, population*) vocabulary. The key difference between texts written by older and younger children was not the overall repertoire of words, but the distribution of those words in the text. That is, younger children tended to repeat high-frequency words extensively, while older children tended to repeat register appropriate words more often. These repetitions led to a significant decrease in the mean frequency and an increase in the register appropriateness of word *tokens*. Changes in sophistication were, therefore, inseparable from changes in diversity. On this view, sophistication is not so much a property of individual words as something that emerges across the length of a text.

Another strand of evidence on the relationships between vocabulary richness measures comes from empirical studies that have researched the relationships between large numbers of vocabulary measures using principal components or factor analysis. However, these analyses, carried out for different types of writing (Durrant et al., 2019; Kim et al., 2018) and also for speech (Eguchi & Kyle, 2020), have not yet revealed a consistent picture of how measures relate to each other.

3.4.5 Vocabulary knowledge depth

In Section 3.2.2, I mentioned the important conceptual distinction between breadth and depth of vocabulary knowledge. The former, I noted, refers to the range of different words that a learner knows, whereas the latter refers to what a learner knows about those words. A striking limitation of most measures discussed in this chapter is that they access only a very shallow type of vocabulary knowledge. Whether we are measuring diversity, word length, mean frequency, or the psychological or semantic properties of words, learners are credited with using a word whenever they are able to recall the form of that word and write it down. This is regardless of whether they have used the word correctly in terms of meaning, syntax, collocation, or register. Thus, a writer who simply listed all the least frequent words they know without repeating them would end up with very high scores for both diversity and sophistication.

This is clearly unsatisfactory, and a key goal for future research should be to develop measures that give a more rounded picture of knowledge depth. Three types of measures currently hold promise for this. One is the measure of register appropriateness, described in Section 3.3.3, which aims to evaluate whether learners are using words appropriate to a particular context. Another is measures originating in usage-based models of language that evaluate the relationship between words and the syntactic contexts in which they are used. These will be discussed in Chapter 5 (Section 3.4). The third is measures of formulaic language, which aim to evaluate whether words are used in an appropriate collocational context. These will be discussed in Chapter 7.

3.5 Conclusion

The study of word use can give us a powerful window into writing development. Learner vocabulary is a key aspect of overall proficiency; it is strongly predictive of learners' overall language abilities (e.g., M. Daller & Yixin, 2017; Sinclair, 2020) and of their broader academic attainment, both in first (e.g., Spencer et al., 2017; Townsend et al., 2012) and second (e.g., M. Daller & Yixin, 2017; Trenkic & Warmington, 2019) language education. Research has also found many measures of vocabulary use to be strongly associated with both perceptions of quality and development over time in first and second language writing (Durrant et al., 2021). It is, therefore, a key area of study and one that will continue to provide important insights into how learner writing develops.

As we saw in Section 3.4.2, researching vocabulary raises some tricky practical and theoretical issues; indeed, getting to grips with these issues is part of the intellectual excitement of working in this area. However, an impressive array of tools and concepts have now been developed and, despite the challenges, it is possible for even novice researchers to do useful vocabulary research, as I hope the next chapter will demonstrate.

3.6 Taking it further

Perhaps the most directly relevant book-length discussion of the issues discussed in this chapter is:

Leńko-Szymańska, A. (2020). *Defining and assessing lexical proficiency*. Routledge.

Also highly relevant is the collection of studies published in:

Jarvis, S., & Daller, M. (Eds.). (2013). *Vocabulary knowledge: Human ratings and automated measures*. John Benjamins.

For a broader perspective, there are a number of excellent general introductions to researching vocabulary learning and use. Key recent examples include:

Durrant, P., Siyanova-Chanturia, A., Kremmel, B., & Sonbul, S. (2022). *Research Methods in Vocabulary Studies*. John Benjamins.
Schmitt, N. (2020). *Vocabulary in language teaching* (2nd ed.). Cambridge University Press.
Webb, S. (Ed.). (2020). *The Routledge handbook of vocabulary studies*. Routledge.

Notes

1 Kyle and Crossley (2015) actually group concreteness together with these other measures, counting them all as examples of psycholinguistic measures.
2 As accessed on 21 October 2021.
3 https://readoxford.org/our-research/leverhulme.
4 Note that there are some differences in the number of factors, their names, and definitions that Jarvis uses in different papers.

References

Bauer, L., & Nation, P. (1993). Word families. *International Journal of Lexicography, 6*(4), 253–79. https://doi.org/10.1093/ijl/6.4.253
Berman, R. A., & Nir-Sagiv, B. (2007). Comparing narrative and expository text construction across adolescence: A developmental paradox. *Discourse Processes, 43*(2), 79–120. https://doi.org/10.1080/01638530709336894
Biber, D., & Conrad, S. (2009). *Register, genre, and style*. Cambridge University Press. https://doi.org/10.1017/CBO9780511814358
Brown, D., Stoeckel, T., McLean, S., & Stewart, J. (2020). The most appropriate lexical unit for L2 vocabulary research and pedagogy: A brief review of the evidence. *Applied Linguistics*, 1–7. https://doi.org/10.1093/applin/amaa061
Bulté, B., & Housen, A. (2014). Conceptualizing and measuring short-term changes in L2 writing complexity. *Journal of Second Language Writing, 26*, 42–65. https://doi.org/10.1016/j.jslw.2014.09.005

Bulté, B., Housen, A., Pierrard, M., & Van Daele, S. (2008). Investigating lexical proficiency development over time – the case of Dutch-speaking learners of French in Brussels. *French Language Studies*, *18*, 277–98. https://doi.org/10.1017/S0959269508003451

Carter, R. (2004). *Language and creativity: The art of common talk*. Routledge.

Chapelle, C. (1994). Are C-tests valid measures for L2 vocabulary research? *Second Language Research*, *10*(2), 157–87. https://doi.org/10.1177/026765839401000203

Clendon, S. A., & Erikson, K. A. (2008). The vocabulary of beginning writers: Implications for children with complex communication needs. *Augmentative and Alternative Communication*, *24*(4), 281–93. https://doi.org/10.1080/07434610802463999

Coltheart, M. (1981). The MRC psycholinguistic database. *Quarterly Journal of Experimental Psychology*, *33*, 497–505. https://doi.org/10.1080/14640748108400805

Cook, G. (2000). *Language play, language learning*. Oxford University Press.

Corson, D. (1984). The lexical bar: Lexical change from 12 to 15 years measured by social class, region and ethnicity. *British Educational Research Journal*, *10*(2), 115–33. https://doi.org/10.1080/0141192840100201

Covington, M. A., & McFall, J. D. (2010). Cutting the Gordion knot: The moving-average type-token ratio. *Journal of Quantitative Linguistics*, *17*(2), 94–100. https://doi.org/10.1080/09296171003643098

Coxhead, A. (2000). A new academic wordlist. *TESOL Quarterly*, *34*(2), 213–38. https://doi.org/10.2307/3587951

Daller, H., Milton, J., & Treffers-Daller, J. (2007). Editors' introduction: Conventions, terminology and an overview of the book. In H. Daller, J. Milton, & J. Treffers-Daller (Eds.), *Modelling and assessing vocabulary knowledge* (pp. 1–32). Cambridge University Press. https://doi.org/10.1017/CBO9780511667268.003

Daller, H., Turlik, J., & Weir, I. (2013). Vocabulary acquisition and the learning curve. In S. Jarvis & H. Daller (Eds.), *Vocabulary knowledge: Human ratings and automated measures* (pp. 185–215). John Benjamins. https://doi.org/10.1075/sibil.47.09ch7

Daller, M., & Yixin, W. (2017). Predicting study success of international students. *Applied Linguistics Review*, *8*(4), 355–74. https://doi.org/10.1515/applirev-2016-2013

Davies, M. (2008–). *The corpus of contemporary American: 450 million words, 1990-present*. Retrieved 8 August 2022 from http://corpus.byu.edu/coca/

Deane, P., & Quinlan, T. (2010). What automated analyses of corpora can tell us about students' writing skills. *Journal of Writing Research*, *2*(2), 151–77. https://doi.org/10.17239/jowr-2010.02.02.4

Douglas, S. R. (2015). The relationship between lexical frequency profiling measures and rater judgements of spoken and written general English language proficiency on the CELPIP-General Test. *TESL Canada Journal* (Special Issue 9), 43–64. https://doi.org/10.18806/tesl.v32i0.1217

Durrant, P., & Brenchley, M. (2019). Development of vocabulary sophistication across genres in English children's writing. *Reading and Writing*, *32*(8), 1927–53. https://doi.org/10.1007/s11145-018-9932-8

Durrant, P., Brenchley, M., & McCallum, L. (2021). *Understanding development and proficiency in writing: Quantitative corpus linguistic approaches*. Cambridge University Press. https://doi.org/10.1017/9781108770101

Durrant, P., & Durrant, A. (2022). Appropriateness as an aspect of lexical richness: What do quantitative measures tell us about children's writing? *Assessing Writing*, *51*, 1–19. https://doi.org/10.1016/j.asw.2021.100596

Durrant, P., Moxley, J., & McCallum, L. (2019). Vocabulary sophistication in first-year composition assignments. *International Journal of Corpus Linguistics*, *24*(1), 33–66. https://doi.org/10.1075/ijcl.17052.dur

Durrant, P., Siyanova-Chanturia, A., Kremmel, B., & Sonbul, S. (2022). *Research methods in vocabulary studies*. John Benjamins.

Egbert, J. (2017). Corpus linguistics and language testing: Navigating unchartered waters. *Language Testing, 34*(4), 555–64. https://doi.org/10.1177/0265532217713045

Eguchi, M., & Kyle, K. (2020). Continuing to explore the multidimensional nature of lexical sophistication: The case of oral proficiency interviews. *The Modern Language Journal, 104*(2), 381–400. https://doi.org/10.1111/modl.12637

Fellbaum, C. (Ed.) (1998). *WordNet: An electronic lexical database*. The MIT Press. https://doi.org/10.7551/mitpress/7287.001.0001

Gardner, D. (2008). Validating the construct of word in applied corpus-based vocabulary research: A critical survey. *Applied Linguistics, 28*(2), 241–65. https://doi.org/10.1093/applin/amm010

Gilquin, G. (2022). The *process corpus of English in education*: Going beyond the written text. *Research in Corpus Linguistics, 10*(1), 31–44. https://doi.org/10.32714/ricl.10.01.02

Godfroid, A. (2020). Sensitive measures of vocabulary knowledge and processing. In S. Webb (Ed.), *The Routledge handbook of vocabulary studies* (pp. 433–53). Routledge. https://doi.org/10.4324/9780429291586-28

Goldberg, A. E. (2006). *Constructions at work: The nature of generalization in language*. Oxford University Press.

Gries, S. T., & Ellis, N. C. (2015). Statistical measures for usage-based linguistics. *Language Learning, 65*(S1), 228–55. https://doi.org/10.1111/lang.12119

Halliday, M. A. K., & Hasan, R. (1976). *Cohesion in English*. Longman.

Hoffman, P., Lambon-Ralph, M. A., & Rogers, T. T. (2013). Semantic diversity: A measure of semantic ambiguity based on variability in the contextual usage of words. *Behavior Research Methods, 45*, 718–30. https://doi.org/10.3758/s13428-012-0278-x

Hou, J., Verspoor, M., & Loerts, H. (2016). An exploratory study into the dynamics of Chinese L2 writing development. *Dutch Journal of Applied Linguistics, 5*(1), 65–96. https://doi.org/10.1075/dujal.5.1.04loe

Hyland, K. (2008). Academic clusters: Text patterning in published and postgraduate writing. *International Journal of Applied Linguistics, 18*(1), 41–62. https://doi.org/10.1111/j.1473-4192.2008.00178.x

Jarvis, S. (2013a). Capturing the diversity in lexical diversity. *Language Learning, 63*, 87–106. https://doi.org/10.1111/j.1467-9922.2012.00739.x

Jarvis, S. (2013b). Defining and measuring lexical diversity. In S. Jarvis & M. Daller (Eds.), *Vocabulary knowledge: Human ratings and automated measures* (pp. 13–43). John Benjamins. https://doi.org/10.1075/sibil.47.03ch1

Jarvis, S. (2017). Grounding lexical diversity in human judgments. *Language Testing, 34*(4), 537–53. https://doi.org/10.1177/0265532217710632

Kim, M., Crossley, S. A., & Kyle, K. (2018). Lexical sophistication as a multidimensional phenomenon: Relations to second language lexical proficiency, development, and writing quality. *The Modern Language Journal, 102*(1), 120–41. https://doi.org/10.1111/modl.12447

Kojima, M., & Yamashita, J. (2014). Reliability of lexical richness measures based on word lists in short second language productions. *System, 42*, 23–33. https://doi.org/10.1016/j.system.2013.10.019

Koutsoftas, A. D., & Gray, S. (2012). Comparison of narrative and expository writing in students with and without language-learning disabilities. *Language, Speech and Hearing Services in Schools, 43*, 395–409. https://doi.org/10.1044/0161-1461(2012/11-0018)

Kyle, K. (2020). Measuring lexical richness. In S. Webb (Ed.), *The Routledge handbook of vocabulary studies* (pp. 454–76): Routledge. https://doi.org/10.4324/9780429291586-29

Kyle, K. (2021). Lexis. In N. Tracy-Ventura & M. Paquot (Eds.), *The Routledge handbook of second language acquisition and corpora* (pp. 332–44). Routledge. https://doi. org/10.4324/9781351137904-29

Kyle, K., & Crossley, S. A. (2015). Automatically assessing lexical sophistication: Indices, tools, findings, and application. *TESOL Quarterly, 49*(4), 757–86. https://doi.org/10.1002/tesq.194

Kyle, K., & Crossley, S. A. (2016). The relationship between lexical sophistication and independent and source-based writing. *Journal of Second Language Writing, 34*, 12–24. https:// doi.org/10.1016/j.jslw.2016.10.003

Kyle, K., Crossley, S. A., & Berger, C. M. (2018). The tool for the automatic analysis of lexical sophistication (TAALES): Version 2.0. *Behavior Research Methods, 50*, 1030–46. https://doi.org/10.3758/s13428-017-0924-4

Laufer, B., & Nation, P. (1995). Vocabulary size and use: Lexical richness in L2 written production. *Applied Linguistics, 16*(3), 307–22. https://doi.org/10.1093/applin/16.3.307

Leńko-Szymańska, A. (2020). *Defining and assessing lexical proficiency*. Routledge. https://doi. org/10.4324/9780429321993

Lorenzo, F., & Rodríguez, L. (2014). Onset and expansion of L2 cognitive academic language proficiency in bilingual settings: CALP in CLIL. *System, 47*, 64–72. https://doi. org/10.1016/j.system.2014.09.016

Malvern, D., & Richards, B. (1997). A new measure of lexical diversity. In A. Ryan & A. Wray (Eds.), *Evolving models of language* (pp. 58–71). Multilingual Latters.

McCarthy, P. M., & Jarvis, S. (2010). MTLD, voc-D, and HD-D: A validation study of sophisticated approaches to lexical diversity assessment. *Behavior Research Methods, 42*(2), 381–92. https://doi.org/10.3758/BRM.42.2.381

Meara, P., & Bell, H. (2001). P-Lex: A simple and effective way of describing the lexical characteristics of short L2 texts. *Prospect, 16*(3), 5–19.

Nation, P. (2013). *Learning vocabulary in another language*. Cambridge University Press. https:// doi.org/10.1017/CBO9781139858656

Nation, P. (2016). *Making and using word lists for language learning and testing*. John Benjamins. https://doi.org/10.1075/z.208

Olinghouse, N. G., & Leaird, J. T. (2009). The relationship between measures of vocabulary and narrative writing quality in second- and fourth-grade students. *Reading and Writing, 22*, 545–65. https://doi.org/10.1007/s11145-008-9124-z

Olinghouse, N. G., & Wilson, J. (2013). The relationship between vocabulary and writing quality in three genres. *Reading and Writing: An Interdisciplinary Journal, 26*, 45–65. https://doi.org/10.1007/s11145-012-9392-5

Perfetti, C. A., & Hart, L. (2002). The lexical quality hypothesis. In L. Verhoeven, C. Elbro, & P. Reitsma (Eds.), *Precursors of functional literacy* (pp. 189–213). John Benjamins. https:// doi.org/10.1075/swll.11.14per

Peters, E. (2020). Factors affecting the learning of single-word items. In S. Webb (Ed.), *The Routledge Handbook of Vocabulary Studies* (pp. 125–42): Routledge. https://doi. org/10.4324/9780429291586-9

Richards, B., & Malvern, D. (2010). Validity and threats to the validity of vocabulary measurement. In H. Daller, J. Milton, & J. Treffers-Daller (Eds.), *Modelling and assessing vocabulary knowledge* (pp. 79–92). Cambridge University Press. https://doi.org/10.1017/ CBO9780511667268.007

Richards, J. C. (1976). The role of vocabulary teaching. *TESOL Quarterly, 10*(1), 77–89. https://doi.org/10.2307/3585941

Roessingh, H., Douglas, S., & Wojtalewicz, B. (2016). Lexical standards for expository writing at grade 3: The transition from early literacy to academic literacy. *Language and Literacy, 18*(3), 123–44. https://doi.org/10.20360/G2W59P

Schmitt, N. (2014). Size and depth of vocabulary knowledge: What the research shows. *Language Learning, 64*(4), 913–51. https://doi.org/10.1111/lang.12077

Segalowitz, N., & Hulstijn, J. H. (2005). Automaticity in bilingualism and second language learning. In J. F. Kroll & A. M. B. De Groot (Eds.), *Handbook of bilingualism: psycholinguistic approaches* (pp. 371–88). Oxford University Press.

Sinclair, J. (2020). *Using machine learning to predict children's reading comprehension from lexical and syntactic features extracted from spoken and written language.* [Doctoral dissertation, University of Toronto].

Spencer, S., Clegg, J., Stackhouse, J., & Rush, R. (2017). Contribution of spoken language and socio-economic background to adolescents' educational achievement at age 16 years. *International Journal of Language & Communication Disorders, 52*(2), 184–96. https://doi.org/10.1111/1460-6984.12264

Townsend, D., Filippini, A., Collins, P., & Biancarosa, G. (2012). Evidence for the importance of academic word knowledge for the academic achievement of diverse middle school students. *The Elementary School Journal, 112*(3), 497–518. https://doi.org/10.1086/663301

Treffers-Daller, J., Parslow, P., & Williams, S. (2018). Back to basics: How measures of lexical diversity can help discriminate between CEFR levels. *Applied Linguistics, 39*(3), 302–27.

Trenkic, D., & Warmington, M. (2019). Language and literacy skills of home and international university students: How different are they, and does it matter? *Bilingualism: Language and Cognition, 22*(2), 349–65. https://doi.org/10.1017/S136672891700075X

Verspoor, M., Lowie, W., Chan, H. P., & Vahtrick, L. (2017). Linguistic complexity in second language development: Variability and variation at advanced stages. *Recherches en Didactique des Langues et des Cultures, 14*(1), 1–27. https://doi.org/10.4000/rdlc.1450

Wilson, M. (1988). MRC psycholinguistic database: Machine-usable dictionary, version 2.00. *Behavior Research Methods, Instruments & Computers, 20*(1), 6–10. https://doi.org/10.3758/BF03202594

4

VOCABULARY RESEARCH IN PRACTICE

Diversity and academic vocabulary

4.1 Introduction

In this chapter, we will see how two different types of vocabulary analysis can be carried out using R. If you have downloaded the GiG corpus (see Chapter 2, Sections 2.5), it will be possible to follow along with the steps set out for each analysis. However, it should also be possible to adapt the methods in this chapter to any appropriately formatted learner corpus you are using (see Chapter 2, Sections 2.4, 2.5, and 2.6 for guidance on preparing your own corpus). Section 4.2 will look at measuring vocabulary diversity, something that can be achieved using only a learner corpus. Section 4.3 will then show how corpus-external information can be integrated into an analysis. Specifically, it employs a reference list of academic words to explore the use of those words in a learner corpus.

In this chapter and in Chapters 6 and 8, I will present R scripts broken down into chunks for ease of explanation. Screenshots of the scripts themselves appear in hierarchically numbered boxes (e.g., *Script 4.2.1.a*). The first number in the boxes' titles (e.g., *4.2.1.a*) refers to the chapter in which the script appears. The second number (*4.2.1.a*) refers to the section within the chapter. So, 4.2.1.a is within Section 2 of Chapter 4. Each section discusses a different analysis. In the current chapter, for example, all scripts starting *4.2* are part of an analysis of vocabulary diversity, while all scripts starting *4.3* are part of an analysis of academic vocabulary. I would advise creating a separate script in RStudio for each of these main sections. So, in the current chapter, I would suggest creating one script for the analysis of diversity and then creating a second script when you get to the analysis of academic vocabulary (see Chapter 2, Section 2.3.2 if you need to revise opening a new script).

Each main section is further broken down into a series of tasks that need to be accomplished within the analysis. Section 4.2, for example, comprises four subsections: "Getting the Metadata and Corpus Filenames," "Generating CTTR Scores,"

DOI: 10.4324/9781003152682-6

"Recording the Results," and "Analyzing Vocabulary Diversity." These subsections are reflected in the third digit in the script numbers (e.g., *4.2.1.a*). These should be thought of as coherent sections within a script, rather than as separate scripts. Finally, individual commands or groups of commands that need explanation within each subsection are represented (where they exist) with a lower-case letter (e.g., *4.2.1.a*). These make it easier to refer to individual commands in the script that I want to explain.

As well as the hierarchically numbered *scripts*, the text includes some additional snippets of R commands, either in the main text or in numbered *figures*. These additional snippets are not part of the main scripts that we are creating and so should not be entered as such. If you want to try these out to confirm how they work (which I would recommend), you can enter them in the Console window, rather than in the script window, where the main action will be happening (see Chapter 2, Section 2.3.2 if you need to revise the different ways of entering commands into R).

Finally, remember that it is very easy to make mistakes when copying code into R. A missing comma, apostrophe, or parenthesis; an incorrectly entered symbol; or a letter entered as upper, rather than lower, case can be very difficult to spot but is likely to stop your script from working or to make it work in unexpected ways. It is therefore important to check your code carefully. If you get stuck, I would advise running the script line by line to identify where the problem is. If you really hit a brick wall, complete versions of the scripts are available for download (see the supplementary materials at www.routledge.com/9780367715786 for information on accessing these).

4.2 Measuring vocabulary diversity

This section will illustrate how lexical diversity can be studied in a learner corpus using R. As discussed in Chapter 3 (Section 3.2.1), lexical diversity is one of the most widely used and reliable indicators of development in learner writing, and many different measures have been proposed. Here, we will use the CTTR to quantify diversity in the GIG corpus.

4.2.1 Getting the metadata and corpus filenames

We will use metadata for two main purposes in this analysis. First, we will use it to identify the filenames of the corpus texts we want to look at. Second, we will use it to classify texts according to their text type (genre) and learner level (year group) so that we can look for differences across those variables. At this point, it will be worth revisiting Chapter 2 (Sections 2.4 and 2.5) to make sure you have a metadata file that is correctly formatted and that includes the necessary information.

You will recall from Chapter 2 (Section 2.2) that I recommended storing your metadata file in a subfolder called 'corpora', which itself should be placed within the overall CLWD' folder. On my (MacOS) computer, I have placed the CLWD folder directly into my home directory. We can make life easier for ourselves at later stages in the process by specifying that CLWD should be our 'working directory' – the starting place from which we direct R to find all files. In Script 4.2.1.a, I have used the *setwd()* function to do this. Note that the '~' mark is shorthand that directs R to my home directory, so '~/CLWD' means 'the CLWD folder, within the home directory'.

SCRIPT 4.2.1.a   SET THE WORKING DIRECTORY

```
setwd('~/CLWD')
```

My metadata is stored in the 'corpora' folder in .csv format, so to read the metadata into R, we use the *read.csv()* function, as illustrated in Script 4.2.1.b. Note that this function has taken two arguments. The first is the pathname and filename of the metadata spreadsheet. Because the working directory has already been set as 'CLWD', we can start from there and specify the pathname as 'corpora/metadata. csv'. The second argument is *header = T*. This is used to indicate that the first row in the metadata spreadsheet contains column headings. The assignment operator ('<-') is then used to store the metadata under the name *metadata*. Once this step has been performed, typing *metadata* into the Console will show you the full contents of the metadata.

SCRIPT 4.2.1.b   READ CORPUS METADATA INTO R

```
metadata <- read.csv('corpora/metadata_gig.csv', header = T)
```

Note that *metadata* is stored as a type of structure we have not seen before, but that we will use a lot throughout this book: a data frame. You will recall that our metadata has been read from a spreadsheet. Data frames are a good way of handling such data. Data frames can be thought of as a series of vectors placed side by side, with each vector representing one column in the spreadsheet (now might be the time to revise Chapter 2, Section 2.3.4 if you need a reminder about vectors). So the *metadata* data frame comprises the vectors 'batch_id', 'text_id', 'file_id', 'year_group', etc.

We can access individual columns in the data frame using that frame's name (in the current case, *metadata*), followed by a dollar sign ($) and the name of the column. For example, the *year_group* column could be accessed by typing *metadata$year_group*. Script 4.2.1.c uses this to create a new vector (called *filenames*) that stores the contents of the *file_id* column.

SCRIPT 4.2.1.c   RETRIEVE FILE NAMES FOR THE CORPUS FROM THE METADATA

```
filenames <- metadata$file_id
```

If you type *filenames* into the Console after executing 4.2.1c, you will see that this vector now contains the names of each text in the corpus (note that these file-names do not include the file extension.*txt*. We will get to that shortly). If your corpus is large, this will output a long list of filenames that would be tedious to scroll through. It is possible to look at just one filename, or a set of filenames, by asking R to show you the names at particular places in the vector. For example, the command *filenames[1]* will return just the first item in the vector, as shown in Figure 4.1.

```
> filenames[1]
[1] "1_1"
```

FIGURE 4.1   Viewing the first element in the *filenames* vector

Returning to our analogy of these vectors as columns in a spreadsheet, the first position in this vector corresponds to the first row in the *file_id* column. Note that, as well as accessing individual entries, it is possible to access ranges of entries (e.g., rows 3 to 6) by typing the positions of the beginning and end of the range, separated by a colon (Figure 4.2).

```
> filenames[3:6]
[1] "1_3"   "1_4"   "1_5"   "2_6a"
```

FIGURE 4.2   Viewing elements 3 to 6 in the *filenames* vector

Or we can access several non-sequential entries using the *c()* (*combine*) function. The following, for example, gives us the first, third, and sixth rows (Figure 4.3).

```
> filenames[c(1,3,6)]
[1] "1_1"   "1_3"   "2_6a"
```

FIGURE 4.3   Viewing elements 1, 3, and 6 in the *filenames* vector

Accessing parts of a vector using square brackets like this is known as *subsetting* and will be important in much of what follows.

4.2.2 Generating CTTR scores

Our first move in generating CTTR scores is to create a new (empty) vector, called *CTTR*, as shown in Script 4.2.2.a. This will be used to store the diversity values for each text. It can be thought of as an additional (currently empty) column that will be appended to the metadata. Like the other columns, each row (i.e., each position in the vector) will include information about one text (i.e., that text's CTTR value).

SCRIPT 4.2.2.a   CREATE AN EMPTY VECTOR TO STORE CTTR SCORES

```
CTTR <- vector()
```

We now get to the core of our task – generating CTTR values for each text. CTTR is calculated as:

$$CTTR = \frac{types}{\sqrt{2 * tokens}}$$

We, therefore, need to find the number of types and the number of tokens in each text in the corpus, perform the calculation, and record the outcome in the new *CTTR* vector. The chunk of script used to do this takes several lines and will enable us to learn about several important functions. I will first present the chunk in full (Script 4.2.2.b–h) and then discuss each of its parts in more detail. For ease of reading, I would recommend entering the whole chunk as it is shown in 4.2.2b-h before reading the explanation that follows.

SCRIPT 4.2.2.b–h   CALCULATE AND RECORD CTTR FOR EACH TEXT

```
# b) start a loop so the process below is repeated for each text
for (i in 1:length(filenames)){
    # c) open the text
    text <- scan(file=paste('corpora/GIG_texts/', filenames[i], '.txt', sep=''),
            what = 'char', sep='\n')
    # d) divide the text into tokens
    tokens <- unlist(strsplit(text, '\\W+'))
    # e) convert the text to lower case
    tokens_lower <- tolower(tokens)
    # f) group tokens into types
    types <- unique(tokens_lower)
    # g) calculate CTTR
    CTTR[i] <- length(types) / sqrt (2 * length (tokens))
    # h) close the loop
}
```

You should keep a few things in mind when doing this:

- When you open the curly brackets at Point b, RStudio will automatically create the close bracket immediately to its right. Points c–g should be entered between these open and close brackets so that the close bracket is the final point in this Script (Point h).
- You will note that Points c–g are indented from the left-hand side. When you put your curser between the curly brackets and press Enter to move to the next line, your curser should indent automatically.
- Do not attempt to run this script until you have entered all of b–h. Once the chunk is complete, R will be able to work with it as a single chunk.
- I have included comments (accompanied by a #) to introduce each point. Although these are not essential to the running of the script, it is good practice to include them so that you (and any others who read the script) can see what each part is intended to do.

This chunk uses a concept that will be essential throughout the remainder of this book: looping. Loops tell R to repeat the same set of procedures a given number of times. In the current case, we need this because we want to carry out the procedures for calculating CTTR separately for each text. This is achieved using the *for()* function, which has the structure:

```
for (i in a range of values){
        carry out this procedure for i
        }
```

If, for example, the 'range of values' is set as 'from 1 to 10', this loop will first carry out the procedures within the curly brackets while taking the value of 'i' to be 1. This means that, wherever we write 'i' in our script, R will understand us to mean 1. Once the procedures have been completed, it will then carry out the same procedures taking the value of 'i' to be 2, then 3, and so on up to i = 10. Once it has carried out the procedures with i=10, R will exit the loop and move on to the next part of the script.

In the current case, we want to calculate CTTR once for every file listed in the *filenames* vector we have already created (that is, for each text in the corpus). We have seen that we can access the name of each file by entering *filenames[1]*, *filenames[2]*, etc. So, what we want is a loop that will first set 'i' as 1, use this to access the first filename and calculate CTTR for that file, then do the same thing for i=2, i=3, etc., until it gets to the last text in the corpus.

This presents the question of how we know when the loop should end: what is the number of the final item in *filenames*? To learn this, we could just look at the corpus to check the number of files. For example, I know that there are 2,825 files in my corpus, so the range of values for the for-loop should be 'i = 1:2825'. The problem with doing it this way is that I will need to go back and change this part of the function each time I use a different corpus (or if I need to add or remove items from my current corpus). This is both annoying and easy to forget, so it can lead to mistakes. It is therefore helpful if we can build an automatic way of checking the number of files into our function. This can be done using the *length()* function, which we met in Chapter 2. The command *length(filenames)* will return the number of items in *filenames* – that is, 2,825. Thus, rather than using *for(i in 1:2825)*, our function looks like this:

```
for(i in 1:length(filenames)){
  carry out this procedure
  }
```

The first line of this function appears in the script at Point b.

We now move to the part within curly brackets, which tells R what the actual procedure is. The first line (labelled *b* in the script) opens a corpus file. As we know, within our loop, 'i' represents a number: first 1, then 2, etc., up to 2,825. We can use this fact to access each of the corpus texts in turn using subsetting. Specifically, the command *filenames[i]* will mean *filenames[1]* on the first iteration of the loop, *filenames[2]* on the second, etc. As we saw earlier, each of these will return one filename from the corpus (in the current case, '1_1', '1_2', etc.).

To open each text, however, it will not be enough simply to tell R the name of that text. We also need to give it a file extension ('.txt') and a pathname so that it knows in which folder on our computer the text can be found. Thus, the full reference needed for text '1_1' on my computer is 'corpora/GiG_texts/1_1.txt'.

This can be achieved using the *paste()* function. *paste()* allows us to combine a series of items into a single string, as Figure 4.4 illustrates.

```
> paste('one', 'two', 'three', sep = ' ')
[1] "one two three"
```

FIGURE 4.4 The *paste()* function

This has taken the three separate items 'one', 'two', and 'three', and combined them into a single string 'one two three'. Note that the *sep* = ' ' argument tells R what should be placed between the items – in the current case, a single whitespace. Thus, if we change this to, '_', or if we put nothing between the two quotation marks (*sep* = '') we get the results shown in Figure 4.5.

```
> paste('one', 'two', 'three', sep='_')
[1] "one_two_three"
> paste('one', 'two', 'three', sep='')
[1] "onetwothree"
```

FIGURE 4.5 The effects of changing the *sep* argument

For our task of specifying a path + filename, we need to combine a pathname with a specified filename and a file extension, with no spaces between them.

The pathname and file extension are the same for all texts, whereas the filename will be different (*1_1*, *1_2*, etc.). We saw in Figures 4.1–4.3 that filenames can be retrieved from the vector *filenames* using square brackets and the position of the required name in that vector. Thus, we could create the required pathname + filename + file extension for the first file in the corpus using the code shown in Figure 4.6.

```
> paste('corpora/GIG_texts/', filenames[1], '.txt', sep='')
[1] "corpora/GIG_texts/1_1.txt"
```

FIGURE 4.6 Specifying path + filename for the first corpus file

A similar combination could be specified for the second file in the corpus by changing the number in square brackets, as shown in Figure 4.7.

```
> paste('corpora/GIG_texts/', filenames[2], '.txt', sep='')
[1] "corpora/GIG_texts/1_2.txt"
```

FIGURE 4.7 Specifying path + filename for the second corpus file

We saw in Script 4.2.1.b that '.csv' files can be opened using the *read.csv()* function. For .txt files containing text corpora, we instead use the *scan()* function. As arguments, we need to include the pathname, information about 'what' type of data is contained in the files (in the current case, this is 'characters' – i.e., letters, numbers, and symbols), and information about how the text should be separated into units. For our purposes, it is best to divide units wherever there is a newline ('\n') marker. We could therefore open the first text in our corpus and assign it to the vector 'text' with the command shown in Figure 4.8.

```
> text <- scan(file = 'corpora/GIG_texts/1_1.txt', what = 'char', sep = '\n')
```

FIGURE 4.8 Reading a corpus text into R

Combining this with what we learned about pasting material and about using the value 'i' to represent a number from 1 to 2,825, depending on where the loop has reached, we get the line shown at Point c in Script 4.2.2 and reproduced in Figure 4.9.

```
# c) open the text
text <- scan(file=paste('corpora/GIG_texts/', filenames[i], '.txt', sep=''),
             what = 'char', sep='\n')
```

FIGURE 4.9 Reading a corpus file with a loop (Script 4.2.2.c)

We can paraphrase this command as *scan* the file that results from pasting 'filenames[i]' into the pathname/file extension, and assign that text to the vector 'text'.

Now that we have our text loaded, the next step is to divide it into tokens (Point d). As we discussed in Chapter 3 (Section 3.1), the question of how word tokens should be identified is a complex one. Here, we will take the relatively straightforward approach of dividing the text wherever something other than a letter or number appears. That is, the text will be divided at all blank spaces and at punctuation marks. Forms like *can't* and *part-time* will, therefore, be counted as two words each. We can do this using the *strsplit()* function. This takes two arguments: the text to be split and the character at which we should split it. We know that the text to be split is called 'text', so this will be the first argument. But what of the second argument? How do we tell R to make the split wherever it finds something other than a non-letter? To understand this, we need a basic understanding of *regular expressions*.

Regular expressions are special codes that R will understand to represent specific items, or sets of items, in a text. To take a simple example, in regular expressions, the full-stop character has the meaning *any character except a newline*. So the regular expression *s..p* would identify any letter string in which *s* is followed by two further characters, then by *p*. So, it would find, for example, *shop, slip, soup, ship* and *swap*. Note that it will find this letter combination even if it doesn't form a whole word. It would identify, for example, the *sapp* found in the middle of *disappear* and the *scip* in *discipline*.

In this book, we will use a very limited repertoire of regular expressions (for a fuller treatment, I would urge readers to check the excellent introduction in Gries, 2017; a quick internet search will also yield many detailed guides). In addition to the items mentioned in the previous paragraph, we will use '+', '*', '\\W', and '^'.

- '+' means that the previous expression may occur once or may appear more than once. Thus, *s..f+* would mean '*s*, followed by two other characters, then at least one appearance of *f*. This would identify, for example, *self, stuff,* and *staff*.
- '*' (asterisk) means that the previous expression may occur zero or more times. Thus *likes** would identify *like, likes,* and even *likesss*.
- '\\W' means anything other than a letter or number. So, this will find, for example, punctuation marks, symbols, and white space.
- '^' marks the beginning of a line of text. So, '^John' will only find the word 'John' if it is at the start of a new line.

We said previously that we want to tokenize by splitting the text wherever a non-alphanumeric character appears. We can use the '\\W' character (i.e., 'anything other than a letter or number') for this job. Because more than one such character may occur in succession (e.g., a sentence break is usually marked by both a punctuation mark and a white space), we also use '+' so that multiple splits aren't made in such cases. Thus, our *strsplit()* command is as shown in Figure 4.10.

```
strsplit(text, '\\W+')
```

FIGURE 4.10 Using *strsplit()* to identify word tokens

This command will not give us exactly what we need, however. So far, we have been storing our text in R as a vector. However, the output of *strsplit()* is a different type of structure (a list, which we will learn more about later). Therefore, to convert this output back into a vector, we embed *strsplit()* inside a second function, *unlist()*, which will convert its output back into the vector format we want. Thus, the full command is as shown in Figure 4.11 (which reproduces Point d from the script).

```
# d) divide the text into tokens
tokens <- unlist(strsplit(text, '\\W+'))
```

FIGURE 4.11 Dividing a text into tokens (Script 4.2.2.d)

This will give us a vector, called *tokens*, in which each item is a word token from the text. Thus, the start of *tokens* for the final text in the GiG corpus looks like Figure 4.12 (note that I've used the final text in the corpus as my example because if you run the whole for-loop shown in Script 4.2.2b–h, this will be the text that R has open after the loop has completed).

```
> tokens[1:5]
[1] "Should"    "children" "walk"     "to"       "school"
```

FIGURE 4.12 Tokens from a GiG text

To calculate CTTR, we need to know the number of tokens and the number of types in the text. We can use the *length()* function that we encountered in Chapter 2 to find out how many tokens there are, as shown in Figure 4.13.

```
> length(tokens)
[1] 150
```

FIGURE 4.13 Using *length()* to count the word tokens in a text

But what about types? To find the number of types, we want to know how many unique items there are in the *tokens* vector. Before taking things any further though, it is important to remember that R is very literal in the way it treats text. If it came across the tokens *The* (at the start of a sentence) and *the* (in the middle of the sentence), for example, these would be treated as two different items because they are not identical (i.e., one is capitalized and the other is not). Before telling R to find unique types, therefore, it is a good idea to convert all tokens to lower case. R has a handy function, *tolower()*, that will do this for us (Point e in the script, reproduced in Figure 4.14).

```
# e) convert the text to lower case
tokens_lower <- tolower(tokens)
```

FIGURE 4.14 Converting tokens to lower case (Script 4.2.2.e)

We can now use this to find types. The function *unique()* removes duplicate entries in a vector to provide a new vector of unique types (Point f in the script, reproduced in Figure 4.15).

```
# f) group tokens into types
types <- unique(tokens_lower)
```

FIGURE 4.15 Using *unique()* to create a vector of word types (Script 4.2.2.f)

Like tokens, the total number of types can then be calculated using the *length()* function, as shown in Figure 4.16.

```
> length(types)
[1] 62
```

FIGURE 4.16 Using *length()* to count the word types in a text

Now that we have vectors for both tokens and types, we are ready to calculate CTTR. We know that this is done using the formula:

$$CTTR = \frac{types}{\sqrt{2 * tokens}}$$

We also know the commands that will give us the numbers to fill out this formula: i.e., *length(tokens)* and *length(types))*. We can bring all of this together to create a single command to find CTTR for the text, as shown in Figure 4.17.

```
> length(types) / sqrt(2* length(tokens))
[1] 3.579572
```

FIGURE 4.17 Calculating CTTR

Remember that we want to record this value into the 'CTTR' vector that we created in Script 4.2.2.a. Specifically, we want to record it to the i'th position in that vector. That is, for the first text, we record it to the 1st position (CTTR[1]), for the second text we record it to the second position (CTTR[2]) etc. Because the variable 'i' is keeping tabs on which text we have gotten to, we can ask R to record the result to 'CTTR[i]', as shown in Figure 4.18 (which reproduces Point g in the script).

```
# g) calculate CTTR
CTTR[i] <- length(types) / sqrt (2 * length (tokens))
```

FIGURE 4.18 Calculating CTTR (Script 4.2.2.g)

This brings us to the end of the procedure for finding CTTR for the text. We finally close the loop using a right-hand curly bracket, which indicates that R should return to the beginning and start working on the next text listed in the *filenames* vector.

4.2.3 Recording the results

Having generated our CTTR scores, we can now append these to our metadata as an additional column. This can be done using the *cbind()* function, as shown in Script 4.2.3.a.

SCRIPT 4.2.3.a   APPEND CTTR SCORES TO THE METADATA

```
output <- cbind(metadata, CTTR)
```

Finally, we save our results to the *outputs* folder ready for further analysis (Script 4.2.3.b). For this, we can use the function *write.csv()*, which will save our output in a typical spreadsheet format. Once you have executed this, it is worth going to the outputs folder on your computer and opening the newly created file (.csv files are best opened in Microsoft Excel or similar) to make sure it looks right. I would recommend doing this each time you write a file in R.

SCRIPT 4.2.3.b   SAVE THE RESULTS TO THE *OUTPUTS* FOLDER FOR USE IN FUTURE ANALYSES

```
write.csv (output, file = 'output/lexical_diversity_CTTR.csv', row.names = F)
```

4.2.4 Analyzing vocabulary diversity

In the previous section, we created a spreadsheet that combined the metadata for our corpus with CCTR values for each text. We can now use this to study how CTTR differs across the variables we are interested in. Script 4.2.4.a starts by retrieving the data we created in Section 2.1.

SCRIPT 4.2.4.a   READ CTTR DATA FROM THE *OUTPUTS* FOLDER

```
data <- read.csv(file = 'output/lexical_diversity_CTTR.csv')
```

In Script 4.2.4.b, we give R some extra information to ensure it understands the order in which our level groups should be ranked. By default, R places groups in alphabetical/numeric order. So, for example, if the groups were *beginner, intermediate*, and *advanced*, the default order would be alphabetical (i.e., *advanced, beginner, intermediate*) which is unlikely to be what we want. The metadata from the GiG corpus mark learner groups as *Year_2*, *Year_6*, *Year_9*, and *Year_11*. Because the letters at the start of these names are identical, it would order them according to their numbers. At first glance, this looks fine, until we realize that R understands *11* as two ones, rather than as eleven. Thus, R would assume we want the order *Year_11*, *Year_2*, *Year_6*, *Year_9*.

To avoid this issue, we can tell R the order in which groups should appear using the *factor()* function. Specifically, we need to tell it that the *year_group* column should be treated as a factor (that is, a set of groups) with the levels: *Year_2*, *Year_6*, *Year_9* and *Year_11*, in that order.

SCRIPT 4.2.4.b   MAKE SURE THE LEVELS OF THE GROUPING VARIABLE ARE IN THE RIGHT ORDER

```
data$year_group <- factor(data$year_group,
                    levels = c('Year_2', 'Year_6', 'Year_9', 'Year_11'))
```

An effective way of uncovering patterns in data of this sort is to create a graph showing the mean value of CTTR at each learner level (in this case, the four year groups), like that shown in Figure 4.19. Because I expected the two different text genres in my corpus to differ in their vocabulary diversity, I have created different sets of means for each genre (note that the school writing in this corpus was divided into two genres: *literary*, which refers to children's creative writing, such as stories and poems, and *non-literary*, which refers to everything else – historical recounts, lab reports, book analyses, etc. See Durrant & Brenchley, 2019 for more information).

It is important to remember that mean scores by themselves can be misleading if there is a large amount of variation within a group. When variation is high, the mean can be a poor guide to the group as a whole and so differences between group means may not be meaningful. For this reason, I have also included error bars. These are the I-shaped vertical lines in the figure and show the 95% confidence interval of each mean value (that is, we can be 95% sure that the true value of the mean for the population that these texts were drawn from falls within this range).

Figure 4.19 shows that, as we had expected, CTTR tends to increase across year groups, with the largest increase from Year 2 to Year 6. We can also see that the increase is greatest in literary writing. Moreover, whereas CTTR in non-literary appears to level off after Year 6, it continues to increase in literary writing. It seems that these children exercised a much wider repertoire of vocabulary, and continued to expand that repertoire over a longer developmental period, in their stories than in their non-literary writing.

This figure was created using the *ggplot2* package. This is a powerful and flexible package for creating graphics in R that is well worth getting to grips with. Wickham (2016) is an excellent, easy-to-follow introduction to its features,

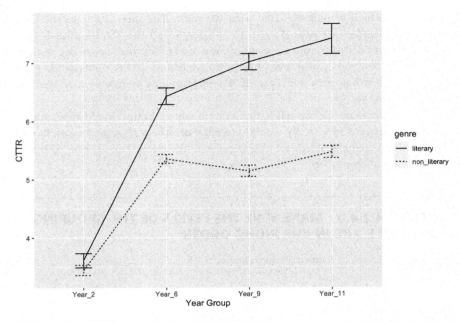

FIGURE 4.19 CTTR across year groups and genres

which is freely available online (https://ggplot2-book.org) and which I would urge readers to explore.

The script used to create Figure 4.19 starts by installing and loading the two packages (*ggplot2* and *Hmisc*) that are required for it to run. It will be recalled from Chapter 2 that a package is a suite of functions that can be added into R on request. Installing a package involves downloading it from an internet server and integrating it into R. This can be done within RStudio using the *install.packages()* function. Once a package has been installed, you will need to load it to make its functions available. This is achieved using the *library()* function (Script 4.2.4.c).

SCRIPT 4.2.4.c   INSTALL AND LOAD THE NECESSARY R PACKAGES

```
install.packages('ggplot2')
install.packages('Hmisc')
library(ggplot2)
library(Hmisc)
```

The code for creating Figure 4.19 is shown in Script 4.2.4.d. Executing this script will output the graph in the Plots tab, which is usually found in the bottom-right-hand corner of the RStudio window. The script involves four main elements that will:

- Give R basic information about the graph and the data that will go into it
- Create the lines that run from left to right, connecting the year group means
- Create the vertical error bars
- Create the x -and y-axis labels

SCRIPT 4.2.4.d   CREATE THE VISUAL

```
ggplot(data, aes(x = year_group, y = CTTR, linetype=genre)) +
    stat_summary(fun='mean', geom='line', aes(group=genre)) +
    stat_summary(fun.data='mean_cl_boot', geom='errorbar', width=.2) +
    labs(y="CTTR")+labs(x="Year Group")
```

The first line tells R that we will create a ggplot graph based on the information in *data* (which we loaded Script 4.2.4.a). It also tells it that the graph will be based on the *year_group*, *CTTR*, and *genre* columns, such that year_group is shown on the x (horizontal) axis, CTTR is on the y (vertical) axis, and genre is shown using different types of line (as can be seen in Figure 4.19, literary texts are shown with an unbroken line, non-literary texts with a broken line).

The second line uses the *stat_summary()* function to express that we do not want to display the individual CTTR scores of each text, but rather summarize those values by calculating their mean. It also specifies that these mean values should be calculated separately for each genre and that they should be represented in the graph using lines (as opposed to points, bars, etc.).

The third line adds in the error bars. It again shows that we want to summarize the data, but this time using a calculation labelled *mean_cl_boot*. This is a method for obtaining confidence intervals for a mean that will work even if our data are not normally distributed. The line also shows that this summary should be displayed in the form of error bars (i.e. I-shaped lines around the mean) and that the width of the horizontal bars at the top and bottom of these should be *.2*. I have used this last option because the default width setting produces much wider horizontal bars that made this particular graph look distractingly crowded (try omitting the width argument to see what I mean).

Finally, the fourth line shows that the x- and y-axes should be labelled *Year Group* and *CTTR*, respectively. If this line is left out, R will default to labelling the axes using the variable names (i.e., *CTTR*, and *year_group*). Adding this information is especially useful when the variable names in your data may not be meaningful to your readers or may be in a format that you don't want to use in your graph (e.g., *year_group* did not look very pretty on the graph, so I decided to specify the label as *Year Group*).

As noted, the graph will appear in the 'Plots' tab on the right-hand side of the RStudio window. Usually, we will also want to save a copy of the graph so that we can re-use it in presentations or publications. The *ggsave()* function shown in Script 4.2.4.e allows us to do this – in this case saving the graph in .jpeg format.

SCRIPT 4.2.4.e   SAVE THE VISUAL TO THE *OUTPUTS* FOLDER

```
ggsave('output/CTTR_lem_line_graph.jpeg')
```

This section has aimed to illustrate how one type of lexical diversity analysis can be used to give insights into a corpus of learner writing. There is, of course, much more to explore on this topic. As Chapter 3 described, there is a lively ongoing debate about how diversity is best quantified. In a fuller analysis, therefore, a range of different measures might be implemented, and their effectiveness in capturing the construct of diversity evaluated. As throughout this book, I have also not touched on the topic of statistical analysis, which requires a book-length treatment in its own right. However, I hope this section has given a practical introduction to how diversity analyses can be performed. Perhaps more importantly, it has introduced several key R functions and techniques that will be used throughout the book and that should serve as a good foundation for your own learner corpus research. The next section will build on what we have learned here to introduce a rather different type of vocabulary analysis, focusing on academic vocabulary.

4.3 Studying academic vocabulary

In this section, we will add two important techniques to our repertoire: working with a POS-tagged corpus and integrating information from an outside reference source into our analyses. The particular reference source we will use is the list of academic vocabulary created by Gardner and Davies (2014), available from https://www.academicwords.info.[1] We will use this list to identify which words in our learner corpus are 'academic'. This will enable us to track changes in how much academic vocabulary is used across learner levels and text types. It will also enable us to create lists of which academic words are used at each level and in each text type. While our focus is on academic words, similar methods could be used to integrate any type of word list into an analysis (e.g., high-frequency words, discipline-specific words, words characteristic of conversational speech). The functionality of the R scripts that follow is similar to that of tools like Range and AntWordProfiler,[2] but they have the advantages of enabling us to customize the way we identify words, and to directly integrate our corpus searches into the subsequent graphical and statistical analysis.

	A	B	C	D	E	F	G
1	word	PoS					
2	study	n					
3	group	n					
4	system	n					
5	social	j					
6	provide	v					
7	however	r					
8	research	n					
9	level	n					
10	result	n					

FIGURE 4.20 Academic words in a spreadsheet

4.3.1 Preparing the list of academic vocabulary

We need first to access our reference list. As I noted in the previous section, the analysis here will use Gardner and Davies's *Academic Vocabulary List* (AVL), which at the time of writing is available from https://www.academicwords.info. Note that several different versions of the list are available on this site. We will be working with the *Academic "core" list*. The AVL arrives as a spreadsheet, with a row for each word and many columns giving different sorts of information for each word (you can find an explanation of each column in the spreadsheet's 'introduction'). For our purposes, however, the frequency information is not needed; we simply want to know what words appear on the list. We therefore only need the second and third columns – i.e., those showing *word* and *POS* (part of speech). To simplify our work, we can copy and paste these two columns into a new spreadsheet (see Figure 4.20), which should then be saved as a '.csv' file (in Microsoft Excel, this can be done by selecting 'csv' as the 'File Format' when saving). I have saved my copy of this file with the filename 'AVL_lemmas.csv' and stored it in the 'reference' folder on my computer (revisit Chapter 2, Section 2.2 if you need a reminder of the folder structure I am using).

Once the list of academic words has been stored in the reference folder, we can set our working directory and read the list into R, as shown in Script 4.3.1.a.

SCRIPT 4.3.1.a   READ VOCABULARY LIST FROM THE REFERENCE FOLDER

```
setwd('~/CLWD')
AVL <- read.csv('reference/AVL_lemmas.csv', header = T)
```

An important feature of this academic word list is that the words listed in the first column have been *lemmatized* (see Chapter 3, Section 3.4.2). Thus, the noun *group*, which is seen in the first row of Figure 4.3 refers to both the singular (*group*) and plural (*groups*) forms. Moreover, it is distinct from the verb form of *group*. The verb *group* gets its own separate entry (which can be found in the 1,251st row in the original spreadsheet). For our task of finding academic words in the learner corpus, this has two important consequences. First, we need to match the academic words with lemmatized versions of each word form in our corpus. There is no point in checking, for example, whether the word *groups* in our learner corpus is on the academic list. So, we will need to make sure such forms in the learner corpus are transformed into their headword forms. Second, it is not sufficient to check whether a particular headword form appears in the academic list. We need also to ensure that the POS of that headword matches what is on the list. For example, although the noun *study* appears on the academic list (see the first row of Figure 4.3), the verb *study* does not. This means that any procedure that marked every occurrence of *study* in the learner corpus as academic would be incorrect; we only want to count *study* when it appears as a noun. The crucial information we need, therefore, is not what items appear in the 'word' column of Figure 4.3, but what word + pos combinations are found in each row. In other words, to identify lemmas in our learner corpus that match the items on this list, we need to know both that they are spelled the same as the words in column A and that their POS match the code in column B. To do this, we will create a single vector that combines these two pieces of information. Script 4.3.1.b achieves this using the *paste()* function that we met earlier to join the two columns together, separated by an underscore. The resulting combinations are stored as 'AVL$lemma_pos'. Figure 4.21 shows the first ten entries. These are the items we will look for in the learner corpus.

```
> AVL$lemma_pos[1:10]
 [1] "study_n"    "group_n"    "system_n"   "social_j"   "provide_v"  "however_r"  "research_n"
 [8] "level_n"    "result_n"   "include_v"
```

FIGURE 4.21 Combined word + pos vector

SCRIPT 4.3.1.b CREATE A SINGLE VECTOR THAT COMBINES WORD AND POS

```
AVL$lemma_pos <- paste(AVL$word, AVL$PoS, sep='_')
```

4.3.2 Converting the parsed corpus to an easier-to-use format

Because we are working with lemmas, we need a version of the corpus that will show the headword form of each lemma, along with its POS. This will enable us to match the corpus content with the academic lemma list illustrated in Figure 4.21. For this purpose, the version of the corpus we used in Section 4.2 will not be sufficient. We need, rather, to use a corpus that has been annotated with POS information and that shows lemma headwords. To this end, I will use a version that has been parsed and tagged using the CoreNLP tool, as described in Chapter 2. The format in which the parsed corpus is provided has a few features that will make our analysis (and future analyses in this book) a little awkward, so it will be worth spending some time now converting this into a more convenient format. Specifically, we will add some meaningful column names, simplify the POS codes, and save the texts as .csv, rather than .conll files. I will present the full script segment first and then unpack its details. As in the previous section, you may find this section easier to follow if you first enter the full script and then read the explanation. Before getting into the script itself though, you will need to create a new, empty, folder within your 'corpora' folder. We will use this to store the new version of the corpus. This new folder should be named 'GiG_parsed'.

SCRIPT 4.3.2   CONVERT PARSED CORPUS

```
# a) get learner corpus metadata and file names
metadata <- read.csv('corpora/metadata_gig.csv', header = T)
filenames <- metadata$file_id
# b) start a loop to go through all files in the corpus
for (i in filenames){
  # c) read the corpus file
  text <- read.delim(paste('corpora/GiG_conll/', i, '.txt.conll', sep=''),
                sep='\t', header=F)
  # d) add column names
  colnames(text) <-c ('word_number', 'word', 'lemma', 'pos', 'ner', 'dep_on', 'dep')
  # e) simplify part of speech codes
  text$pos <- gsub('^J.*', 'j', text$pos)
  text$pos <- gsub('^N.*', 'n', text$pos)
  text$pos <- gsub('^RB.*', 'r', text$pos)
  text$pos <- gsub('^V.*', 'v', text$pos)
  # f) save the revised corpus file in a new folder
  write.csv(text, file=paste('corpora/GiG_parsed/', i, '.csv', sep=''),
          row.names=F)
# g) close the loop
}
```

This script starts in a way that should be familiar by now. That is, by opening the metadata and extracting a vector of file names. It then introduces a for-loop so that the following commands will be repeated for each text in the corpus separately.

It is important to note that the for-loop has been set up slightly differently here from previous examples. Up until now, we have used loops that cycle through a sequence of number values ('i = 1', 'i = 2', 'i = 3', etc.). This has been useful because we have been using the 'i' value for two different purposes: to identify the text that should be opened (the first text, second text, third text, etc.) and to identify at which position in a vector we should record results for that text. For example, in Section 4.2 of this chapter (Script 4.2.2), 'i' was used to show where in the 'CTTR' vector the CTTR score of each text should be recorded. This dual use of 'i' allowed us to ensure that the order of the new vector matched the order of the texts that we are studying. This, in turn, allowed us to confidently combine the new vectors/lists with information in our metadata.

In the present case, however, we are not creating any new vectors or lists. We are simply opening texts and creating a new version of them. We, therefore, do not need a single number to refer to both text and position. This enables us to use a simpler version of the for-loop. Rather than looping through a sequence of numbers, we loop through the file names themselves. Thus, rather than the familiar line shown in Figure 4.22.

```
for (i in 1:length(filenames)){
```

FIGURE 4.22 For-loop with numbers

we use the simpler version shown in Figure 4.23.

```
for (i in filenames){
```

FIGURE 4.23 For-loop without numbers

In this style of loop, the sequence is not '1', '2', '3', etc., but rather the names of the files, in the order they appear within the vector 'filenames'. For my corpus, that means '1_1', '1_2', '1_3', etc. Because the values of i are these filenames, rather than numbers indexing filenames, this allows us to simplify the instructions to read and write files. Thus, rather than specifying the filename in the way shown in Figure 4.24.

```
paste('corpora/GiG_parsed/', filenames[i], '.csv', sep=''), row.names=F)
```

FIGURE 4.24 Creating a file reference when 'i' represents a number

we can use the simpler version in Figure 4.25.

```
paste('corpora/GiG_parsed/', i, '.csv', sep=''), row.names=F)
```

FIGURE 4.25 Creating a file reference when 'i' represents a file name

Thus, Point c in the script is as shown in Figure 4.26.

```
# c) read the corpus file
text <- read.delim(paste('corpora/GiG_conll/', i, '.txt.conll', sep=''),
                   sep='\t', header=F)
```

FIGURE 4.26 Opening a file when 'i' represents a file name (Script 4.3.2.c)

You will notice that we are using a new function here (*read.delim()*). This performs a similar role to the *read.csv()* function we've been using up until now, but is more flexible, and so will work with our .conll files, whereas *read.csv()* will not. Like *read.csv()*, this function will store the file contents as a data frame. Note also that, whereas the files we have been working with until now have had column headings, the parsed texts do not; hence, the *header* argument is set to *F*(alse).

With the file open, the first change we will make is to add column names. This can be achieved using the *colnames()* functions, as shown in Point d. In the analysis that follows, only two of these columns ('lemma' and 'pos') will be relevant, but, for the sake of completeness, the full list is:[3]

- word_id: the number of the word within its sentence
- word: the original word form
- lemma: the headword of the word's lemma
- pos: the word's part of speech
- ner: named entities
- dep_on: the number of the word on which this word is dependent
- dep: the dependency relationship into which the word enters.

A slight issue with this parsed version of the corpus is that it uses a different set of POS codes from those in the AVL. Specifically, the parsed corpus uses Penn Treebank[4] codes, which make some fine-grained distinctions that aren't used in the AVL. On the Penn Treebank system, 'adjectives', for example, are divided into three different types: 'Adjective' (JJ), 'adjective, comparative', (JJR), and 'adjective, superlative' (JJS). The AVL, in contrast, uses a much simpler system, with a single code for each of the four lexical POS: 'j' = adjective; 'n' = noun; 'r' = adverb; 'v' = verb. Point b uses the regular expressions that we encountered in Section 4.2 (Script 4.2.2) to simplify the codes in the corpus, bringing them into line with the AVL's system.

It does this in conjunction with an extremely useful function that we haven't yet seen: *gsub()*. This performs a similar task to the 'find and replace' function of a word processor. Thus, for example, imagine the vector 'a' contains the names of students in my class, as in Figure 4.27.

```
> a <- c('Ann', 'Bob', 'Colin', 'Christopher', 'Debbie')
```

FIGURE 4.27 Vector of student names

Imagine I then discover that 'Bob' prefers to be known as *Robert*. We can update the list accordingly using *gsub()*. Within this function, we first specify the string we are looking for ('Bob'), then the string we would like to replace it with ('Robert'), and then the structure with which we are working ('a'). Thus Figure 4.28.

```
> b <- gsub('Bob', 'Robert', a)
```

FIGURE 4.28 Using *gsub()* to change an element

This will create a new vector ('b') with our revised student names, as shown in Figure 4.29.

```
> b
[1] "Ann"          "Robert"        "Colin"         "Christopher" "Debbie"
```

FIGURE 4.29 The revised vector

Point e in our script combines the *gsub()* function with regular expressions to identify any POS code starting with 'J' (including 'JJ', 'JJR', and 'JJS') and replacing them with the AVL-style code 'j'. Codes starting 'J' are identified with the expression '^J*' (see Section 4.2.2 if you need to revise regular expressions). Similar replacements are then made for codes starting 'R' (adverbs), 'N' (nouns), and 'V' (verbs).

With these adjustments made, we can save the text in .csv format using the *write. csv()* function (Point f in the script). I have decided to store the converted texts in a new subfolder within my corpus folder called 'GiG_parsed'. This will be the version of the corpus I use for the rest of the analysis.

4.3.3 Identifying AVL words in the learner corpus

To carry out the analysis, we first need to read in the corpus metadata and list the filenames, as shown in Script 4.3.3.a.

SCRIPT 4.3.3.a   READ CORPUS METADATA INTO R AND RETRIEVE FILENAMES

```
metadata <- read.csv('corpora/metadata_gig.csv', header = T)
filenames <- metadata$file_id
```

We then create two empty structures to store the results of our analyses (Script 4.3.3.b). The first ('AVL_percent') is a vector where we can record quantitative information about the number of AVL words in each text. This will work in the same way as the 'CTTR' vector we used in Section 4.2. The second is a type of structure we came across only briefly earlier: the list. Lists are very flexible structures in which each element can be a structure of another type. For example, the elements within a list might be vectors, data frames, or other lists. In the present analysis, we will use the 'text_AVL_lemmas' list to record which academic words were found in each text. That is, each element in the list will correspond to one text and each will comprise a vector showing which academic words were found in that text.

SCRIPT 4.3.3.b   CREATE EMPTY OUTPUT VECTOR AND LIST TO STORE RESULTS

```
AVL_percent <- vector()
text_AVL_lemmas <- list()
```

Script 4.3.3.c–k. is the real core of our task, where we identify the percentage of words in each text that are 'academic' and record those words so that we can inspect them later. This is a rather long section, so I will first present it in full and then unpack its parts.

SCRIPT 4.3.3.c–k IDENTIFY AND RECORD ACADEMIC WORDS IN EACH TEXT

```
# c) start a loop to go through all files in the corpus
for (i in 1:length(filenames)){
# d) read text
  text <- read.csv(paste('corpora/GiG_parsed/', filenames[i], '.csv', sep=''),
               stringsAsFactors = F)
# e) identify lexical words
  lexical_words <- c(which(text$pos == 'j' |
                           text$pos == 'n' |
                           text$pos == 'r' |
                           text$pos == 'v'))
# f) reduce text to lexical words only
  text <- text[lexical_words,]
# g) create lemma_pos combinations
  text$lemma_pos <- paste(tolower(text$lemma), text$pos, sep = '_')
# h) identify which lemmas are found on reference list
  AVL_lemmas <- which(text$lemma_pos %in% AVL$lemma_pos)
# i) quantify percentage of lemmas found on reference list
  AVL_percent[i] <- length(AVL_lemmas)/length(text$lemma_pos)
# j) save matching lemmas to list
  text_AVL_lemmas[[i]] <- text$lemma_pos[AVL_lemmas]
# k) close the loop
}
```

Because the analysis is carried out separately for each text, we start (Point c) by initiating a for-loop that will conduct all the following steps for each text in our corpus in turn. With the loop initiated, we first need to read each corpus text into R, using the *read.csv()* function (Point d). Note that this function has an additional argument that we haven't met before: *stringsAsFactors = T*. By default, when R finds character strings in a .csv file, it will assume that these represent group names (in R's jargon *factors*). So far, this has worked well for us. We saw in Section 4.2.4 how the strings 'Year_2', 'Year_6', etc., were treated as group names, which is exactly what we wanted. Now that we are reading in corpus texts, however, we want to treat the contents of the texts as just strings of characters, not as group names. By specifying that strings should not be treated as factors, we ensure that this doesn't happen.

Because the AVL only includes lexical words (adjectives, nouns, adverbs, and verbs), our analysis will use only these words in the learner corpus. We can identify lexical words using the *which()* function (Point e). This identifies which elements in a vector meet a specified condition. For example, we can ask which elements in the 'POS' column of a given text are adjectives (i.e., have a pos code of 'j') using the command in Figure 4.30.

```
> which(text$pos == 'j')
```

FIGURE 4.30 Identifying adjectives in a text

For the first text in my corpus, this gives the response shown in Figure 4.31, which indicates that the 16th, 34th, 89th, etc., words in the text are marked as adjectives. If you are following along with the GiG corpus and want to duplicate this, you can do so by first setting 'i' to 1 by entering **i <- 1** in the Console window, then running Point d in Script 4.3.3 to open the first text and, finally, executing the command in Figure 4.30.

```
[1]  16  34  89 103 138 139 157 164 173 200 215 224 250 256 268 272 273 287 294 321 333 337 363 397
[25] 401
```

FIGURE 4.31 Positions of adjectives in a text

Point e uses a slightly elaborated version of this technique to identify which words are *either* adjectives, *or* nouns, *or* adverbs, *or* verbs, as shown in Figure 4.32.

```
# e) identify lexical words
lexical_words <- c(which(text$pos == 'j' |
                         text$pos == 'n' |
                         text$pos == 'r' |
                         text$pos == 'v'))
```

FIGURE 4.32 Identifying lexical POS in a text (Script 4.3.3.e)

The ' | ' mark (note that this vertical line, or *pipe*, is usually located on the same key as the backslash on US or UK QWERTY keyboards) has the meaning of *or* and is used to separate the four possible conditions. The vector of numbers that is returned (and stored as 'lexical words') indicates the positions of words that meet any one of these conditions.

We can now use the vector of word positions in 'lexical_words' to specify that 'text' should be reduced only to these words using subsetting. Up to this point, we have used subsetting only to access parts of a vector. Thus, for example, if we have a vector 'a' comprising the names of students in a class, we can access specific elements in this vector, as shown in Figure 4.33.

```
> a <- c('Ann', 'Bob', 'Colin', 'Christopher', 'Debbie')
> a[2]
[1] "Bob"
```

FIGURE 4.33 Accessing part of a vector

However, in the present case, we are dealing not with a vector but with a data frame. This is different because, unlike a vector, a data frame has two dimensions. That is, it has both columns and rows. When specifying which elements of a data frame we want to access, we therefore, need to state both a column number and a row number. Figure 4.34 shows the first few rows of the data frame for the first text

```
> head(text)
  word_number    word  lemma pos ner dep_on      dep
1           1    Dear   Dear   n   0      2 compound
2           2  Editor Editor   n   0      6    nsubj
3           3       ,      ,       0      6    punct
4           4       I      I PRP   0      6    nsubj
5           5      am     be   v   0      6      aux
6           6 writing  write   v   0      0     ROOT
```

FIGURE 4.34   Text in a data frame

in my corpus (again, this is what you will get if you set **i <− 1** and then run Point d before executing the command in Figure 4.34).

If I wanted to access only the word 'be', in the lemma column, I would need to give both a row number (5) and a column number (3) (since the lemma column is the third from the left), as shown in Figure 4.35. Note that the row number comes first, the column number second.

```
> text[5,3]
[1] "be"
```

FIGURE 4.35   Accessing part of a data frame

What if I want to access an entire row or an entire column? We can do this by leaving one side of the comma blank. That is, if a row number is specified on the left of the comma but no column number is specified on the right, R will access the entire row, as shown in Figure 4.36.

```
> text[5,]
  word_number word lemma pos ner dep_on dep
5           5   am    be   v   0      6 aux
```

FIGURE 4.36   Accessing an entire row in a data frame

Conversely, if a column number is specified on the right of the comma but no row number is specified on the left, R will access the entire row, as shown in Figure 4.37 (I have included only the first few rows of the resultant output here).

```
> text[,3]
 [1] "Dear"       "Editor"      ","      "I"
 [5] "be"         "write"       "to"     "express"
 [9] "my"         "opposition"  "to"     "the"
```

FIGURE 4.37   Accessing an entire column in a data frame

In our current case, what we want to do is access all the rows in *text* that contain lexical words – that is, the rows with the numbers that we stored in the vector *lexical_words* at Point e. This is done as shown in Figure 4.38, which reproduces Point f from the script.

```
# f) reduce text to lexical words only
text <- text[lexical_words,]
```

FIGURE 4.38 Accessing lexical words from a text (Script 4.3.3.f)

After applying Points e and f, the first few rows for the first text in my corpus look like Figure 4.39.

```
> head(text)
     word_number        word      lemma pos ner dep_on      dep
1              1        Dear       Dear   n   0      2 compound
2              2      Editor     Editor   n   0      6    nsubj
5              5          am         be   v   0      6      aux
6              6     writing      write   v   0      0     ROOT
8              8     express    express   v   0      6    xcomp
10            10  opposition opposition   n   0      8     dobj
```

FIGURE 4.39 Lexical words accessed from a text

Moving on, you will recall that, in Script 4.3.1, we used the *paste()* function to create a vector of academic items in which the headword of each lemma is combined with its POS, in the format 'lemma_pos' ('study_n', 'group_n', etc. – see Figure 4.21). We can now do exactly the same thing for lexical words in the study corpus, as shown in Figure 4.40 (Point g).

```
# g) create lemma_pos combinations
text$lemma_pos <- paste(tolower(text$lemma), text$pos, sep = '_')
```

FIGURE 4.40 Creating lemma + pos combinations (Script 4.3.3.g)

We now have two lists of lemma_pos combinations: the academic word list (which we've stored in the vector AVL$lemma_pos) and the list of lexical words from our corpus text (stored in the vector text$lemma_pos). The next step is to find out where these two vectors overlap; that is, which items in text$lemma_pos are also in AVL$lemma_pos. This is achieved at Point h using the *which()* function that we met earlier and the *%in%* operator, as shown in Figure 4.41.

```
# h) identify which lemmas are found on reference list
AVL_lemmas <- which(text$lemma_pos %in% AVL$lemma_pos)
```

FIGURE 4.41 Identifying academic lemmas in a text (Script 4.3.3.h)

As an intuitive reading of the command suggests, this will tell us *which* items from text$lemma_pos are *in* AVL_lemma_pos. As we saw previously, this will return a vector of position numbers. We store these as the vector 'AVL_lemmas'.

With this vector in hand, we can now calculate the percentage of lexical words in our text that are academic. We do this (Point i) by dividing the length of the AVL_lemmas vector (which has one entry for every AVL word in the text) by the length of the text$lemma_pos vector (which has one entry for every lexical word in the text). The outcome of this division is stored in the AVL_percent vector that we created way back in Script 4.3.3.b. As in previous sections, '[i]' is used to place this score in the position corresponding to the text that is currently being analyzed, as shown in Figure 4.42.

```
# i) quantify percentage of lemmas found on reference list
    AVL_percent[i] <- length(AVL_lemmas)/length(text$lemma_pos)
```

FIGURE 4.42   Record the percentage of lemmas in a text that are academic words (Script 4.33.i)

This gives us a quantitative record of the prevalence of AVL words in the text, but for further analysis, it would be useful also to keep a note of which academic words were found. At Point j, the lemma_pos combinations from the AVL list are stored in the text_AVL_lemmas list that we created at Script 4.3.3.b. It will be recalled that lists take other structures as their elements. Here, we specify that element i in the list (i.e. the element corresponding to the current text) should be a vector of academic words found in the text (Figure 4.43).

```
# j) save matching lemmas to list
    text_AVL_lemmas[[i]] <- text$lemma_pos[AVL_lemmas]
```

FIGURE 4.43   Record academic lemmas for each text (Script 4.3.3.j)

This brings us to the end of the procedures we need to carry out separately for each text, so the loop is then closed (Point k). Once all texts have been processed, the final two lines of the Script (4.3.3.l) use cbind to combine the quantitative results with our metadata and store the resulting file in the outputs folder under the name 'AVL.csv'.

SCRIPT 4.3.3.l   CREATE AN OUTPUT TABLE AND SAVE IT TO THE OUTPUTS FOLDER

```
output <- cbind(metadata, AVL_percent)
write.csv (output, file = 'output/AVL.csv', row.names = F)
```

4.3.4 Visualizing variation in measures

A graph can be created to show the overall quantitative outcomes of this analysis in the same way as we did for diversity (see Script 4.2.4). The code for this is shown in Script 4.3.4. The key difference from the graph created by Script 4.2.4 is that, rather than showing results separately for each genre, I have decided to look also at academic disciplines. Use of academic vocabulary is known to differ across disciplines (Durrant, 2014), so there is good reason to think that this might be a relevant variable. I have also kept the distinction between literary and non-literary writing. The 'discipline_genre' column of my metadata classifies texts based on these two variables, so the 'linetype' and 'group' attributes in the *ggplot()* function now refer to this column, rather than the 'genre' column used in Script 4.3.4.

SCRIPT 4.3.4   VISUALIZE VARIATION IN ACADEMIC VOCABULARY

```
library(ggplot2)
library(Hmisc)
data <- read.csv(file = 'output/AVL.csv')
data$year_group <- factor(data$year_group,
                levels = c('Year_2', 'Year_6', 'Year_9', 'Year_11'))
ggplot(data, aes(year_group, AVL_percent, linetype=discipline_genre)) +
    stat_summary(fun='mean', geom='line', aes(group=discipline_genre)) +
    stat_summary(fun.data='mean_cl_boot', geom='errorbar', width=.2) +
    labs(y="AVL %")+labs(x="Year Group")
ggsave('output/AVL_line_graph.jpeg')
```

The graph created by this script for my data can be seen in Figure 4.44. This shows that use of academic vocabulary increases in all disciplines and genres as children progress through school. However, this increase is steepest in non-literary writing (English literary writing showed only a small increase[5]), especially non-literary science writing.

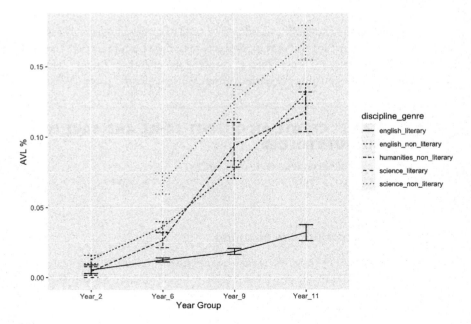

FIGURE 4.44 Academic words in child writing

4.3.5 Investigating the patterns

In Chapter 1, I emphasized the importance of complementing broad-brush quantitative findings with more detailed analyses to help us interpret any overall patterns. The precise nature of such follow-up analyses will depend on your research goals and the nature of the quantitative patterns. They are also likely to involve some degree of interpretive engagement with texts and so introduce an element of subjectivity into the research process. Analysis of this sort is therefore difficult to exemplify in full here (for a full example of an analysis of this sort, see Durrant & Durrant, 2020). Rather than detailing a complete analysis, therefore, the current section will give some ideas as to how we might get started on an analysis to follow up on the results shown in Figure 4.44.

The first step is likely to be to formulate some questions about the patterns we have found. With respect to Figure 4.44, for example, we might want to ask questions such as the following:

- Why does the use of academic words increase in literary writing, despite this not being an academic genre?
- Why is the increase in academic words seen in science writing so much steeper than that seen in other disciplines?
- Given that adults are known to use different sets of academic vocabulary in different disciplines (Hyland & Tse, 2007), are the increases seen for non-literary all due to increases in the use of a single set of words, or are different sets of academic vocabulary being learned in each discipline?

Once a question has been clearly formulated, we can start thinking about practical ways of answering it. In answering any of these questions, a likely first step will be to identify exactly which academic words learners are using and how often. Script 4.3.5 demonstrates one way of retrieving the words for one particular group of texts: non-literary science texts written by Year 11 students. The overall aim will be to create a spreadsheet showing the number of times each AVL word appears in this group of texts and the number of different texts in which it is found.

It will be recalled that, in Script 4.3.3, the academic words from each text were recorded in a list called *text_AVL_lemmas*, with each element corresponding to the words found in one text. What we want to do now, therefore, is to retrieve the elements corresponding to Year 11, non-literary science texts. To do this, we can exploit the fact that the numbers of the texts in our list match the numbers of those texts in the metadata: for the GiG corpus, the first text is 1_1.txt; the second is 1_2.txt; etc. So, if we can find the numbers of rows in the metadata that correspond to Year 11 non-literary science writing, we can then use these numbers to identify the appropriate rows in the text_AVL_lemmas list.

This is achieved in Script 4.3.5a using the *which()* function. We used this function in Script 4.3.3 along with the '|' ('or') operator to find items meeting *at least one* of multiple conditions. This time, we use the '&' ('and') operator to identify items that meet *both* of two specified conditions: i.e. year_group == '11' AND discipline_genre == 'science_non_literary'. The numbers of the rows meeting these conditions are then saved in the vector 'year_11_science'.

SCRIPT 4.3.5.a   IDENTIFY POSITION OF YEAR 11, NON-LITERARY SCIENCE TEXTS

```
metadata <- read.csv(file = 'corpora/metadata_gig.csv')
year_11_science <- which(metadata$year_group == 'Year_11' &
                     metadata$discipline_genre == "science_non_literary")
```

The next step is to retrieve the academic words that were used in these texts (Script 4.3.5b). The positions in this list correspond to the positions in our metadata spreadsheet (position one in the list contains words from the text that are found in the first row of the metadata, etc.). We can, therefore, use the *year_11_science* vector we have just created, together with subsetting, to identify those elements corresponding to the texts we are interested in. These are then stored in the new list *text_AVL_lemmas_sample*. We also create a second version of this, as a vector rather than a list (*text_AVL_lemmas_sample_unlisted*). These two different versions will be used in different ways later in the script.

SCRIPT 4.3.5.b   RETRIEVE AVL WORDS FROM EACH TEXT

```
text_AVL_lemmas_sample <- text_AVL_lemmas[year_11_science]
text_AVL_lemmas_sample_unlisted <- unlist(text_AVL_lemmas_sample)
```

As noted, we want to find both the frequency of each AVL word and the number of texts in which each appears. In Script 4.3.5.c, we create vectors to store each of these two pieces of information for each word.

SCRIPT 4.3.5.c   CREATE EMPTY VECTORS TO RECORD FREQUENCY AND RANGE

```
range <- vector(length = length(AVL$lemma_pos))
frequency <- vector(length = length(AVL$lemma_pos))
```

In Script 4.3.5.d., we then set up a loop that goes through each item in the AVL and for each, firstly, checks how frequently it occurs in the texts (this uses the unlisted version of the words, created in 4.3.5.b) and, secondly, checks in how many different texts it appears (using the list version from 4.3.5.b).

SCRIPT 4.3.5.d   RETRIEVE FREQUENCY AND RANGE FOR EACH AVL ITEM

```
for (i in 1:length(AVL$lemma_pos)){
  frequency[i] <- length(grep(AVL$lemma_pos[i], text_AVL_lemmas_sample_unlisted))
  range[i] <- length(grep(AVL$lemma_pos[i], text_AVL_lemmas_sample))
}
```

Finally, in Script 4.3.5.e, this information is compiled into a data frame, with the AVL items in the first column, the frequency of each item in the second, and the number of texts in which each appears in the third. The items are ordered according to the number of texts in which they appear. This table is then saved as a. csv file to our output folder. Figure 4.45 shows the first few lines of the resulting spreadsheet. The next step in our analysis would probably be to use a concordancer to understand how the most common words are used in context (which, you will be relieved to hear after this long adventure, I will not attempt to describe here.

SCRIPT 4.3.5.e   COMPILE THE INFORMATION TO A DATA FRAME AND SAVE TO THE OUTPUT FOLDER

```
output <- data.frame(AVL$lemma_pos, frequency, range)
output <- output[order(output$range, decreasing = T),]
write.csv(output, file = 'output/AVL_Year_11_Sci.csv', row.names = F)
```

	A	B	C	D	E	F
1	AVL.lemma_pos	frequency	range			
2	result_n	121	30			
3	however_r	48	23			
4	increase_v	57	23			
5	hypothesis_n	62	23			
6	thesis_n	62	23			
7	support_v	61	21			
8	compare_v	33	20			
9	rate_n	54	18			
10	graph_n	45	18			

FIGURE 4.45   Part of the frequency/range list of AVL words

4.4 Conclusion

This chapter has aimed to show how the analyses of vocabulary diversity and sophistication introduced in Chapter 3 can be put into practice to study a real corpus of learner writing. It has also introduced some key aspects of using R for corpus research. The functions and techniques described here will be essential in the other hands-on chapters later in the book, so the work done here will be foundational for those. Key points that you should now be familiar with are:

- Setting a working directory using *setwd()*;
- Loading and saving data, using *read.csv()*, *write.csv()*, *scan()*, and *read.delim()*;
- Creating data structures using *vector()*, *list()*, *unlist()*, and *data.frame()*;
- Editing a data frame using *colnames()* and *cbind()*;
- Editing a vector using *c()*, *tolower()*, *strsplit()*, *gsub()*, *unique()*, and *paste()*;
- Accessing elements within a vector or data frame using *which()*, *%in%*, and subsetting (square brackets);
- Accessing columns within a data frame using *$*;
- Searching for text strings using regular expressions;
- Repeating procedures for each text in a corpus using *for()*;
- Installing and loading packages into R using *install.packages()* and *library()*;
- Telling R how grouping variables should be interpreted using *factor()*; and
- Creating a graph using *gglot()*.

These have been amongst the most important and frequently used elements of R in my own research, and getting to grips with the scripts in this chapter should set a good foundation for your studies of writing development.

Notes

1 This and other URLs in this section were last accessed on 5 March 2022.
2 Range: https://www.wgtn.ac.nz/lals/resources/paul-nations-resources/vocabulary-analysis-programs; AntWordProfile: https://www.laurenceanthony.net/software/antwordprofiler/.
3 We will see the meanings of these column names in more detail in Chapter 6.
4 See https://www.ling.upenn.edu/courses/Fall_2003/ling001/penn_treebank_pos.html for a full list of codes
5 Although the legend refers also to 'science_literary' writing, this is not clearly visible in the graph because this genre was only encountered in a small group of texts at Year 2.

References

Durrant, P. (2014). Discipline and level specificity in university students' written vocabulary. *Applied Linguistics, 35*(3), 328–56. https://doi.org/10.1093/applin/amt016

Durrant, P., & Brenchley, M. (2019). Development of vocabulary sophistication across genres in English children's writing. *Reading and Writing, 32*(8), 1927–53. https://doi.org/10.1007/s11145-018-9932-8

Durrant, P., & Durrant, A. (2020). Appropriateness as an aspect of lexical richness: what do quantitative measures tell us about children's writing? *Assessing Writing, 51*. https://doi.org/10.1016/j.asw.2021.100596

Gardner, D., & Davies, M. (2014). A new academic vocabulary list. *Applied Linguistics, 35*(3), 305–327. https://doi.org/10.1093/applin/amt015

Gries, S. T. (2017). *Quantitative Corpus Linguistics with R: A Practical Introduction* (2nd ed.). Routledge.

Hyland, K., & Tse, P. (2007). Is there an 'academic vocabulary'? *TESOL Quarterly, 41*(2), 235–53. https://doi.org/10.1002/j.1545-7249.2007.tb00058.x

Wickham, H. (2016). *ggplot2: Elegant graphics for data analysis*. Springer. https://doi.org/10.1007/978-3-319-24277-4

## PART THREE

Studying grammar in writing development

5

UNDERSTANDING GRAMMAR IN LEARNER WRITING

5.1 Introduction

Over the last 80 years, grammar has been the single most common focus of corpus studies of writing development (Durrant et al., 2021). There are several possible reasons for this popularity. Perhaps most central is the fact that grammar is such a core part of the way that language has been described and understood, with a tradition stretching back to antiquity, and work on the grammar of English dating from the sixteenth century (McCarthy, 2021). This tradition has provided researchers with both a rich and detailed repertoire of grammatical features to explore and an exciting array of theoretical ideas about how grammar relates to education, society, and cognition. Of all our lenses on writing development, therefore, grammar is the most thoroughly developed. Not coincidentally, grammar also represents a central concern of both first and second language teaching, occupying a privileged place in curricula and assessment criteria (e.g., Cambridge Assessment English, 2012; Department for Education, 2014; Standards and Testing Agency, 2015). This makes it a natural focus for educationally oriented researchers who want to inform such curricula or assessments. Finally, there is good evidence that several grammatical measures are reliable indices of writing development (Durrant et al., 2021; Wolfe-Quintero et al., 1998). This makes them fertile ground for those wishing to understand such development.

The first part of this chapter will briefly discuss some broad principles of grammar research. It will focus on choosing between different models of grammar to work with, identifying specific grammatical features to study, and thinking about how to interpret those features. The remainder of the chapter will then discuss in detail three approaches to studying grammar: approaches based on grammatical complexity, approaches based on multi-dimensional analysis, and approaches based

DOI: 10.4324/9781003152682-8

on usage-based models of language. We will see how each of these approaches is based on different ways of thinking about grammar and highlights different aspects of writing development.

5.2 Studying development through grammar

5.2.1 Models of grammar

For researchers new to studying the grammar of learner writing, an essential starting point is to understand that there is no single agreed-upon grammar of English. At one level, this is seen in the fact that different linguists have theorized grammar in fundamentally different ways. Some see it as a formal system that can be described and explained without reference to meaning; others see meaning as an important constituent part of grammatical categories. Some see the structure of grammar as arising from properties of the human mind; others see it as arising from patterns of social interaction. Differences of this sort have led to quite different approaches to describing grammar, and hence quite different sets of grammatical categories and structures. Even a cursory glance at the set of terms used in Systemic Functional Grammar (Halliday & Matthiessen, 2014), for example, makes clear that it differs in important ways from that in more traditional treatments (e.g., Crystal, 2010).

Even when grammarians take a broadly similar theoretical approach, they can disagree about which categories should be used and how they should be defined. Moreover, when different grammars do use categories that are nominally 'the same', they sometimes turn out to define them in different ways. This is reflected even in such a fundamental grammatical unit as the *clause*[1] (Bulté & Housen, 2012). Such differences of definition are important because they can lead to marked differences in the outcomes of our analyses and confusion over how findings should be interpreted and synthesized across different studies.

The implication of this for our purposes is that researchers cannot assume that there is a universally accepted set of grammatical categories or ideas that they can adopt in their studies. This is not to say that researchers need to decide which is the universally *best* or *most valid* grammar. However, it does mean that we should select our grammatical frameworks in a principled and thoughtful way. For some researchers, a framework may follow from the context they are studying. If they aim to inform practice in a particular educational programme, for example, they may choose a grammar that is consistent with what is already used within that programme. Researchers interested in the social functions of language are often influenced by Systemic Functional Grammar (Halliday & Matthiessen, 2014). Those focusing on language's relationship to cognition may prefer to draw on Cognitive Grammar (Langacker, 1987) or Construction Grammar (Goldberg, 2006). Another consideration is the level of description provided by individual grammars. Corpus-based grammars such as the *Longman Grammar of Spoken and Written English* (Biber et al., 1999) or the *Cambridge Grammar of English* (Carter & McCarthy, 2006), for example, provide detailed information about the typical frequencies of particular forms and their distributions across contexts that can provide an excellent backdrop and point of comparison for studies of learner writing.

A researcher's choice of a grammatical framework is also likely to be influenced by practical considerations. Some frameworks will simply be easier to implement than others in a corpus study. One reason for this may be that their categories are more clearly defined or explained, and so easier to identify in a reliable way. Another may be that automated parsers annotate a corpus in line with a particular framework. As we discussed in Chapter 2, it can be impractical to study a large corpus without such tools, and this may lead researchers to simply adopt whatever grammar happens to be implemented in a parser to which they have access. While this is an understandable tendency, it is important that researchers who decide to use a parser have, at the very least, a clear understanding of what framework their chosen parser implements and consider the implications for how they interpret their findings.

An example of why this matters can be seen in the way that the widely used *Coh-Metrix* (McNamara et al., 2014) tool analyses the central category of *noun phrase*. Its measure of *modifiers per noun phrase* is markedly out of step with most mainstream grammatical models in that it includes determiners as a category of modifier and excludes features such as relative clauses and appositional structures. This should lead researchers who use this tool to question whether the measure genuinely tells us something about noun phrase modification and to what extent their results are comparable with those of other studies.

The Stanford CoreNLP tool that we have been using in this book is not immune to such considerations.[2] One example can be seen in its use of a category called *open clause complement*, which is applied to a range of structures that more traditional models might label as subject predicatives (*you look* great), object predicatives (*I painted it* black), and non-finite clauses (*she asked me* to come).

5.2.2 Selecting and interpreting grammatical features

I have suggested that one reason for the popularity of grammar as a research focus may be the rich array of descriptive categories that it provides. As any reader who has carried a comprehensive grammar book home from the library will attest, these routinely weigh in at well over a thousand tightly packed pages, and so offer researchers a seemingly endless repertoire of things to measure. While these riches are enticing, they can also be overwhelming when it comes to choosing specific features to study. For research to be meaningful, it is important to think through this choice in a careful and principled way, with a clear idea of what chosen features represent, why they are worth studying, and how differences in their use should be interpreted.

Unfortunately, some of the existing literature is less than helpful in this regard. As Bulté and Housen (2012) have argued, many studies appear to have given little consideration to the theoretical interpretation of their measures. Perhaps because of this, it is not uncommon for studies to include multiple measures of the same thing. In key methodological reviews of the area, Norris and Ortega (2009) and

Bulté and Housen (2012) note a tendency for a relatively limited range of measures (mostly concerning use of subordinate clauses) to dominate the field, while many other, potentially important, features are neglected. Publications sometimes leave the critical reader with the impression that features have been chosen primarily because they can be readily quantified, and/or because they have been used in previous studies.

Like the choice of an overall grammatical model (discussed in the previous section), principled selection of features to study should be primarily based on the goals of your research. If you are interested in studying the effects of a particular programme of study, for example, you might choose to focus on grammatical forms that are explicitly targeted by that programme (e.g., those cited in a syllabus) or that you have reason to believe will be important for students on that programme. Researchers interested in tracking the effects of an English for Academic Purposes programme, for example, will probably choose to focus on features that previous research has shown to be important in the types of academic writing for which students are preparing. Reference works such as the *Longman Grammar of Spoken and Written English* (Biber et al., 1999), which describe the frequency and use of grammatical categories in specific types of texts (e.g., how frequent is the passive voice in academic writing?) can be invaluable in providing this sort of information.

Researchers with more theoretical aims might wish to test the predictions of a given developmental model and hence focus on features that are most relevant to those predictions. An example of this approach can be seen in recent studies inspired by Biber and his colleagues (Biber et al., 2011; Biber et al., 2020), who claim that maturing writers shift from elaborating their sentences with finite dependent clauses that function as clause constituents to elaborating them with phrases that function as noun phrase modifiers. Their framework proposes five stages of development, along with specified emerging features expected at each, that can provide a clear framework for empirical testing (see Section 5.3.2). Another example (discussed in more detail in Section 5.3.4) is work inspired by usage-based models of language development, which make predictions about the relationships between grammatical structures and the vocabulary that is used in them.

The aims that motivate your study will also influence the ways in which you think about your findings, and hence the ways in which you interpret them. A researcher interested in the outcomes of a particular programme, for example, might (in the simplest case) interpret an increase in the use of a particular target feature as indicating that the programme has been successful in one of its aims. Researchers interested in testing the predictions of usage-based developmental models are likely to be more interested in seeing writing as a reflection of writers' cognitive processes and so interpret findings as providing evidence for constructs such as *entrenchment* or *abstraction* (see Section 5.3.4). Others are often interested in what the prevalence of particular features tells us about the types of meanings that are expressed in texts. For example, shifts in the frequencies of relevant grammatical forms (or sets of forms) might be interpreted as telling us that writing deals with more or less abstract content, focuses more or less on personal opinion, engages in more or less narration, and so on (see Section 5.3.3).

5.3 Approaches to grammatical development

5.3.1 Varieties of grammatical approaches

In this section, we will look at three approaches to studying writing development through grammar that have been prominent in the research literature. We will see how each gives very different sorts of insights into writing development and leads to very different sorts of analysis.

5.3.2 Development in grammatical complexity

Grammatical complexity has been usefully defined as "the addition of structural elements to 'simple' phrases and clauses" (Biber et al., 2020, p. 5). This can be illustrated by sentences A–C.

A. Rover barked.
B. Rover, who was getting much too excited, barked.
C. Rover barked when he heard the post arrive.

Sentence **A** is grammatically simple because it contains only elements that are grammatically obligatory. It comprises two phrases that include only their head-words (the noun phrase *Rover* and the verb phrase *barked*), and these phrases are combined into a clause comprising only a subject and a verb. Sentences **B** and **C** are more complex in that they add non-obligatory elements, either to the original phrases or to the original clause. Specifically, sentence **B** elaborates on the noun phrase *Rover* by adding a postmodifying relative clause (*who was getting much too excited*). Sentence **C** elaborates on the original clause by adding an adverbial clause (*when he heard the post arrive*).

Many ways of quantifying grammatical complexity have been proposed, and it can be difficult for researchers to know which one(s) to choose or what the differences between them might be. To help us navigate this maze of options, a helpful starting point is to categorize measures according to how *generic* or *specific* they are.

The idea of measures as being more generic or more specific is based on the hierarchical relationships that exist between grammatical features. By *hierarchical* here, I mean that some features are *types of* other features. Noun, verbs, and adjectives, for example, are all types of words. We can therefore picture a hierarchy in which words exist at the top of a tree that branches down into nouns, verbs, adjectives, and other parts of speech. Descending further down this tree, nouns, verbs, adjectives, etc., could be divided into a range of still finer-grained categories: abstract vs. non-abstract nouns; countable vs. uncountable nouns; derived vs. base nouns, etc.

To take a slightly different type of example, the generic category of *phrase* can be divided into more specific categories, such as *noun phrase, verb phrase, adjective phrase,* etc. These in turn might be divided into finer categories such as *postmodified noun phrase, noun phrase functioning as the subject of a verb,* etc. As these examples make clear, there are many different ways in which a tree might be split into finer categories. The general point, however, is that grammatical measures based on units relatively high up in a tree (e.g., words, phrases) are more generic, while those lower down a tree (e.g., abstract nouns, noun phrases postmodified with a relative clause) are more specific.

Much work on grammatical complexity has been based on a small set of measures involving highly generic categories, most commonly: *words per t-unit,*[3] *words per clause, words per sentence,* and *clauses per t-unit.* These measures are relatively simple to calculate, and previous research has shown that they correlate strongly both with proficiency and with development over time in first and second language writing (Durrant et al., 2021; Wolfe-Quintero et al., 1998). For researchers aiming to provide a simple way of indexing writing development or ascertaining learners' proficiency levels, such measures are, therefore, very attractive.

If our aim is to *understand* writing development, however, generic measures can be less useful (Biber et al., 2020; Durrant et al., 2021). The core problem with these measures is that their scores can be influenced by a range of quite different linguistic factors. Words per t-unit, for example (probably the most frequently used measure of grammatical complexity) can be increased either by greater use of complex phrases (as in example B) or by greater use of subordinate clauses (as in example C). This is problematic because, as Biber et al. (2020) have shown, phrasal complexity and clausal complexity are importantly different constructs in writing development. Whereas clausal complexity is characteristic of spoken language and tends to be used in lower-level writing, phrasal complexity reflects patterns of mature academic writing and tends to be used by more advanced learners. By conflating these different types of complexity, therefore, generic measures run the risk of presenting a distorted picture of development.

The *clauses per t-unit* measure partially addresses this problem in that increases in the measure must reflect increases in subordination, rather than in phrasal complexity. However, for many purposes, this will still not be sufficient. One problem relates to the nature of development. Durrant et al. (2020), for example, show how different types of subordinate clauses can follow very different developmental patterns in children's writing. A measure that conflates different types of subordination may, therefore, provide a misleading overall picture. Another reason is more pragmatic: if we want our research to inform education, we need to deal with features that can be meaningfully used in a pedagogical setting. The broad category of *subordination,* which subsumes finite and non-finite adverbial, complement, and noun modifier clauses may simply be too vague for such purposes.

Kellog Hunt (1965), who developed the notion of the *t-unit,* and to whom much of the subsequent use of generic indices can ultimately be traced, was well aware of this issue. He used such indices only as a first step in his analysis and followed them up with a range of more granular measures to throw light on the reasons for changes at the generic level. For researchers aiming to understand (rather than merely to index) writing development and to provide useful guidance to language teachers and learners, this is an important example to follow.

For researchers wanting to study complexity in terms of the development of specific features of language, a useful starting place is the framework suggested by Biber et al. (2020) and reproduced (with minor changes) in Table 5.1. Biber et al. propose that development in grammatical complexity involves learners shifting away from the structures near the top of this table and towards those near the bottom. The major trends in this model are that

- elaboration with non-finite subordinate clauses (*Rover barked **to get our attention***) is more complex than elaboration with finite subordinate clauses (*Rover barked **because he wanted our attention***);
- elaboration with phrases (*Rover barked **at the sound of the postman***) is more complex than elaboration with finite subordinate clauses (*Rover barked **when he heard the postman***); and
- elaboration of phrases (*Rover, **the mad dog,** barked*) is more complex than elaboration of clauses (*Rover barked **like a mad dog***).

These developments mark a shift from a more spoken to a more written form of language and, Biber et al. propose, a move towards greater written complexity. It is important to remember, however, that this model is not intended to predict *categorical* shifts. That is, we should not expect advanced writers to stop using finite clauses and instead use only phrasal modifiers or to stop elaborating on clauses and only elaborate on phrases. Rather, they are *quantitative* tendencies. Writers will come to use less of the former and more of the latter.

5.3.3 Multi-dimensional analysis

Multi-dimensional analysis (MDA) was originally developed by Biber (1988, 2019) as a method for studying variation between linguistic registers (e.g., for understanding how conversational speech differs from academic writing), but many researchers now apply it to studying writing development. As we will see, MDA is an attractive method in that it has a strong theoretical basis and in that it enables us to combine many different linguistic features into a single analysis. Biber et al. (2016) thus argue that it offers a way of creating holistic indices of linguistic complexity that are more satisfactory than the generic measures discussed in Section 5.3.2.

Three ideas are central to understanding MDA. First, it posits that registers are best characterized not by their use of individual linguistic features (e.g., how much they use first person pronouns; how much they use passive voice), but rather by *sets of features* that tend to group together. In his pioneering study of variation between spoken and written English, Biber (1988) finds that a range of features including contractions, present tense verbs, first and second person pronouns, *be* as a main

TABLE 5.1 Biber et al.'s (2020) framework for grammatical complexity features in English

Structural type	Syntactic function within structural type	Specific structural/syntactic features	Examples
Finite dependent clauses	1. Finite adverbial clause	Causative clauses: *because* + clause	*She won't narc on me, because she prides herself on being a gangster.*
		Conditional clauses: *if* + clause	*Well, if I stay here, I'll have to leave early in the morning.*
		Concessive clauses: *although* + clause	*If I don't put my name, she doesn't know who wrote it, although she might guess.*
	2. Finite complement clause	Verb controlled *that*-clause	*I would hope that we can have more control over them.*
			(with ZERO complementizer): yeah, I think I probably could.
		Verb controlled *wh*-clause	*I don't know how they do it.*
		Adjective controlled *that*-clause	*It is evident that the virus formation is related to the cytoplasmic inclusions.*
		Noun controlled *that*-clause	*The fact that no tracer particles were found in or below the tight junction (zonula occludens) indicates that these areas are not a pathway for particles of this size in the toad bladder.*
	3. Finite noun modifier clause	Relative clause with *that*	*The results from a large number of cloze tests were used to estimate the amount of experimental error that could be expected to result from using cloze tests of various lengths*
		Relative clause with *wh*-relativizer	*Their nucleoid is formed by dense granules and rods composing a ring which limits a central electrontransparent space.*

Category	Feature	Subtype	Example
Non-finite dependent clauses	4. Non-finite adverbial clause	*to*-clause indicating 'purpose'	*To verify our conclusion that the organic material is arranged as a coating around the silica shell components, thin sections of fixed cells were also examined.*
	5. Non-finite complement clause	Verb controlled *to*-clause	*I really want to fix this room up.*
		Verb controlled *ing*-clause	*I like watching the traffic go by.*
		Adjective controlled *to*-clause	*It was important to obtain customer feedback.*
		Noun controlled *to*-clause	*The project is part of a massive plan to complete the section of road…*
	6. Non-finite noun modifying clause	Noun + *ing*-clause (non-finite relative clause)	*Transfer tests following over-training indicated individual variability.*
		Noun + *ed*-clause (non-finite passive relative clause)	*The results shown in Tables IV and V add to the picture…*
Dependent phrases (non-clausal)	7. Adverbial phrase (i.e., a phrase modifying a clause)	Adverbial phrase as adverbial	*I raved about it afterwards.*
		Prepositional phrase as adverbial	*Alright, we'll talk to you in the morning.*
	8. Phrasal modifier (i.e., a phrase modifying another phrase)	Modifier of a noun phrase — Attributive adjective as noun pre-modifier	*emotional injury, conventional practices aviation security committee, fighter pilot training*
		Noun as noun pre-modifier	*Class mean scores were computed by averaging the scores for male and female target students in the class.*
		Prepositional phrase as noun post-modifier	*Two Stuart monarchs (Charles I and Charles II) were strongly suspected of Romish sympathies.*
		Appositive noun phrase as noun post-modifier	*James Klein, president of the American Benefits Council*
		Modifier of an adjective phrase — Adverb phrase as adjective modifier	*That cat was surprisingly fast.*
		Modifier of an adverb phrase — Adverb phrase as adverb modifier	*We will see those impacts fairly quickly.*

verb, emphatics, and amplifiers tend to occur together in the sense that when one is frequent in a text, the others are also likely to be frequent. Similarly, features such as use of nouns, long words, prepositional phrases, and a diverse vocabulary also tend to occur together. Moreover, these two sets of features contrast with each other. That is, texts with large numbers of contractions, present tense verbs, etc., tend to have fewer nouns, long words, etc. These contrasting feature sets are identified using *factor analysis*, a statistical technique which identifies groups of variables that correlate (either positively or negatively) with each other. It combines these correlating variables into *factors*: latent variables that are hypothesized to underlie the groups of correlated features. In MDA, these factors are referred to as *dimensions*. A text can be positioned on a dimension according to the prevalence in that text of the groups of features that define that dimension.

The second key idea of MDA is that dimensions are functionally motivated. That is, the reason that contractions, present tense verbs, etc., tend to occur together, and to stand in contrast to nouns, long words, etc., is that these groups of features collaborate to perform textual roles that are distinctive of different registers. To continue with our previous example, Biber (1988) argues that the group of features including contractions, etc., invokes what he calls an *involved* style of language. That is, language that is interactive, that takes place in a concrete local context (e.g., friends together in the same room) and that is mainly affective in its aims (e.g., focused in promoting good feeling between participants, rather than passing on essential information). In contrast, the group including nouns, etc., invokes an *informational* style. These features are found when we have specific information to convey. Because of this difference in function, the former set of features is more prevalent in conversations, and the latter more prevalent in official documents and academic writing.

The third key idea of MDA is that registers differ from each other in multiple ways. We have just seen that Biber (1988) found that conversation and academic writing differ in that the former focuses on interaction and the latter on information. But this, of course, is not the only way in which these registers differ. Conversation, for example, is more likely than academic prose to depend on the local context to convey meaning (*pass me that thing over there!*); it is more likely to refer to concrete than abstract entities; it is more transient; it allows speakers less time to plan (or understand) messages, etc. Potentially, each difference between registers could be associated with distinctive sets of co-occurring features. It is in this sense that Biber's analysis is *multi-dimensional*. It recognizes that understanding the differences between registers involves understanding their use of multiple dimensions, each of which is a response to a particular set of communicative needs. As Biber puts it,

> [N]o single parameter or dimension is adequate in itself to capture the full range of variation among registers in a language. Rather, different dimensions are realized by different sets of co-occurring linguistic features, reflecting different functional underpinnings (e.g., interactiveness, planning, informational focus).

(Biber, 2019, p. 13)

Although the original aim of MDA was to understand differences between text registers, many researchers now apply it to the study of learner writing. One such application has been in language test validation, where MDA has been used to determine whether purportedly different writing tasks (e.g., the *independent* and *integrated* parts of the TOEFL writing exam) genuinely elicit different types of writing (e.g., Biber & Gray, 2013). Several researchers have also used MDA to study how learner writing changes over time (Crossley et al., 2014; Crosthwaite, 2016; Friginal & Weigle, 2014; Gray et al., 2019) and/or across texts that have been rated at different levels of quality/proficiency (Biber & Gray, 2013; Biber et al., 2016; Crossley et al., 2014; Friginal & Weigle, 2014). These studies have either borrowed dimensions from previous studies (e.g., Crosthwaite, 2016) or created new sets of dimensions based on the learner corpus itself (e.g., Friginal & Weigle, 2014) and then positioned learner texts on, and traced how those positions vary across, the variables of time or quality/proficiency.

It is possible to distinguish *strong* and *weak* versions of this extension of MDA. The strong version extends MDA's original functionalist logic to claim that, analogous to different registers, "linguistic differences among…proficiency levels have a functional basis" (Biber et al., 2016, p. 641). In other words, much as the sets of linguistic features prevalent in conversation differ from those in academic prose because of the different communicative functions of those two registers, the writing of advanced learners differs from that of beginner or intermediate learners because of differences in the meanings expressed by those groups. An example of such differences is found in a study by Crosthwaite (2016). In direct parallel to the conversation/academic writing contrast previously discussed, he finds that the writing of university-level second language learners becomes less *involved* and more *information-oriented* as they progress through an English for Academic Purposes programme.

Not all researchers have adhered to such a strong functional interpretation of proficiency differences, however. In what I have called the *weak* version of MDA, the strategy of identifying multiple dimensions of co–occurring features is adopted, but differences across dimensions are not interpreted functionally. In their study of first language learner writing, for example, Crossley et al. (2014) interpret functions purely in terms of how effectively they distinguish texts that have been rated at different levels of quality. MDA is an attractive approach to studying proficiency differences, even when stripped of its functional interpretations, because it is highly plausible that, as Biber et al. (2016, p. 657) state, "instructors/raters and students/ examinees are much more tuned in to constellations of linguistic features used effectively than they are to the use of any individual linguistic feature". Indeed, it seems likely that many individual features are not markers of sophistication when used on their own, but only when used in combination with a wider set of compatible features to create an overall effect (Durrant et al., 2021).

5.3.4 Usage-based models of development

A third approach to understanding grammatical development is found in studies adopting a *usage-based* (UB) model of language. As Wulff (2021) explains, UB models rest on two key ideas: that language learning is shaped by the language to which learners are exposed and that it is achieved using the same cognitive mechanisms as other types of learning (e.g., forming categories, drawing inferences, automatizing frequently used processes). UB researchers have been particularly drawn to corpus research because they are interested in understanding how quantitative properties of language influence development, how language ability unfolds over time, and what factors moderate language performance (Wulff, 2021), questions which corpus methods are ideally suited to address. A UB approach to studying writing development has a more explicitly cognitive focus than the approaches discussed so far. Perhaps because of this, UB research has been notable for developing innovative methods of analysis and especially for combining corpus data with experimental data, primarily from elicitation and acceptability judgement tests (e.g., Jo & Oh, 2021; Römer et al., 2014; Sung & Kim, 2020).

While several different theories subscribe to UB principles, writing development research has been most influenced by Construction Grammar (Goldberg, 2006). This holds that individuals' language systems comprise structured inventories of *constructions*: that is, form-meaning combinations at different levels of abstraction. These include individual morphemes (e.g., the combination of the form -*s* with the meaning PLURAL), words (e.g., the combination of the form *dog* with the meaning of a four-legged friend), and syntactic structures (e.g., the combination of the form Verb-Object-Object with the meaning of causing someone to receive something, as the in the sentence *He gave the dog a bone*). Because constructions can exist at any level of abstraction, they include not only the classic levels of description just mentioned but also form-meaning pairs that cut across levels. For example, a speaker might store the sequence *give*-Object-Object as a construction, alongside the constructions of the word *give* and the more abstract sentence pattern Verb-Object-Object. Form-meaning pairs are likely to be stored as constructions if they are so frequent that their storage makes for efficient language processing (a likely hypothesis in the case of *give*-Object-Object) or because there are aspects of their use that could not be predicted on the basis of other aspects of the language system (Goldberg, 2006). For example, knowledge of the words *think* and *about* and of the grammar of verbs and prepositions may not allow a speaker to predict that we *think about* (rather than, say, *think towards*) something.

Because constructions cut across traditional linguistic levels of description and allow for (semi-)concrete instantiations of abstract grammatical patterns to be stored alongside the patterns themselves, they are often studied under the heading of formulaic language (Wulff, 2019). Collocations, sentence stems, and formulaic phrases of the sort discussed in Chapters 7 and 8 can be usefully theorized under this heading. However, a UB approach also gives us interesting ways of thinking about the development of grammar.

A particularly important focus of attention in this type of research has been on Verb Argument Constructions (VAC). VACs include a range of forms, such as the Verb-Object-Locative (e.g., *put it in the box*), Verb-Locative (e.g., *go home*), and Verb-Object-Object (also known as the *ditransitive*; e.g., *give me the ball*). On a UB view, abstract constructions of this sort are acquired through multiple encounters with specific examples and with variations on those examples (*give baby milk; give baby ball; give Johnny a kiss; pass me the salt*, etc.). During this process, speakers store frequently encountered examples as constructions, and processes of analogy and abstraction lead gradually to more abstract representations (Lieven & Tomasello, 2008; Tomasello, 2003). While a potentially unlimited range of different verbs can be used in these constructions, each construction tends to be strongly associated with a particular verb that is both highly frequent in it and that is *prototypical* of its meaning. Thus, for example, the Verb–Object–Locative construction is most frequently realized with the verb *put*, Verb–Locative with the verb *go*, and Verb–Object–Object with *give*. These high-frequency versions of the constructions are described in UB terminology as *pathbreaking* verbs and are held to give learners important clues as to the construction's abstract meaning (e.g., Ellis & Ferreira-Junior, 2009a; Sung & Kim, 2020).

This model makes a number of quantitative predictions about the course of grammar development (Ellis & Ferreira-Junior, 2009b), and corpus researchers have developed several methods of analysis for testing these predictions. One set of predictions relates to the *token* and *type* frequencies of constructions (Wulff, 2021). In this context, token frequency refers to the number of times a particular version of a construction appears. Type frequency refers to the number of distinct variants of a construction. For example, imagine a corpus containing the following examples of the ditransitive (Verb–Object–Object) construction:

- *gave him a coffee*
- *sent him a letter*
- *played him a tune*
- *sent him a letter*
- *gave him a coffee*
- *gave him a coffee*

Here, we have three types of the ditransitive construction (*gave him a coffee, sent him a letter, played him a tune*). We also have three tokens of *gave him a coffee*, two tokens of *sent a letter*, and one token of *played him a tune*. Repetition of a particular version of a construction (i.e., high token frequency) is hypothesized to make a learner more likely to store that version in their memory. So, learners exposed to input like that shown in the bullet points might end up memorizing *gave him a coffee*. High type frequency, on the other hand, makes a learner more likely to abstract away from specific versions of a construction and hence learn the abstract pattern than underlies them. In this case, that would be Verb–Object–Object with the meaning of transferring an object to a recipient.

With this model in mind, UB researchers have been especially interested in tracking type and token frequencies in learner writing. In particular, learners' use of a wide range of different verbs within a particular construction (i.e., a high type frequency) is taken as evidence that they have achieved an abstract representation of that construction. The token frequency of particular versions of a construction, on the other hand, is taken to give information about pathbreaking verbs. UB models predict that pathbreaking verbs for learners will be those that are most prototypical of the meaning of a given construction. Researchers have traced the influence of pathbreaking verbs through a method known as *construction growth analysis* (e.g., Jo & Oh, 2021; Römer & Berger, 2019) in which the frequencies of each verb used within a construction are traced across time or proficiency levels.

UB models have also tried to understand the relationship between learners' and native speakers' use of specific constructions. One approach has been to calculate the correlations between the frequencies with which learners use verbs within a construction and the frequencies found in a reference corpus. Römer and Berger (2019), for example, show how the frequencies with which learners at all levels of proficiency use verbs are significantly correlated with those verbs' frequencies in a native corpus, which they interpret as showing that learning is, as UB models hypothesize, influenced by the frequencies with which particular versions of a construction are encountered. They also find that the correlation increases with increasing proficiency, which they take to show progress towards native norms.

A rather different use of native speaker reference corpora is found in the work of Kris Kyle and his colleagues (Kyle & Crossley, 2017; Kyle et al., 2020). Using the Tool for the Automatic Analysis of Syntactic Sophistication and Complexity (TAASSC) tool, they identify the VACs and VAC + verb combinations found in learner texts and look up their frequency in a reference corpus. As with measures of word frequency in vocabulary studies (see Chapter 3, Section 3.5.3.3), they then calculate mean frequency measures for each learner text. Just as use of low-frequency vocabulary is taken to indicate lexical sophistication, use of low-frequency VACs and VAC + verb combinations is taken to indicate syntactic sophistication. In line with this, Kyle and Crossley (2017) find negative correlations between these frequencies and the scores assigned to texts by raters, while Kyle et al. (2020) find frequencies to decrease over time.

The same researchers also calculate the association between verbs and VACs in the reference corpus using association measures. As we will discuss further in the context of collocation in Part Four of this book, association measures are statistics which quantify the strength of *attraction* between two linguistic features (Gries & Durrant, 2021). In the current case, they quantify the attraction between verbs and the VACs in which they are found. Use of strongly associated verb + VAC combinations is taken to indicate more appropriate word choice and fewer grammatical errors. In line with this, association measures are found to be positively correlated with quality scores (Kyle & Crossley, 2017).

5.4 Conclusion

The various models of grammar offer researchers an array of rich descriptive concepts that can be used to understand development in learner writing, providing insights into writing from social, cognitive, and discourse perspectives.

While the sheer volume of concepts available can appear overwhelming, pioneering work by scholars such as Kellog Hunt, Douglas Biber, and Ute Römer have provided excellent foundations and guidelines on which other researchers can now build. While, as we will see in the next chapter, researching grammar can pose practical methodological challenges, these are far from intractable, and developments in automated parsing make the study of grammar in learner writing ever more accessible.

5.5 Taking it further

For researchers wanting to get to grips with the grammatical frameworks that can be used to study writing development, a good starting point is the student books that often accompany major grammar works. Key examples are:

Biber, D., Conrad, S., & Leech, G. (2002). *Student grammar of spoken and written English*. Longman.

Huddleston, R., & Pullum, G. K. (2005). *A students' introduction to English grammar*. Cambridge University Press.

For a review of the ways that traditional grammatical categories have been used to study writing development, see Chapter 3 of:

Durrant, P., Brenchley, M., & McCallum, L. (2021). *Understanding development and proficiency in writing: quantitative corpus linguistic approaches*. Cambridge University Press.

An alternative approach to the types of analysis discussed in this chapter is studies that use the categories of Systemic Functional Grammar. A key book-length example is:

Christie, F., & Derewianka, B. (2008). *School discourse: Learning to write across the years of schooling*. Continuum.

For an interesting general discussion of different theories of grammar and their relevance to language learning, see:

McCarthy, M. (2021). *Innovations and challenges in grammar*. Routledge.

Notes

1 That is, whereas some researchers have required a clause to include both a subject and a finite verb, others have only required a verb.
2 A list of grammatical categories used by the Stanford parser can be found at http://universaldependencies.org/docsv1/en/dep/index.html. Last accessed 15 April 2022.
3 A *t-unit* can be defined as a main clause and the subordinate clauses attached to it. This term was introduced by Hunt (1965) as a way of indexing writing maturity in children's writing. It was a response to the problem that young children's erratic use of punctuation made comparison of sentence lengths unreliable.

References

Biber, D. (1988). *Variation across speech and writing*. Cambridge University Press. https://doi.org/10.1017/CBO9780511621024

Biber, D. (2019). Multi-dimensional analysis: A historical synopsis. In T. B. Sardinha & M. V. Pinto (Eds.), *Multi-dimensional analysis: Research methods and current issues* (pp. 11–26). Bloomsbury Academic. https://doi.org/10.5040/9781350023857.0009

Biber, D., & Gray, B. (2013). Discourse characteristics of writing and speaking task types on the TOEFL iBT test: a lexico-grammatical analysis. *TOEFL iBT Research Report, 19*. https://doi.org/10.1002/j.2333-8504.2013.tb02311.x

Biber, D., Gray, B., & Poonpon, K. (2011). Should we use chracteristics of conversation to measure grammatical complexity in L2 writing development? *TESOL Quarterly, 45*(1), 5–35. https://doi.org/10.5054/tq.2011.244483

Biber, D., Gray, B., & Staples, S. (2016). Predicting patterns of grammatical complexity across language exam task types and proficiency levels. *Applied Linguistics, 37*(5), 639–68. https://doi.org/10.1093/applin/amu059

Biber, D., Gray, B., Staples, S., & Egbert, J. (2020). Investigating grammatical complexity in L2 English writing research: Linguistic description versus predictive measurement. *Journal of English for Academic Purposes, 46*, 1475–1585. https://doi.org/10.1016/j.jeap.2020.100869

Biber, D., Johansson, S., Leech, G., Conrad, S., & Finegan, E. (1999). *Longman grammar of spoken and written English*. Longman.

Bulté, B., & Housen, A. (2012). Defining and operationalising L2 complexity. In A. Housen, K. Kuiken, & I. Vedder (Eds.), *Dimensions of L2 performance and proficiency: Complexity, accuracy and fluency in SLA* (pp. 21–46). John Benjamins. https://doi.org/10.1075/lllt.32.02bul

Cambridge Assessment English. (2012). Cambridge English qualifications: C1 advanced handbook for teachers. Retrieved from https://www.cambridgeenglish.org/Images/167804-cambridge-english-advanced-handbook.pdf (Accessed: 22 February 2020).

Carter, R., & McCarthy, M. (2006). *Cambridge grammar of English*. Cambridge University Press.

Crossley, S. A., Allen, L. K., & McNamara, D. (2014). A Multi-dimensional analysis of essay writing: What linguistic features tell us about situational parameters and the effects of language functions on judgments of quality? In T. B. Sardinha & M. V. Pinto (Eds.), *Multi-dimensional analysis, 25 years on: A tribute to Douglas Biber* (pp. 197–233). John Benjamins Publishing Company. https://doi.org/10.1075/scl.60.07cro

Crosthwaite, P. (2016). A longitudinal multidimensional analysis of EAP writing: Determining course effectiveness. *Journal of English for Academic Purposes, 22*, 166–78. https://doi.org/10.1016/j.jeap.2016.04.005

Crystal, D. (2010). *Rediscover grammar*. Pearson Longman.

Department for Education. (2014). *The national curriculum in England. Framework document*. Retrieved from https://www.gov.uk/government/publications/national-curriculum-in-england-framework-for-key-stages-1-to-4 on 22 April 2018.

Durrant, P., Brenchley, M., & Clarkson, R. (2020). Syntactic development across genres in children's writing: The case of adverbial clauses. *Journal of Writing Research, 12*(2), 419–52. https://doi.org/10.17239/jowr-2020.12.02.04

Durrant, P., Brenchley, M., & McCallum, L. (2021). *Understanding development and proficiency in writing: Quantitative corpus linguistic approaches*. Cambridge University Press. https://doi.org/10.1017/9781108770101

Ellis, N. C., & Ferreira-Junior, F. (2009a). Construction learning as a function of frequency, frequency distribution, and function. *The Modern Language Journal*, *93*(3), 370–85. https://doi.org/10.1111/j.1540-4781.2009.00896.x

Ellis, N. C., & Ferreira-Junior, F. (2009b). Constructions and their acquisition: Islands and the distinctiveness of their occupancy. *Annual Review of Cognitive Linguistics*, 7, 187–220. https://doi.org/10.1075/arcl.7.08ell

Friginal, E., & Weigle, S. (2014). Exploring multiple profiles of L2 writing using multi-dimensional analysis. *Journal of Second Language Writing*, *26*, 80–95. https://doi.org/10.1016/j.jslw.2014.09.007

Goldberg, A. E. (2006). *Constructions at work: The nature of generalization in language*. Oxford: Oxford University Press.

Gray, B., Geluso, J., & Nguyen, P. (2019). The longituindal development of grammatical complexity at the phrasal and clausal levels in spoken and written responses to the TOEFL iBT® test. *TOEFL Research Report*, *90*. https://doi.org/10.1002/ets2.12280

Gries, S. T., & Durrant, P. (2021). Analyzing co-occurrence data. In M. Paquot & S. T. Gries (Eds.), *Practical handbook of corpus linguistics*. Springer.

Halliday, M. A. K., & Matthiessen, C. M. I. M. (2014). *Halliday's introduction of functional grammar* (4th ed.). Routledge. https://doi.org/10.4324/9780203783771

Hunt, K. W. (1965). *Grammatical structures written at three grade levels. NCTE research report No.3*. National Council of Teachers of English.

Jo, R., & Oh, S.-Y. (2021). A usage-based study of L2 constructional development: Combining learner corpus and experimental data. *English Teaching*, *76*(1), 3–31. https://doi.org/10.15858/engtea.76.1.202103.3

Kyle, K., & Crossley, S. A. (2017). Assessing syntactic sophistication in L2 writing: A usage-based approach. *Language Testing*, *34*(4), 513–35. https://doi.org/10.1177/0265532217712554

Kyle, K., Crossley, S. A., & Verspoor, M. (2020). Measuring longitudinal writing development using indices of syntactic complexity and sophistication. *Studies in Second Language Acquisition*. https://doi.org/10.1017/S0272263120000546

Langacker, R. W. (1987). *Foundations of cognitive grammar: Volume 1 theoretical prerequisites*. Stanford University Press.

Lieven, E. V. M., & Tomasello, M. (2008). Children's first language acquisition from a usage-based perspective. In P. Robinson & N. C. Ellis (Eds.), *Handbook of cognitive linguistics and second language acquisition* (pp. 168–96). Routledge.

McCarthy, M. (2021). *Innovations and challenges in grammar*. Routledge. https://doi.org/10.4324/9780429243561

McNamara, D., Graesser, A. C., McCarthy, P. M., & Cai, Z. (2014). *Automated evaluation of text and discourse with Coh-Metrix*. Cambridge University Press. https://doi.org/10.1017/CBO9780511894664

Norris, J. M., & Ortega, L. (2009). Towards and organic approach to investigating CAF in instructed SLA: The case of complexity. *Applied Linguistics*, *30*(4), 555–78. https://doi.org/10.1093/applin/amp044

Römer, U., & Berger, C. M. (2019). Observing the emergence of constructional knowledge: Verb patterns in German and Spanish learners of English at different proficiency levels. *Studies in Second Language Acquisition*, *41*, 1089–110. https://doi.org/10.1017/S0272263119000202

Römer, U., Roberson, A., O'Donnell, M. B., & Ellis, N. C. (2014). Linking learner corpus and experimental data in studying second language learners' knowledge of verb-argument constructions. *ICAME Journal*, *38*, 115–35. https://doi.org/10.2478/icame-2014-0006

Standards and Testing Agency. (2015). National curriculum tests key stage 2: English grammar, spelling, and punctuation – mark schemes. Retrieved from https://dera.ioe.ac.uk/23390/3/Sample_ks2_EnglishGPS_markscheme.pdf (Accessed: 13 March 2020).

Sung, M.-C., & Kim, H. (2020). Effects of verb–construction association on second language constructional generalizations in production and comprehension. *Second Language Research.* https://doi.org/10.1177/0267658320932625

Tomasello, M. (2003). *Constructing a language: A usage-based theory of language acquisition.* Harvard University Press.

Wolfe-Quintero, K., Inagaki, S., & Kim, H. Y. (1998). *Second language development in writing: Measures of fluency, accuracy and complexity.* University of Hawaii Press.

Wulff, S. (2019). Aquisition of formulaic language from a usage-based perspective. In A. Siyanova-Chanturia & A. Pellicer-Sánchez (Eds.), *Understanding formulaic language: A second language acquisition perspective* (pp. 19–37). Routledge. https://doi.org/10.4324/9781315206615-2

Wulff, S. (2021). Usage-based approaches. In N. Tracy-Ventura & M. Paquot (Eds.), *The Routledge handbook of second language acquisition and corpora* (pp. 175–88). Routledge. https://doi.org/10.4324/9781351137904-16

6

GRAMMAR RESEARCH IN PRACTICE

Evaluating parser accuracy

6.1 Introduction

If you are conducting grammar research on a finite budget, you are likely sooner or later to use automated syntactic parsing. As we have seen elsewhere (Chapter 1, Section 1.6.2), this raises important issues as to the accuracy of such parses. The central focus of this chapter will be on the crucial step of checking this accuracy. Although this can seem a daunting task, it is an essential part of ensuring the quality of research findings so is worth devoting some time to. We will see that there are practical techniques for checking and increasing the accuracy of a syntactic parse that can be carried out even within a modestly resourced project.

The chapter will start by reviewing a parsed corpus to understand its structure before moving on to an extended worked example that demonstrates how the accuracy of a parse for a given feature (adjectives which premodify nouns) can be checked and improved. Finally, we will revisit the techniques used in Chapter 4 to create a visualization to summarize the frequency of this feature across learner levels and genres.

6.2 Reading a parsed corpus

In Chapter 2, we saw how to create a parsed version of a corpus using the Stanford CoreNLP programme (Manning et al., 2014). Applying this parser to a text produces an output like that in Figure 6.1 (this is also the format of the parsed corpora that I have recommended downloading – as described in Chapter 2, Section 2.6.5).

Outputs like this will be central to the work we discuss in this chapter so before going any further, it is important to get a good understanding of how they work. Figure 6.1 shows a parse for the sentence *Furthermore, your reporter has neglected to*

DOI: 10.4324/9781003152682-9

1 Furthermore	furthermore	r	O	6	advmod
2 ,	,	,	O	6	punct
3 your	you	PRP$	O	4	nmod:poss
4 reporter	reporter	n	O	6	nsubj
5 has	have	v	O	6	aux
6 neglected	neglect	v	O	0	ROOT
7 to	to	TO	O	8	mark
8 include	include	v	O	6	xcomp
9 many	many	j	O	11	amod
10 positive	positive	j	O	11	amod
11 effects	effect	n	O	8	dobj
12 of	of	IN	O	14	case
13 the	the	DT	O	14	det
14 experience	experience	n	O	11	nmod
15 .	.	.	O	6	punct

FIGURE 6.1 Sample output from Stanford CoreNLP parser

include many positive effects of the experience. The first column assigns a number to each word in this sentence. The second column shows the text in its original form. The third column again shows the text, but each word is now converted to its lemmatized form (see Chapter 3, Section 3.4.2.3 if you need to remind yourself about lemmas), without inflections or capitalization. Thus, *Furthermore* becomes *furthermore*, *your* becomes *you*, *neglected* becomes *neglect*, and *effects* becomes *effect*. The fourth column assigns a POS tag to each word. RB indicates an adverb, PRP$ indicates a possessive pronoun, NN indicates a singular or mass noun, and so on. A full list of the POS tags used by this parser can be found at https://www.ling. upenn.edu/courses/Fall_2003/ling001/penn_treebank_pos.html.[1] Column five indicates any named entities (e.g., person or company names that are recognized by the parser). You will see that there are none in this excerpt, so each row has a value of 'O'.

When studying grammar, the sixth and seventh columns are of special interest as these show how the sentence has been parsed. Column six links each word to the word with which it has its main syntactic relationship. In the terminology of dependency parsing, these are the words on which they are *dependent*. Thus, in this example, *Furthermore* (word 1) is dependent on *neglected* (word 6), *your* (word 3) is dependent on *reporter* (word 4), and so on. Column seven states what this dependency relationship is (a full list of the dependency relationships used in this parser can be found at https://universaldependencies.org/u/dep/index.html). So, for example:

- *Furthermore* is an *adverbial modifier* (*advmod*) of *neglected*;
- *your* is a *possessive nominal modifier* (*nmod:poss*) of *reporter*; and
- *reporter* is a *nominal subject* (*nsubj*) of *neglected*.

A special case that should be noted is the main verb *neglected*. This is the *root* of the sentence, the core to which all dependencies ultimately lead. Words that are not directly dependent on *neglected* are dependent on it via other words. For example, the word *of* (row 12) is dependent on *experience*, which is dependent on *effects*, which is dependent on *include*, which is dependent on *neglected*. Because it is the endpoint of all dependencies, the root is not itself dependent on any other word, so gets the number 0 in column six.

6.3 Accuracy evaluation and fixtagging: an introduction

Once we have a parsed text, we can use it to identify and count the grammatical features in which we are interested. As we saw in Chapter 2, automated parsers are always prone to error, so before making any counts, it is essential to check that our chosen features have been identified with a reasonable degree of accuracy. This section will discuss principles for checking accuracy. Section 6.4 will then work through an extended example of how these principles can be put into practice with a learner corpus.

Though automated annotators are powerful tools, they are rarely completely accurate (at least in our current state of technology). For learner writing, this problem is compounded by the fact that annotators are typically trained on corpora of published native speaker writing so may not be ideally suited to working with learner texts. Despite this, some learner corpus studies have reported promising accuracy figures. Gilquin (2020) describes 92%–99% accuracy for POS tagging across different learner corpora. Figures for parsing syntactic relationships between words are slightly lower but still give cause for optimism. Huang et al. (2018) find 86% of words in their learner corpus were correctly parsed by the Stanford parser (compared to 88% for a native speaker corpus). However, these positive-sounding figures come with some important caveats.

First, overall accuracy figures tend to be skewed by high-frequency features. POS accuracy, for example, is strongly influenced by the fact that many of the words in any corpus will be frequent items that are easy to tag (e.g., *the, a, of, and*). The 100% accuracy achieved for such words can often disguise much poorer performance for other items. This is problematic as it may be precisely these poorer performing items that we want to study. With this in mind, we should heed Gray's (2019) warning that to evaluate the accuracy of our findings, we need to know how well a parser performs on the features that we are counting, rather than its overall accuracy for our corpus as a whole.

Similarly, the relatively high overall accuracy of parsing for learner corpora is partly due to learner corpora tending to include large numbers of short sentences, which are relatively easy to parse. Accuracy for longer learner sentences tends to be much poorer (Huang et al., 2018). If we are interested in studying the developing complexity of learner language, this is clearly problematic as it might mean that we miss the very sentences in which we are most interested.

It is also important to note that the linguistic errors that are often prevalent in learner writing can have a significant impact on parsing. Huang et al. (2018) found that over 60% of learner errors led to at least one parsing error in their corpus of learner English. Interestingly, however, most error-induced parsing issues in Huang et al.'s study could be attributed to errors of punctuation, spelling, and capitalization (2018). This suggests that parsing could be much improved if errors of this sort are corrected in the corpus before the parse takes place. Of course, this will only make sense if any such changes do not affect the things that we want to study. If our research focused on how learners use punctuation, for example, correcting sentence boundaries before the parse would give us misleading results.

The take-home message from all of this is that, although automated annotators can be invaluable tools, they will almost certainly introduce some errors into your findings. Moreover, overall accuracy figures reported in the literature for a particular annotator may not be a good guide to the size of this error, both because the accuracy achieved in one corpus may not transfer to another, and because overall accuracy does not necessarily imply accuracy for the features we are studying. For these reasons, it is important to evaluate how accurately the things you are interested in have been annotated in your texts. As Gray (2019) has observed, the process of evaluating an annotation is a painstaking and resource-intensive one, but it is a crucial part of the research process. It enables us to make informed decisions about which annotator (if any) to use, about which features can be validly studied, about what manual corrections might be needed to an annotator's output, and about how findings should be interpreted.

Examples of a feature that a parser correctly identifies are referred to in technical terms as *true positives*. Alongside these correctly identified items, there are two main types of errors that a parser might make. If we are trying to identify adjectives, for example, one type of mistake would be for it to incorrectly tag words as adjectives even though they aren't adjectives. In other words, it might claim that something is an adjective when it isn't (e.g., it might tag a noun as an adjective). Mistakes of this sort are known as *false positives*. Another type of mistake would be for the parser *not* to tag a word that really *is* an adjective. That is, it might miss some genuine adjectives (e.g., it might tag an adjective as a noun). Mistakes of this sort are known as *false negatives*.

When evaluating the accuracy of an annotation, we attempt to quantify both of these types of mistakes. The measure of false positives is known as *precision*. This tells us what percentage of tags in the annotated texts are correct. To continue with our adjective example, I would get a figure for precision by looking at all the items it has marked as adjectives and deciding how many of these really were adjectives. The measure of false negatives is known as *recall*. This refers to the percentage of actual cases of a feature in the corpus that the annotator has found. To continue our example, I would look at all the items in the corpus that really are adjectives and check what percentage of these the annotator has identified.

To calculate precision and recall, we, therefore, need to know the numbers of:

- *true positives*: e.g., the number of items that the annotator has identified as adjectives and that really are adjectives;

- *false positives*: e.g., the number of items that the annotator has identified as adjectives but that actually are not adjectives; and
- *false negatives*: e.g., the number of items that are adjectives but that the annotator has not identified as adjectives.

Using these definitions, precision is calculated as:

$$precision = \frac{true\ positives}{true\ positives + false\ positives}$$

And recall is calculated as:

$$recall = \frac{true\ positives}{true\ positives + false\ negatives}$$

In practice, checking precision can be easier than checking recall. To check precision, we simply need to search for all cases of a given tag and decide if we think they are correct or not. Recall is trickier because we need to trawl through the corpus to find all cases of the feature we are interested in. In both analyses (but especially analysis of recall), it may not be practical to check annotations for a whole corpus. For this reason, accuracy checks are often performed on a manageable sample of texts. Biber and Gray (2013), for example, checked the accuracy of their annotator with a 5% sample of the 3,839 texts in their corpus (i.e., approximately 190 texts). It is important that the sample chosen is large enough for the features we are checking to appear a reasonable number of times and for the sample to be chosen from across the major learner and text types that make up the corpus (Gray, 2019).

Once precision and recall figures have been determined, we need to interpret them and make decisions about our research. There are no firm rules about what levels of accuracy are acceptable, so researchers need to draw conclusions based on the aims of their own study. Before coming to a final decision, however, it is important to consider whether making some adjustments will improve the accuracy figures. To take a simple example, the Stanford parser systematically tags words such as *other, many*, and *latter* as adjectives, whereas many grammarians would describe them as determiners (e.g., Biber et al., 1999). If we adopt the latter definition, these items will introduce errors into our adjective counts. These items are not *wrong* in an objective sense, since the parser is correct according to its own definition of *adjective*, but they cause the count to include items that I as the researcher do not want to identify as adjectives. From the perspective of my project, therefore, they can be considered erroneous. Because this error is systematic, however, it is relatively easy to correct. As we will see in Section 6.4, an R script can be written to identify these items and re-tag them as determiners. This is an example of what researchers call *fixtagging* (Gray, 2019).

If you have a manually annotated version of the corpus to compare with the computer-parsed version, systematic errors of this sort can be identified by examining cases where the two versions do not align. If you do not have parallel corpora of this sort, errors of precision can be identified by manually inspecting examples of items that have been tagged with a feature of interest. This could be done, for example, by searching for the relevant grammatical tag in a concordancing programme. Errors of recall may be identifiable by trying alternative ways of locating a feature. For example, passives might be found by searching for past participle verbs that haven't been identified as passives (Gray, 2019).

Of course, not all annotation errors will be obviously systematic and so not all can be corrected with simple fixes of the sort described earlier. If accuracy is not at a level that you deem reasonable, you may decide to correct these types of errors individually.

6.4 Accuracy evaluation and fixtagging: a worked example

To illustrate how the processes discussed in the previous section can work in practice, this section will work in detail through an example of accuracy evaluation and fixtagging using data from the GiG project.

6.4.1 Hand-annotating a sample of texts

One of the aims of the GiG project was to trace the development of grammar in terms of noun phrase complexity and subordination (Durrant & Brenchley, in press; Durrant et al., 2020). To determine how well an automated parser could identify relevant features, we sampled 240 texts equally across the four different age groups and two major genre types found in the corpus (as shown in Table 6.1). These texts were then hand-coded for features of noun phrase complexity and subordination by a team of six annotators. To ensure our hand-coding was as accurate as possible, each text was coded independently by two annotators. A member of our core research team then compared the two sets of codes for each text. Whenever there

TABLE 6.1 Corpus sampled for manual annotation

Level	Genre	Texts
Year 2	Literary	30
	Non-literary	30
Year 6	Literary	30
	Non-literary	30
Year 9	Literary	30
	Non-literary	30
Year 11	Literary	30
	Non-literary	30

was a discrepancy between the two annotators, the core research team member decided on the correct coding.

As we were interested specifically in noun phrases and subordinate clauses, only features of the text relevant to those constructs were coded. This reduced the amount of work required as annotators did not have to spend time coding parts of the texts that would not be used in the analysis. Because grammarians can differ in how they define particular grammatical features (see Chapter 5, Section 5.2.1), we prepared an annotation guide that defined and illustrated the features that needed to be coded.[2] It is important to note that this guide was based on definitions that met the aims of our project (i.e., that would be meaningful for informing language pedagogy in England). They were not intended to match the definitions used by the parser. We have already seen that our definitions differed from those of the Stanford parser in at least one way – i.e., that several items that we wished to classify as determiners were classified as adjectives by the parser. If our aim had been to undertake a neutral evaluation of the parser, this would have been unfair. Such an evaluation should be performed using the terms of the parser's own grammar. However, our aim was not to evaluate the parser in general, but rather to evaluate how well it enabled us to achieve our own research aims. That is, we wanted to know how accurately it identified features as they were defined for the purposes of our research.

To compare our coding with that of the parser, we needed to ensure that the two sets of codes could be systematically aligned and compared. For this reason, texts were prepared for hand-coding by first running them through the parser to create spreadsheets similar to those in Figure 6.1. The codes assigned by the parser were then deleted so that texts could be coded by hand. We also added sentence numbers to each text for ease of reference (see Figure 6.2. We will see how sentence numbers can be added to parsed texts of this sort using R in Chapter 8, Section 8.2.1).

A sample hand-coded text can be seen alongside the automatically parsed version in Figure 6.3. The next stage in our analysis was to check to what extent these two sets of codes matched up. As we saw earlier, the crucial information is not the overall match between the two sets of codes, but rather how accurately the parser identifies the features that we wanted to count.

To illustrate with a simple example, one feature of noun complexity in which we were interested was premodification by adjectives. We needed, therefore, to determine how closely the parser matched our manually coded texts in identifying this feature. The following sections will describe this process in detail. If you wish to follow these steps using the original data, instructions for accessing the relevant files can be found in Chapter 2.

6.4.2 Getting metadata and filenames

Our next step is to read the metadata into R. As always, we start by setting the working directory. Because only a subsample of the corpus has been hand-annotated, we next need to retrieve the names of those files that are in the subsample.

sentence_id	word_id	word	pos	dep_on	dep
5	1	Suddenly			
5	2	outside			
5	3	he			
5	4	sees			
5	5	a			
5	6	beautiful			
5	7	bird			
5	8	flew			
5	9	down			
5	10	from			
5	11	the			
5	12	clear			
5	13	bright			
5	14	blue			
5	15	sky			
5	16	and			
5	17	into			
5	18	the			
5	19	shop			

FIGURE 6.2 A corpus text ready for hand annotation

We can do this by referring to the metadata. Texts that have been hand-coded have the code '1' in the 'hand_coded' column of the metadata, so we can use this to iden-tify the appropriate texts. Specifically, we can look for rows where hand_coded == 1 and retrieve only the filename ('file_id') entries for those rows (see Script 6.4.2).

SCRIPT 6.4.2   SET WORKING DIRECTORY; GET METADATA AND FILENAMES FOR HAND-CODED TEXTS

```
setwd('~/CLWD')
metadata <- read.csv('corpora/metadata_gig.csv')
filenames <- metadata$file_id[metadata$hand_coded==1]
```

6.4.3 Identifying and counting adjectives

To compare the manual and automated parses, we need to create two lists: one showing which words in each text were identified as pre-modifying adjectives by the hand-annotators, and the other showing the same thing for the computer parser. The next step in our process is, therefore, to create two empty lists, one for each parse type (Script 6.4.3.a). Similar to our use of lists to store academic vocab-ulary in Chapter 4, each element in the lists will correspond to one text, with each element representing the positions (i.e., row numbers) of all the adjectives identified in that text.

Hand-parsed text

	# word	POS	head rel
5	1 Suddenly		
5	2 outside		
5	3 he	pro	4 subj
5	4 sees		7
5	5 a	det	7
5	6 beautiful	adj	7 amod
5	7 bird	noun_com	8 subj_gram
5	8 flew	verb_lex_act	4 obj_fin_gram
5	9 down	prt	10
5	10 from	prep	8
5	11 the	det	15
5	12 clear	adj	15 amod
5	13 bright	adj	15 amod
5	14 blue	adj	15 amod
5	15 sky	noun_com	10 prepobj
5	16 and	conj_coord	17
5	17 into	prep	8
5	18 the	det	19
5	19 shop	noun_com	17 prepobj

Stanford NLP-parsed text

# word	lemma	POS		head rel
1 Suddenly	suddenly	r	0	3 advmod
2 outside	outside	IN	0	3 case
3 he	he	PRP	0	4 nmod
4 sees	see	v	0	0 ROOT
5 a	a	DT	0	7 det
6 beautiful	beautiful	j	0	7 amod
7 bird	bird	n	0	4 nsubj
8 flew	fly	v	0	7 acl:relcl
9 down	down	r	0	8 advmod
10 from	from	IN	0	15 case
11 the	the	DT	0	15 det
12 clear	clear	j	0	13 amod
13 bright	bright	j	0	15 amod
14 blue	blue	j	0	15 amod
15 sky	sky	n	0	8 nmod
16 and	and	CC	0	15 cc
17 into	into	IN	0	19 case
18 the	the	DT	0	19 det
19 shop	shop	n	0	15 conj

FIGURE 6.3 Parallel hand- and computer-parsed texts

SCRIPT 6.4.3.a   CREATE AN EMPTY VARIABLE TO STORE COUNTS OF ATTRIBUTIVE ADJECTIVES FOR EACH TEXT

```
adj_premod_cases_comp <- list()
adj_premod_cases_hand <- list()
```

Script 6.4.3.b–g is a for-loop that finds and counts adjectives in each hand-parsed and computer-parsed text. Points c and e use *read.csv()* to read in the computer- and hand-parsed versions of the text, respectively. Points d and f serve to identify the adjectives in each text. Note that Point c uses the adapted version of the computer-parsed corpus that we created in Chapter 4 and stored in the 'GiG_parsed' folder (Script 4.3.2). If you have not already created that version, you should revisit Script 4.3.2 and do so now.

SCRIPT 6.4.3.b–g   IDENTIFY AND COUNT ADJECTIVES

```
# b) start a loop so the process below is repeated for each text
for (i in 1:length(filenames)){
  # c) open the computer-parsed text
  text <- read.csv(paste('corpora/GiG_parsed/', filenames[i], '.csv', sep=''),
                   header = T, stringsAsFactors = F)
  # d) identify attributive adjectives in the computer-parsed text
  adj_premod_cases_comp[[i]] <- which(text$dep=='amod')
  # e) open the hand-parsed text
  text <- read.csv(file = paste ('corpora/GiG_hand_parsed/', filenames[i], '.csv',
                   sep = ''))
  # f) identify attributive adjectives in the hand-parsed text
  adj_premod_cases_hand[[i]] <- which(text$dep=='amod')
# g) close the loop
}
```

It is worth spending some time to see how Points d and f work. In both versions of the annotation, pre-modifying adjectives are marked with the code *amod* in the 'dep' column (examples can be seen in lines 12, 13, and 14 of Figure 6.3). We, therefore, need a line of R code that will identify all such items. This is achieved at Points d and f using the *which()* function, as reproduced in Figure 6.4.

```
which(text$dep=='amod')
```

FIGURE 6.4 Using *which()* to identify pre-modifying adjectives

This returns a vector showing the row in the text where each example of a pre-modifying adjective is found. In one of our hand-annotated texts, for example, the *amod* tag is found in the 11th, 44th, and 47th rows, so the *which()* function returns the vector shown in Figure 6.5 (note that I have included this figure purely

[1] 11 44 47

FIGURE 6.5   Locations of pre-modifying adjectives

to help you understand the logic of the script. It won't appear when you run the script and you don't need to reproduce this in your own analysis).

To compare the two sets of texts, we want to record a vector like this separately for each text in the sample. As we saw in Chapter 4, lists are an excellent way of doing this as each item in a list can contain a whole vector. In Figure 6.6, for example (which, again, won't appear when you run the script), the first item, headed [[1]], includes a vector with the single number 9, indicating that a single adjective pre-modifier was found in this text, at row 9. The second item [[2]] is empty, showing that there were no adjective pre-modifiers in this text. The third item includes the vector 11, 44, 47, showing that adjective pre-modifiers occurred in these rows.

```
[[1]]
[1] 9

[[2]]
integer(0)

[[3]]
[1] 11 44 47
```

FIGURE 6.6   Locations of pre-modifying adjectives across three texts

In Points d and f, the vector of row numbers for each text is assigned to the relevant item in the output lists using double square brackets.

At the end of this step, we have therefore obtained two parallel lists, each similar to the one shown in Figure 6.6. One list indexes the positions of adjective pre-modifiers in the hand-annotated texts; the other does the same for the computer-annotated texts.

6.4.4 Identifying true positives, false positives, and false negatives

We saw in Section 2.1 that parser accuracy can be evaluated in terms of precision and recall. We also saw that these figures can be calculated from the numbers of true positives, false positives, and false negatives. To evaluate accuracy, we, therefore, need to obtain these three figures for each text. As well as finding the numbers of true/false positives/negatives, it will also be useful to identify where in each text true/false positives/negatives occur so that we can pinpoint what the parser is getting right and where any problems have arisen.

As in Script 6.4.3, we start by creating lists to store results for each text. As before, each element in the lists will correspond to a single text. This time, these elements will be vectors showing the position of each true positive, false positive, and false negative.

SCRIPT 6.4.4.a CREATE LISTS FOR EACH SET OF POSITIONS WE WANT TO RECORD

```
true_positives <- list()
false_positives <- list()
false_negatives <- list()
```

We then start a loop to go through the texts in the sample. It will be recalled from Script 6.4.3 that we have already stored the positions of each adjective pre-modifier in each version of the corpus in the lists *adj_premod_cases_comp* and *adj_premod_cases_hand*. In both lists, each element represents a text from the corpus and includes a vector showing the position of each adjective pre-modifier. The loop in Script 6.4.4.b–d, therefore, goes to each item in the two lists and compares them.

To identify true positives, we need to find what the two lists have in common. That is, which positions recorded in the 'comp' list are also recorded in the 'hand' list. This is done using the *intersect()* function, which identifies overlaps between two vectors. That is, it shows us which positions appear on both lists. To identify false positives, we need to find positions where the 'comp' version records an adjective pre-modifier but the 'hand' version does not. This is done using the *setdiff()* function, which shows us which positions appear in one vector (the first one mentioned in brackets after the function) but not the other. False negatives are the reverse of false positives. That is, we need to find positions where the 'hand' version records an adjective pre-modifier but the 'comp' version does not. This is also achieved using the *setdiff()* function, but the position of the two lists in the brackets that follow the function is reversed.

SCRIPT 6.4.4.b–d CALCULATE PRECISION AND RECALL: RECORD THE POSITION OF EACH TRUE POSITIVE, FALSE POSITIVE, AND FALSE NEGATIVE AND RECORD THESE TO THE APPROPRIATE POINT IN THE LIST

```
# b) start a loop so the process below is repeated for each text
for (i in 1:length(filenames)){
    # c) record the positions of true positives, false positives, false negatives
    true_positives[[i]] <- intersect(adj_premod_cases_comp[[i]],
                                adj_premod_cases_hand[[i]])
    false_positives[[i]] <- setdiff(adj_premod_cases_comp[[i]],
                                adj_premod_cases_hand[[i]])
    false_negatives[[i]] <- setdiff(adj_premod_cases_hand[[i]],
                                adj_premod_cases_comp[[i]])
# d) close the loop
}
```

TABLE 6.2 Positions of true positives, false positives, and false negatives in three texts

True positives	False positives	False negatives
[[1]] [1] 9	[[1]] integer(0)	[[1]] integer(0)
[[2]] integer(0)	[[2]] integer(0)	[[2]] integer(0)
[[3]] [1] 11 44	[[3]] [1] 47	[[3]] [1] 5

The outcome of this process is three lists: *true positives, false positives* and *false negatives*. For the GiG data, the first three items in these lists are shown in Table 6.2 (again, this figure is purely to illustrate the logic of the analysis. You don't need to create similar output).

These show that the first text (represented by item [[1]] in each list) had one true positive (at row 9) and no false positives or negatives. We saw in Figure 6.6 that the second text ([[2]]) did not have any cases of adjective pre-modifiers. For this reason, there are no true positives, false positives, or false negatives. Text three ([[3]]) is slightly more complex. This had two true positives (at rows 11 and 44), one false positive (at row 47), and one false negative (at row 5).

6.4.5 Calculating precision and recall

Using the three lists created by Script 6.4.4, we can now calculate precision and recall. This is done by, firstly, calculating the total number of true positives, false positives, and false negatives across all texts (Point a). To calculate these, we convert the three lists into vectors using the *unlist()* function and then use the *length()* function to find out how many entries each contains. Once we have found the numbers of true/false positives/negatives, we can plug them into the formula discussed in Section 2.1 to find precision and recall (Point b).

SCRIPT 6.4.5   CALCULATE PRECISION AND RECALL ACCURACY

```
# a) count the numbers of true positives, false positives, false negatives
true_positives_count <- length(unlist(true_positives))
false_positives_count <- length(unlist(false_positives))
false_negatives_count <- length(unlist(false_negatives))

# b) calculate precision and recall
precision <- true_positives_count / (true_positives_count + false_positives_count)
recall <- true_positives_count / (true_positives_count + false_negatives_count)
```

The values for precision and recall are now stored as variables called *precision* and *recall*. To see their values, we simply need to type the variable name into the R console and press Enter. Figure 6.7 shows these commands and their output for the data I have been using.

```
> precision
[1] 0.7713718
> recall
[1] 0.8707361
```

FIGURE 6.7 Precision and recall figures for the GiG corpus

As we discussed earlier, there are no set values for what we should consider adequate accuracy. We need to make an educated judgement based on the aims of our research. In the present case, we can see that recall is the higher of the two figures, with the parser managing to capture nearly nine out of every ten cases of pre-modifying adjectives. This suggests that our analysis will capture most of what is happening with this feature. However, it is important to spend some time looking at the cases the parser has missed. If there are important types of adjective pre-modifier that are being systematically left out, this may mean that we are giving a skewed view of its overall use. Also, if absences are systematic, we may be able to fixtag the parser output to make sure these cases are captured.

Precision is lower than recall, with only 77% of cases identified as adjective pre-modifiers by the parser being confirmed as such by the hand annotation. Stated differently, out of every 100 cases identified by the parser, about 23 are 'wrong' in the sense that they aren't considered genuine adjectives pre-modifiers by our human annotators. It will be important to look at these errors in detail to see if performance can be improved.

6.4.6 Identifying matches and differences in hand vs. computer parses

To understand where the parser went wrong, it will be useful to have a spreadsheet showing, for each text in our corpus,

- which words were identified as adjective pre-modifiers by hand-annotators,
- which words were identified as adjective pre-modifiers by the parser,
- which words were *correctly* identified by the parser as adjective pre-modifiers (the true positives),
- which words were *incorrectly* identified by the parser as adjective pre-modifiers (the false positives), and
- which genuine adjective pre-modifiers were missed by the parser (the false negatives).

All this information already exists in the five lists we created in Scripts 6.4.3 and 6.4.4. That is, the lists:

- adj_premod_cases_hand
- adj_premod_cases_comp
- adj_true_positives
- adj_false_positives
- adj_false_negatives

However, the list format in which these are currently stored cannot be easily written into a spreadsheet for further inspection. For this reason, Script 6.4.6 converts these lists into vectors. We start by creating an empty vector corresponding to each list (Point a).

SCRIPT 6.4.6 IDENTIFY MATCHES AND DIFFERENCES IN ANNOTATION

```
# a) create empty variables to store cases
hand_parse_cases <- vector()
comp_parse_cases <- vector()
true_positive_cases <- vector()
false_positive_cases <- vector()
false_negative_cases <- vector()
# b) start a loop so the process below is repeated for each text
for (i in 1:length(filenames)){
    # c) get row numbers for each case (hand- and computer-annotated) and for
    # each true/false positive/negative
    hand_parse_cases[i] <- paste(adj_premod_cases_hand[[i]], collapse = '_')
    comp_parse_cases[i] <- paste(adj_premod_cases_comp[[i]], collapse = '_')
    true_positive_cases[i] <- paste(true_positives[[i]], collapse = '_')
    false_positive_cases[i] <- paste(false_positives[[i]], collapse = '_')
    false_negative_cases[i] <- paste(false_negatives[[i]], collapse = '_')
# d) close the loop
}
# e) create a spreadsheet to store this information
write.csv(data.frame(filenames, hand_parse_cases, comp_parse_cases,
                    true_positive_cases, false_positive_cases, false_negative_cases),
        file = 'output/accuracy_check.csv', row.names = F)
```

In the central part of the script, we then start a loop to go through all texts and use the information from the five lists created in Scripts 6.4.3 and 6.4.4 to create entries in our five vectors. Specifically, for each item in the lists, the *paste()* function is used to combine the various entries for that item into a single string separated by underscores ('_').

To illustrate how Point c works, we have seen that the first three items on the *adj_premod_cases_comp* list are shown in Figure 6.8 (again, don't expect this to appear during your analysis).

Point b will convert these into the items in a vector. Figure 6.9 shows what the first few items look like for my data.

Once the loop has been closed, Point e combines our five vectors into a single table using the *data.frame()* function and saves this table as a .csv file called *accuracy_check.csv*. This can now be opened as a spreadsheet (e.g., using Microsoft *Excel*,

```
[[1]]
[1] 9

[[2]]
integer(0)

[[3]]
[1] 11 44 47
```

FIGURE 6.8   First three elements in *adj_premod_cases_comp*

```
[1] "9"              " "          "11_44_47"
```

FIGURE 6.9   First three elements in *comp_parse_cases*

filenames	hand_parse_cases	comp_parse_cases	true_positive_cases	false_positive_cases	false_negative_cases
2_6b	9	9	9		
2_6c					
2_6d	5_11_44	11_44_47	11_44	47	5
2_8c					
2_9b					
2_13c		39		39	
2_16b	13_20_37	13_20_37	13_20_37		
2_18b	11	11	11		
2_18c					
2_23c					

FIGURE 6.10   Output from Script 6.4.6: identifying matches and mismatches

Apply *Numbers*, or OpenOffice *Calc*). Figure 6.10 shows the first ten rows of this spreadsheet for the GiG data I have been using.

6.4.7 Identifying and fixing parsing errors

To diagnose problems with the parse, we are principally interested in where it has gone wrong. That is, in false positives and false negatives. In the current case, false positives are of particular interest because the chief problem with our accuracy rates was in precision (i.e., the proportion of false positives) rather than recall (the proportion of false negatives).

From Figure 6.10, we can see that the first false positive is found in text 2_6d, at row 47. So, our first step should be to open the hand- and computer-annotated version of that text and see what has happened at row 47. The relevant sections of the two versions are shown in Figure 6.11.

The 47th item in the text is, somewhat confusingly, the 48th row in the Excel sheet. This is because the first row is the column headings. In this case, the relevant item is the word *other*, which occurs in the noun phrase *other things*. We can see that the computer annotator has marked this as an adjective, whereas the hand-annotators have marked it as a determiner.

Hand-annotated

40	5	1 For	NA	1 prepobj
41	5	2 lunch	noun_com	4 subj
42	5	3 I	pro	NA
43	5	4 had	NA	7
44	5	5 a	det	7
45	5	6 big	adj	7 amod
46	5	7 sandwich	noun_com	4 dobj
47	5	8 and	conj_coord	10
48	5	9 other	det	10
49	5	10 things	noun_com	4 dobj
50	5	11 .	NA	

Computer-annotated

40	1 For	for	IN	0	2 case
41	2 lunch	lunch	n	0	4 nmod
42	3 I	I	PRP	0	4 nsubj
43	4 had	have	v	0	0 ROOT
44	5 a	a	DT	0	7 det
45	6 big	big	j	0	7 amod
46	7 sandwich	sandwich	n	0	4 dobj
47	8 and	and	CC	0	7 cc
48	9 other	other	j	0	10 amod
49	10 things	thing	n	0	7 conj
50	11 .	.	.	0	4 punct

FIGURE 6.11 Mismatch in parallel hand- and computer-parsed texts

I have already noted that the Stanford parser classifies as adjectives words that many grammars classify as determiners. This is not necessarily a fault with the Stanford parser per se since the parser is staying faithful to its own definitions, but it is a problem as far as our research is concerned as we do not want to mark these items as adjectives.

Fortunately, this issue is relatively simple to solve. All we need to do is come up with a list of the words that the parser classifies as adjectives but that we wish to classify as determiners and write an R script that changes the annotation for these items. To do this, I consulted the grammar that informed our hand annotation (Biber et al., 1999) to create a list of everything that should be classed as a determiner. I then used concordancing software – specifically, *CasualConc* (Imao, 2021), but any concordancer would do just as well – to recall each of these words from the computer-annotated versions of the texts and see if they had been classified as adjectives. The following words turned out to be problematic:

> *other, first, second, third, fourth, fifth, sixth, seventh, much, many, more*

Script 6.4.7 'fixes' these items in the computer-annotated version of the corpus. As with previous scripts, it first (Point a) reads in the metadata and extracts a list of filenames. It then initiates a loop to run through each file (Point b) and opens them in turn (Point c).

SCRIPT 6.4.7 FIX PROBLEMS WITH THE PARSE

```
# a) read in the metadata and get file names for the corpus
metadata <- read.csv('corpora/metadata_gig.csv')
filenames <- metadata$file_id
# b) start a loop so the process below is repeated for each text
for (i in filenames){
  # c) read in a text
  text <- read.csv(paste('corpora/GiG_parsed/', i, '.csv', sep=''))
  # d) identify the position of any words from the list of items to be corrected
  det <- text$lemma %in% c('other',
                  'first', 'second', 'third', 'fourth', 'fifth', 'sixth',
                  'seventh', 'much', 'many', 'more')
  # e) change the part of speech and dependency relations of these items
  # to determiner
  text$pos[det] <- 'DT'
  text$dep[det] <- 'det'
  # f) save the revised corpus file in a new folder
  write.csv(text, paste('corpora/GiG_parsed_revised/', i, '.csv', sep=''))
# g) close the loop
}
```

With the text open, we next use the *%in%* operator to identify any items in the *lemma* column that match one of the items in our list of problematic words (Point d). This creates a vector called *det*, which records the positions of these words. This vector is then used to tell R to change the pos column to DT and the dep column to 'det' wherever one of these items occurs (Point e). Finally, the revised corpus file is saved (Point f) and the loop closed (Point g). I have opted to save the files to a new folder ('GiG_parsed_revised') rather than the original folder. In this way, the original version can be retained in case I need to revert to it later. Before running the script, it is, therefore, necessary to create a new, empty, folder, called 'GiG_parsed_revised' within the main 'corpora' folder.

Once we have *fixed* the parse in this way, we next cycle back through Scripts 6.4.2–6.4.6 to re-evaluate accuracy and identify any further problems that might need fixing. Note that this time, rather than reading in the parsed corpus from the file from the folder 'GiG_parsed', I need to read it in from 'GiG_parsed_revised', so Point c in Script 6.4.3 will need to be changed accordingly, as illustrated in Figure 6.12.

```
text <- read.csv(paste('corpora/GiG_parsed_revised/', filenames[i], '.csv', sep=''),
            header = T, stringsAsFactors = F)
```

FIGURE 6.12   6.4.3.c revised

If we run through Scripts 6.4.2–6.4.6 again with the new version of the corpus, we find that the precision and recall scores to have changed, though not dramatically (see Figure 6.13).

```
> precision
[1] 0.8115578
> recall
[1] 0.8698384
```

FIGURE 6.13   Accuracy scores after fixtagging

The recall score has dropped slightly (from .871 to .870), suggesting that by changing all the words on our list to determiners, we may have overshot our mark; some of these words are sometimes genuinely used as adjectives. However, this drop in recall can be offset against a rather larger improvement in precision (from .771 to .812). For many purposes, this may be considered a worthwhile trade-off.

6.5 Tracing development in a grammatical feature

Once we are satisfied with the levels of accuracy with which a feature is identified, we can move on to count its occurrences in each text. Frequencies of occurrence can then be used to determine how a feature's use correlates with variables like time or quality, or if we are performing a multi-dimensional analysis (see Chapter 5, Section 5.3.3), how it covaries with other features. We will now look briefly at how frequency of adjective premodification can be traced in the current corpus. This follows the same format as the scripts described in Chapter 4 for quantifying features of vocabulary across year groups, so I will not discuss the elements of these scripts in detail.

6.5.1 Counting a feature in texts

Continuing with our example of adjective pre-modifiers, Script 6.5.1 illustrates how this feature can be counted in texts and the counts saved to a spreadsheet for further analysis. As with previous processes in this chapter, we start by setting the working directory, opening the metadata, and retrieving filenames (Point a). We then create an empty variable (*adj_premod_count*) to store the feature counts for each text (Point b). A loop is then initiated (Point c), which opens each parsed text (Point d). It then counts the instances of 'amod' dependency markers in each using the *sum()* function, which tells us how many times a given condition is met – in this case, how many times the 'dep' column is equal to the value *amod* (Point e). This number is recorded as *adj_premod_counts*. Because older children tend to write longer texts, these counts need to be normalized in some way to enable fair comparisons. One option would be to divide the number of adjectives by the number of nouns in the text (telling us what proportion of nouns are pre-modified).

SCRIPT 6.5.1 COUNT PRE-MODIFYING ADJECTIVES

```
# a) set working directory. Access metadata and get list of file names
setwd('~/CLWD')
metadata <- read.csv('corpora/metadata_gig.csv')
filenames <- metadata$file_id
# b) create an empty variable to store feature counts for each text
adj_premod_count <- vector()
# c) start a loop so the process below is repeated for each text
for (i in 1:length(filenames)){
  # d) open the text
  text <- read.csv(paste('corpora/GiG_parsed_revised/',
                         filenames[i], '.csv', sep=''))
  # e) count attributive adjectives
  adj_premods <- sum(text$dep=='amod')
  # f) normalize adjective count to occurrences per noun
  adj_premod_count[i] <- adj_premods/sum(text$pos == 'n')
# g) close the loop
}
# h) create and save an output table
output <- data.frame(metadata, adj_premod_count)
write.csv(output, file='output/adj_premods.csv', row.names = F)
```

Another option would be to divide by the total number of words in the text (telling us how frequently adjectives occurred). At Point f in the script, I have chosen the first option, dividing the adjective counts by the total number of nouns in the text and recording them in the *adj_premod_count* vector. The loop is then closed at Point g. Finally, the *adj_premod_count* vector is combined with the metadata and saved (Point h).

6.5.2 Visualizing variation across learner groups

In Chapter 4 (Script 4.2.4), we saw how to create a visual that summarizes differences in a measure across learner groups. The same technique can be applied using the file created in Section 5.1 to show how use of adjectives differs across year groups in our child corpus (Script 6.5.2). Note that if you run this script for the GiG corpus, two warning messages will be provided alongside the plot, stating that two rows with non-finite values have been removed. This is because two very short texts written by young learners contained no nouns. The normalized adjective counts (which, you will recall, were created by dividing the number of adjectives by the number of nouns) are therefore not meaningful for

---

SCRIPT 6.5.2   VISUALIZE VARIATION ACROSS LEARNER GROUPS

```
# a) make sure the necessary R packages are loaded
library(ggplot2)
library(Hmisc)
# b) read the data into R
data <- read.csv(file = 'output/adj_premods.csv')
# c) remove unwanted participants (Year 4) and convert grouping
# variable to factor
data$year_group <- factor(data$year_group,
                          levels = c('Year_2', 'Year_6', 'Year_9', 'Year_11'))
# d) create the visual
ggplot(data, aes(year_group, adj_premod_count, linetype=genre)) +
    stat_summary(fun='mean', geom='line', aes(group=genre)) +
    stat_summary(fun.data='mean_cl_boot', geom='errorbar', width=.2) +
    labs(y="adjectives per noun")+labs(x="Year Group")
# e) save the visual to the 'outputs' folder
ggsave('output/adj_premod_line_graph.jpeg')
```

---

these texts. R's warning message shows that it has excluded them when creating the graph.

The resultant graph is shown in Figure 6.14. This suggests quite clearly that adjective pre-modifiers are more frequent in literary than in non-literary writing (at least in Years 2–9). It also seems that, while the mean number of adjectives per noun remains relatively constant across year groups in non-literary writing, there

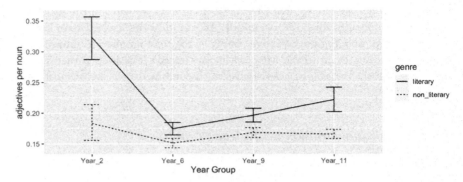

FIGURE 6.14 Frequency of adjective pre-modifiers across discipline*genres and year groups

are substantial differences between year groups for literary writing. Most strikingly, the youngest writers (in Year 2) use far more adjectives than the other year groups. There is a sharp downward correction at Year 6, and then a more gradual increase across year groups up to Year 11.

The high scores at Year 2 may reflect the way that many children at this stage of their education seem keen to premodify almost every noun with at least one (often more!) adjective, as exemplified in Excerpt 1.

1. If you're a **healthy nice** doctor, you use a **comfy soft** trolley bed to check their **unhealthy shocked** patients. If you're a **mad magic** doctor, you use your **earwaxy listening** ear to make sure the **frightened sad** patients is OK.

Figure 6.14 suggests that this tendency has been largely overcome by Year 6.

Further follow-up analysis building on these findings might then look into why an increase is seen from Year 6 to 11 and whether a shift is seen in the types of adjectives that learners are using and the functions for which they are using them (for an example of an analysis along these lines, see Durrant & Brenchley, in press, which looks in detail at premodification in the GiG corpus).

6.6 Conclusion

Researchers of writing development can benefit enormously from the ability to annotate the syntactic features of texts. However, automated annotation also has the potential to produce misleading results if it is not carefully checked. Studying the accuracy of such annotations is therefore one of the most essential steps in corpus studies of development that focus on grammar. It is also one of the most daunting. I hope that this chapter has convinced you that accuracy checks can be achieved in a practical way and are well worth the time spent on them.

The chapter has mostly built on R techniques and functions already learned in previous chapters. However, three key new functions have also been introduced. Specifically, we have seen how to:

- Identify overlaps and differences between two vectors using *intersect()* and *set-diff()*; and
- Count the number of elements in a vector that meet a criterion using *sum()*.

These functions will be put to further use when we come to study collocations in Chapter 8.

Notes

1 This and other URLs cited in this chapter were last accessed on 14 March 2022.
2 This guide can be found at http://phildurrant.net/creating-the-growth-in-grammar-corpus/.

References

Biber, D., & Gray, B. (2013). Discourse characteristics of writing and speaking task types on the TOEFL iBT test: A lexico-grammatical analysis. *TOEFL iBT Research Report, 19.* https://doi.org/10.1002/j.2333-8504.2013.tb02311.x

Biber, D., Johansson, S., Leech, G., Conrad, S., & Finegan, E. (1999). *Longman grammar of spoken and written English.* Longman.

Durrant, P., & Brenchley, M. (2022). Development of noun phrase complexity in children's writing. *Applied Linguistics.*

Durrant, P., Brenchley, M., & Clarkson, R. (2020). Syntactic development across genres in children's writing: The case of adverbial clauses. *Journal of Writing Research, 12*(2), 419–52. https://doi.org/10.17239/jowr-2020.12.02.04

Gilquin, G. (2020). Learner corpora. In M. Paquot & S. T. Gries (Eds.), *A practical handbook of corpus linguistics* (pp. 283–303) Springer. https://doi.org/10.1007/978-3-030-46216-1_13

Gray, B. (2019). Tagging and counting linguistic features for multi-dimensional analysis. In T. Berber Sardinha & M. V. Pinto (Eds.), *Multi-dimensional analysis: Research methods and current issues* (pp. 43–66). Bloomsbury Academic. https://doi.org/10.5040/9781350023857.0011

Huang, Y., Murakami, A., Alexopoulou, T., & Korhonen, A. (2018). Dependency parsing of learner English. *International Journal of Corpus Linguistics, 23*(1), 28–54. https://doi.org/10.1075/ijcl.16080.hua

Imao, Y. (2021). CasualConc (version 2.1.6). Osaka University. Retrieved from Available from https://sites.google.com/site/casualconc/(last accessed 19 April 2021)

Manning, C. D., Surdeanu, M., Bauer, J., Finkel, J., Bethard, S. J., & McClosky, D. (2014). The Stanford CoreNLP natural language processing toolkit. *Proceedings of the 52nd Annual Meeting of the Association for Computational Linguistics: System Demonstrations,* 55–60. https://doi.org/10.3115/v1/P14-5010

PART FOUR
Studying formulaic language in writing development

7
UNDERSTANDING FORMULAIC LANGUAGE IN LEARNER WRITING

7.1 Introduction

Much applied linguistic research relies on analyzing language into smaller constituent parts and placing those parts into general abstract categories. Thus, for example, analyses discussed in Chapter 5 involved breaking sentences into phrases and assigning labels, such as *noun phrase* or *preposition phrase* to those phrases. These might then be broken down further, into determiners, pre- and post-modifiers, complements, and so on. As I hope Chapter 5 has convinced you, a great deal can be learned about writing development by using categories of this sort. Research on formulaic language, however, is based on the idea that additional insights are often available if we consider sequences holistically. This is seen most clearly in polywords, such as *by and large* (meaning *generally*); idioms, such as *on the ball* (meaning *alert*); and phrasal verbs, such as *carry out* (meaning *do*), all of which are difficult to make sense of when broken into their constituent words. Other key categories include pragmatic formulas, such *as nice to meet you*; collocations, such *stiff drink*; and lexical bundles, such as *on the other hand*.

Compared with vocabulary and grammar, formulaic language is a relative newcomer to writing development research. However, interest in this area has developed rapidly over the last two decades, especially in relation to second language writing. As we will see in this chapter, taking a formulaic perspective on writing opens up new types of analyses and enables a range of insights that are not available within the more traditional linguistic approaches. We can therefore confidently expect work in this area to continue to increase in the future.

There are several reasons why learner language researchers have been interested in formulaic language (Durrant et al., 2021). First, many formulaic sequences need to be specifically learned. A student of English who knows the grammatical categories and component words of *by and large* or *on the ball*, is unlikely to

DOI: 10.4324/9781003152682-11

understand or produce these phrases without learning them as wholes. This suggests that they should be explicitly targeted by teaching. Second, many researchers have argued that formulaic sequences are processed in speakers' minds differently from more novel language. Some have suggested that formulaic sequences may be stored holistically in our mental lexicon, others that there are special connections linking their component parts (Siyanova-Chanturia, 2015). Whatever model you prefer, there is widespread agreement that producing and understanding formulaic sequences takes less mental effort than producing and understanding novel language. A learner who masters formulaic sequences is therefore likely to use the language with greater ease and fluency (Pawley & Syder, 1983). Third, some theories of language learning assign formulaic language a key role in the language learning process. UB models, in particular (see Chapter 5, Section 5.2.3), propose that we learn language through processes of abstracting rules from memorized formulaic sequences (Tomasello, 2003; Wulff, 2019). Fourth, many researchers see formulaic language as an important part of sounding like an *insider* in a language community. Within any social group (be it broader, like a nation, or narrower, like communities of academic researchers), members are likely to find themselves facing communicative situations that recur on a regular basis. Recurrent situations at the level of a national community might include meeting a new person, being told that someone is ill, or sitting down to a meal with other people. Recurrent situations faced by academics might include referring to a graph in a text, signalling a contrast from a previous idea, or acknowledging another scholar's work. Communities tend to develop conventional ways of expressing oneself in these situations (*Nice to meet you! Get well soon! Bon appetit! As shown in Figure 1; on the other hand; as* NNN *have argued*, etc.). Such phrases both ease communication and can come to seem *natural* or *appropriate* to community members and therefore mark a speaker or writer as proficient (Hyland, 2008). Finally, because formulaic language is often specific to both contexts and communicative functions within those contexts, analysis of such language can give insights into a writer's orientation to those contexts and the extent to which they express particular meanings. For example, analysis might give clues as to how often academic writers refer to graphs, signal contrasts, or acknowledge other scholars' work.

7.2 Defining formulaic language

Formulaic language has been defined in different ways by researchers with different theoretical and practical aims. A useful catch-all is provided by Wray, who defines a formulaic sequence as "any multiword string that is perceived by the agent (i.e., learner, researcher, etc.) to have an identity or usefulness as a single lexical unit" (Wray, 2019, p. 267). This definition is helpfully flexible because it leaves open the questions of why, and in what ways, someone might perceive a string as having identity or usefulness as a single unit. A polyword like *by and large*, for example, might be seen in this way because it can only be understood or learned as a whole. A pragmatic formula, like *get well soon* might be valued because of its usefulness in negotiating social situations. A high-frequency chunk like *on the other hand* might be valued because it is used so often or because its high frequency facilitates psycholinguistic processing (Siyanova-Chanturia & Pellicer-Sánchez, 2019).

The fact that there are many different reasons for perceiving a sequence as formulaic implies that many different types of sequences can be considered formulaic. Durrant et al. (2022), for example, cite nine categories, as summarized in Table 7.1. As we will see, however, most corpus research into writing development has focused on two types that are particularly well-suited to corpus analysis: collocations and lexical bundles. The sections that follow will focus primarily on these.

TABLE 7.1 Types of formulaic sequence (Durrant et al., 2022)

Formula type	Description	Examples
Phrasal and prepositional verbs	*phrasal* verbs: verbs followed by an adverbial particle, where the phase as a whole is used with a non-literal meaning *prepositional verbs*: verbs followed by a preposition	*blow up; shut down* *approve of; cope with*
Polywords	fixed multiword expressions that function as a single unit	*for the most part; so far* *so good*
Idioms	a relatively fixed sequence of words with a non-literal, typically metaphorical meaning	*over the moon; driving me up the wall*
Proverbs	non-literal sequences, often sentence-length, providing advice, warnings, and commonplace generalizations	*a watched pot never boils*
Binomials	recurrent conventional sequences of two words from the same POS, connected by a conjunction	*black and white; alive and well*
Pragmatic formulas	context-bound phrases that are characteristic of a particular speech community and that have a specific pragmatic function	*bless you; take care*
Collocations	Pairs of words that are syntagmatically associated with each other because either: (a) they are frequently found together; (b) they are *restricted* to each other, in the sense that at least one is rarely found outside of the other's company; or (c) one word takes on a special meaning it does not carry in other contexts. Pairs may be flexible in the sense that their relative positions in an utterance can change and, in some cases, they can be used in different POS: e.g., *that was a **strong argument**; that **argument** was **strong**; she **argued strongly**.*	a) *take time; young people* b) *purse lips; upside down* c) *stiff drink; curry favour*

(Continued)

TABLE 7.1 (Continued) Types of formulaic sequence (Durrant et al., 2022)

Formula type	Description	Examples
Lexical bundles	Contiguous word combinations which occur very frequently in language.	*one the other hand; one of the; and so on*
Lexicalized sentence stems	A conventional expression in which some elements are fixed and others allow for a range of possibilities	Noun Phrase – *think-*TENSE *nothing of* ing-clause: e.g., *Simon thinks nothing of spending £200 on a pair of shoes.*

7.3 How can we study formulaic language in a corpus?

7.3.1 A frequency-based approach to studying formulaic language

We can distinguish two main ways of identifying formulaic language in a learner corpus. The first uses frequency data, either from the learner corpus itself or from a reference corpus, to identify sequences as formulaic. The second relies on the intuition or judgement of the analyst or their informants. At present, the former approach has been the more widely used in corpus research so will be our main focus here (for further discussion of the second approach, see Durrant et al., 2021).

Researchers have been using frequency information to identify formulaic language for several decades (Jones & Sinclair, 1974; Sinclair, 1966 are interesting early examples) and a range of techniques have been developed. Techniques used in contemporary writing research can be categorized in terms of three main distinctions:

- those that focus on *recurrence* vs. those that focus on *co-occurrence*;
- those that focus on fixed word sequences vs. those that focus on flexible word pairings; and
- those based on data from a learner corpus vs. those based on data from a reference corpus.

The distinction between recurrence and co-occurrence is related to whether we see a sequence primarily as a lexical item in its own right or as a combination of separate words that are drawn to each other. Recurrence takes the 'lexical item' approach. It refers to how frequently a particular combination of words occurs in a corpus. Researchers have been interested in this both because a combination that recurs is likely to play an important role in a community's discourse and because it is likely to have a special status (e.g., holistic storage) in writers' mental language systems. Co-occurrence, in contrast, refers to how strongly the component words in a sequence are associated with each other. A good example of this is the collocation *curry favour*. Though not particularly frequent as a unit (i.e., its rate of recurrence is relatively low), its component words are strongly co-occurrent because the verb *curry* is almost always followed by *favour*. In other words, the attraction from one word to the other is strong.

The second distinction, between fixed and flexible sequences, concerns what should be counted as cases of *the same* sequence. Consider the following examples:

1. *She made a* **strong argument** *for her case.*
2. *She made a* **strong** *and persuasive* **argument** *for her case.*
3. *The* **argument** *for her case was* **strong**.
4. *She* **argued strongly** *for her case.*

If our analysis focuses on fixed sequences, an item is counted as recurring only if the same sequence of words is repeated. Thus, the combination *strong argument* would be counted as having occurred once in these examples (i.e., in Sentence 1). A second sequence – *argued strongly* – would also be counted as having occurred once. If we take a more flexible approach by allowing words to shift their positions relative to each other while retaining their identity as the same sequence, the combination *strong + argument* will be counted as occurring three times (in Sentences 1, 2, and 3). A different type of flexibility is to allow sequences that include derivationally or inflectionally related words (see Chapter 3, Section 3.1.2) to be counted as instances of the same type. In this case, *argued strongly* would also be considered an example of the same sequence as *strong argument*.

The final distinction concerns where our frequency data come from. One approach is to identify sequences as formulaic based on their occurrences in the learner corpus we are studying. That is, a sequence is counted as formulaic based on how frequently it is used by the learners whose writing makes up our corpus. This approach can be described as *corpus-internal* because it is based on frequencies within the learner corpus (Durrant et al., 2021). A strength of this approach is that it can identify items that are formulaic *for the learners*, regardless of whether they are formulaic in the broader language they are learning. It, therefore, treats learner writing in its own terms. A limitation is that learner corpora are typically rather small, which can be problematic because many types of formulaic language only show themselves in larger samples. This is especially the case for strongly co-occurring but relatively infrequent collocations like *curry favour*.

A more fundamental issue with a corpus-internal approach is the flipside of the previously noted advantage. We saw that this approach identifies sequences as formulaic regardless of whether they are used in the broader language. But for many research purposes, this is not what we want. Much of the time, it is precisely whether and how learners use sequences that are formulaic in the broader language that we are most interested in. In a school context, for example, we might want to know whether learners use sequences that are typical of mature academic writing. For these purposes, it is better to identify formulas based on their occurrence in a reference corpus that represents the target language we are interested in. This approach can be described as *corpus-external* (Durrant et al., 2021).

Equipped with these distinctions between recurrence vs. co-occurrence, fixed vs. flexible sequences, and internal vs. external approaches, we can now look in detail at the two main types of formulaic sequences that have been studied in writing development research: *lexical bundles* and *collocations*.

7.3.2 Lexical bundles

Fixed sequences of words that recur frequently in a corpus are known as *lexical bundles*. Archetypal examples in written discourse include *on the other hand, as a result of, it is important to,* and *on the basis of.* Sequences of this sort are of interest partly because they can give insights into the discourse functions that learners express in their writing. Bundles often have transparent functions, such as linking ideas (*on the other hand*), showing cause-effect relationships (*as a result of*), and expressing author stance (*it is important to*). So, by looking at writers' use of bundles, we can get a sense of how frequently, and in what ways, they express such functions. Another reason bundles are of interest is that they are relatively context-specific. Typical bundles can differ strikingly between speech and writing, between academic and general writing, and between writing in different academic disciplines, for example (Biber, 2006; Durrant, 2017; Simpson-Vlach & Ellis, 2010). Compare typical spoken bundles such as *and I was like* and *if you know what I mean* with bundles from academic writing, such as *in order to, due to the* and *can be seen*. For this reason, bundles can give important insights into the context-specific use of conventional language that, as we saw earlier, is taken to distinguish expert from novice writing.

A common corpus-internal approach to studying lexical bundles in learner writing is to determine what discourse functions are frequently expressed with lexical bundles by writers at different levels of proficiency (Appel & Wood, 2016; Biber & Gray, 2013; Chen & Baker, 2016; Ruan, 2017; Staples et al., 2013). Such studies have typically based their analysis on the functional framework proposed by Biber et al. (2004), summarized here in Table 7.2. This classifies bundles under three general categories – *stance, text,* and *referential* – and then into several subcategories. Such analysis can give a sense of the extent to which learners express stance, cohesion, etc. in conventionalized forms. While research of this sort has great promise, results to date have been inconsistent, even across relatively similar contexts (Durrant et al., 2021). Possible reasons for this will be discussed later in this section.

Another use of lexical bundles is seen in studies which employ the corpus-external technique of determining how much use learners make of sequences that are attested in a reference corpus. Most frequently, such studies have simply calculated the proportion of word combinations of a specified length (e.g., two words, three words, four words) in learner texts that are attested a given number of times in a suitable reference corpus. This has proved to be a relatively reliable index of proficiency, with most studies finding that more proficient texts make more use of attested sequences (Bestgen, 2017; Bestgen & Granger, 2014; Garner et al., 2019; Kim et al., 2018; Kyle & Crossley, 2016). A slightly more complex approach is to calculate the average frequency with which learners' word combinations appear in a reference corpus (this is analogous to the measures of vocabulary frequency

TABLE 7.2 Functional classification of lexical bundles, based on Biber et al. (2004)

General category	Definition	Sub-category	Sub-category definition	Examples
Stance	Provide a frame for the interpretation of the following proposition	Epistemic	Comment on the knowledge status of the information in the following proposition: certain, uncertain, or probably/possible	the fact that the
		Attitudinal/modality	Express writer attitudes towards the actions or events described in the following proposition. Four major sub-categories: desire; obligation/directive; intention/prediction; ability	it is important to; it is necessary to; to be able to; it is possible to
Discourse	None provided	Topic introduction/focus	Provide overt signals that a new topic is being introduced	None provided
		Topic elaboration/clarification	None provided	on the other hand; as well as the
Referential	Generally identify an entity or single out some particular attribute of an entity as especially important	Identification/focus	focus on the noun phrase following the bundle as especially important	is one of the; one of the most
		Imprecision	indicates imprecise reference	None provided
		Specification of attributes: Quantity	Specify quantities or amounts	the rest of the; per cent of the
		Tangible framing	describe size/form of the following noun	the size of the; in the form of
		Intangible framing	specify abstract characteristics (e.g., in the form of, the nature of the) or to establish logical relationships in a text (e.g., on the basis of, in terms of the)	the nature of the; in the case of; in terms of the; as a result of; on the basis of; in the absence of; the way in which; the extent to which; in the presence of
		Time/place/text reference — Place	None provided	in the United States
		Time	None provided	at the same time; at the time of
		Text deixis	None provided	shown in figure N; as shown in figure
		Multi-functional	None provided	the end of the; the top of the; at the end of; in the middle of

discussed in Chapter 3, Section 3.3). Results have generally shown a positive correlation between proficiency and mean frequency, though there does seem to be some variation depending on the specific task type and grading criteria used (Garner et al., 2019; Kim et al., 2018; Kyle & Crossley, 2016).

Studying lexical bundles in learner writing raises several methodological issues that researchers need to be aware of. One concerns exactly how *lexical bundle* should be defined. A standard definition is that they are word sequences of a specified length that appear more than a specified number of times and/or in a specified number of texts in a corpus. In Biber and Gray's study, for example, lexical bundles are four-word sequences that appear in at least 10 (out of 960) texts in their corpus and with a frequency of at least five per 100,000 words.

Biber and Gray's (2013) focus on four-word sequences is common to much lexical bundle research. Although longer bundles can be (and have been, e.g., Appel & Wood 2016) identified, long bundles tend to be both relatively infrequent and highly context-specific. This can be seen in the right-hand columns of Table 7.3, which list the ten most frequent six-word bundles in the BAWE corpus. Compared to the four-word bundles shown in the middle columns, these are infrequent and mostly tied to very clearly defined contexts (mostly, in this case, medical contexts). As the left-hand columns show, two-word bundles are much more frequent than four-word bundles. However, this can also be problematic since studying such items can produce an overwhelming amount of data that researchers may not be able to handle in a practical way. Moreover, unlike the four- and six-word bundles, these short combinations do not have readily identifiable discourse functions, making them far less interesting for our purposes. Combinations of between three and five words, therefore, appear to represent a *sweet spot* where bundles are abundant but manageable and where many (though not all) combinations have relatively clear functions.

TABLE 7.3 Most frequent two-, four-, and six-word bundles in BAWE corpus

Two-word bundles		Four-word bundles		Six-word bundles	
Bundle	Freq.*	Bundle	Freq.	Bundle	Freq.
of the	66,522	*on the other hand*	839	*it can be seen that the*	58
in the	38,711	*as a result of*	740	*International Journal of Contemporary Hospitality Management*	55
to the	24,630	*in the case of*	613	*the nature of the problem and*	52
and the	17,398	*the end of the*	610	*from the patient about presenting*	50
it is	16,649	*it is important to*	577	*problem and their expectations for treatment*	50
to be	15,388	*at the same time*	508	*and the social and family background*	50
on the	14,341	*as well as the*	503	*and a summary of key information*	50
that the	13,040	*in the form of*	482	*gathered from the patient about the*	50
for the	12,198	*at the end of*	428	*of referral and a summary of*	50
can be	10,491	*it is possible to*	404	*to your clinical problem solving by*	50

Retrieved from sketchengine.eu, 23 November 2021

* Freq = total number of occurrences in the corpus

The other elements of Gray and Biber's definition concern how frequently a combination needs to recur, and in how many different texts it should appear, to be counted as a lexical bundle. In practice, these thresholds are often decided based on the practical concern of what gives researchers a substantial, but manageable, number of bundles to work with. However, Lu et al. (2018) show that variation in thresholds can have a surprisingly large impact on findings. They note that, in their data, when the frequency threshold was set at a low level, non-native English writers were found to use more bundle types than native writers. When the threshold was set to a higher level, however, this finding was reversed, with the native writers evidencing more bundle types. The most appropriate threshold for a given study is likely to depend heavily on design features of the corpus being used (more on this shortly) and on the aims of the research. No single *correct* threshold for lexical bundles is therefore likely to emerge. However, Lu et al.'s (2018) findings imply that it is important for researchers to consider the impact that alternative thresholds might have on their findings.

A further complication is introduced by the fact that the internal structure of a corpus can have a large impact on the number of word sequences that qualify as lexical bundles. Because many bundles are closely related to particular topics, a corpus made up of several texts on the same topic is likely to contain more recurrent sequences than a corpus of texts on a variety of different topics. A corpus of texts on our current topic, for example, is likely to feature sequences like *types of formulaic language* or *English for Academic Purposes* multiple times in multiple texts. However, if a text on this topic were mixed into a broader corpus on a range of academic topics, the same phrases would not be repeated so often and so not qualify as lexical bundles. Similarly, repetition of bundles within a text is more likely than repetition between texts, both because of the unity of topic and because individual writers may have (perhaps unconscious) tendencies to use particular bundles. This means that a million-word corpus made up of 1,000 short texts is likely to feature fewer repeated sequences than a corpus of the same length made up of ten long texts.

Pan et al. (2020) demonstrate that issues of this sort can have a serious impact on research findings. They systematically altered the makeup of their first and second language corpora and found that, when both the number and length of texts were equivalent across corpora, more bundles were found in the L2 corpus, but when the corpora were allowed to differ, such that L1 texts were longer than L2 texts, the pattern was reversed, with more bundles being found in the L1 corpus. This latter pattern held regardless of whether the two corpora were equivalent in terms of the total number of words or in terms of the total number of texts in each corpus. Specific features of corpus design thus have a strong influence on the outcomes of lexical bundle studies. Great care is therefore needed when making comparisons of this sort.

A second set of issues in lexical bundle research concerns the reliability of functional classifications. I have noted that different researchers have come to quite different conclusions about the differences in functional types in learner writing across L2 proficiency levels, despite their having been conducted in similar contexts

(Appel & Wood, 2016; Biber & Gray, 2013; Chen & Baker, 2016; Ruan, 2017; Staples et al., 2013; Vidakovic & Barker, 2010). Two possible reasons suggest themselves for this lack of consistency. The first is that these studies have been based on relatively small corpora, typically 100–200 texts at each proficiency level. Since many lexical bundles are individually relatively infrequent (compared to words), many only emerge from analyses of large numbers of texts. It may be, therefore, that the sample sizes used to date are simply too small to generate reliable findings.

A second possibility concerns the nature of the functional categories themselves. With a few notable exceptions (e.g., Appel & Wood, 2016), research of this sort rarely gives information about the process of assigning bundles to categories or estimates of the reliability of the process. This is problematic because functional classification is heavily dependent on subjective judgement. The issue is all the more acute because, as Table 7.2 illustrates, definitions in the most commonly used framework are somewhat vague, and some categories are not defined at all. A useful priority for future research would be to provide more explicit, operational definitions of these categories and to test how reliably they can be applied by different raters to different types of text.

7.4 Collocations

As with formulaic language in general, collocation has been defined and studied in different ways by different researchers (useful overviews from different perspectives can be found in Barfield & Gyllstad, 2009; Barnbrook et al., 2013; Cowie, 1998; Nesselhauf, 2004). As discussed previously, our main concern will be with what researchers have called a *frequency-based* approach (Nesselhauf, 2004). In this tradition, *collocation* refers to the way that certain words are associated with certain other words, in the sense that they are often found in that word's company (the metaphor of collocation as words 'keeping company' with each other comes from Firth, 1968). We have already noted, for example, that the verb *curry* usually occurs with the noun *favour*. Similarly, *upside* often occurs with *down*, *shrug* with *shoulders*, and *kith* with *kin*.

On this view, collocation is principally concerned with *co-occurrence*, rather than *recurrence*. That is, we are more interested in the association between words than in their overall frequency as a phrase. A wide range of *association measures* have been suggested to quantify this co-occurrence (Gablasova et al., 2017; Gries & Durrant, 2021). Conceptually, the most commonly used measures can be divided into three main groups: hypothesis-testing measures, strength of association measures, and directional measures.

All these measures build on the idea that collocations are pairs of words that appear together more frequently than we would expect by chance alone (an operational definition proposed by Jones & Sinclair, 1974). To understand this idea, we can think of language as if it were produced by drawing words at random from a tombola. Imagine each token in our corpus is written on a slip of paper in the tombola. When a slip is picked out at random, it is more likely to be a high-frequency word than a low-frequency word, since high-frequency words appear on far more of the papers. Indeed, in a tombola replicating the British National Corpus (BNC), the five most frequent words (*the, of, and, to, a*) would cumulatively appear on around 15% of slips. So, our chances of pulling out one of these slips are much higher than our chances of pulling out words like *absent-minded, peapod, inkpot, muckraker,* and *oilcan,* which would cumulatively appear on only 0.0001% of slips.

In the same way, if we pull out two words together, we are more likely to select two high-frequency words than two low-frequency words. With this logic in mind, we would expect high-frequency words like *of* and *to* to appear close to each other very regularly in texts, without any need to say that they are collocates. Indeed, *to* appears within five words of *of* nearly half a million times in the BNC, in contexts like *we kept **to** ourselves for the rest **of** the day,* and *The government subsequently altered its estimate **of** those able **to** claim.* In contrast, if low-frequency words appear together multiple times, this is likely to be due to a collocational attraction between them. The pairing *raw material,* for example, appears in the BNC considerably less frequently than *of-to* (at just over 900 occurrences). However, because the individual words that make it up are relatively infrequent (*raw* is over 1,000 times less frequent than *of* and *to*), these 900 occurrences can be considered to indicate a likely collocational attraction.

The three main types of association measures mentioned all build on this idea of comparing the overall frequency of a word pair with the frequency of its component words. But they make this comparison in importantly different ways. Hypothesis-testing measures (which include *t-score, z-score, chi-square,* and *log-likelihood*) take their logic from tests of statistical significance. They address the question of how confident we can be that two words really do appear together more frequently than we'd expect by chance alone. Because pairs that appear together very frequently give us more confidence in this conclusion, tests of this sort tend to privilege high-frequency combinations. To illustrate, Table 7.4 shows the 20 top collocates of the word *language* in the BAWE corpus, as ranked by t-score.

TABLE 7.4 Collocates of *language* with the highest t-score in the BAWE corpus

Rank	Word	T-score	Rank	Word	T-score
1	the	36.74	11	their	13.11
2	of	33.89	12	s	12.79
3	and	29.10	13	for	12.57
4	in	25.92	14	it	12.12
5	to	24.25	15	with	11.96
6	a	23.16	16	language	11.60
7	is	23.10	17	acquisition	11.16
8	that	18.24	18	this	11.12
9	as	17.32	19	be	10.71
10	use	16.29	20	by	10.55

As with significance tests in other fields of research, hypothesis-testing measures are strongly affected by the size of the sample we are working with. In other words, they will tend to be higher in larger corpora, other things being equal. This makes comparison of these association measures across corpora of different sizes problematic for many purposes.

The second major type of association measure focuses on the strength of association between words. That is, they tell us the extent to which the words in a collocation are exclusive to each other. A pair like *kith – kin*, for example, scores very highly on these measures because each of these words is rarely found without the other. Of the 14 occurrences of *kith* and 808 occurrences of *kin* in the BNC, 12 are within three words of each other.

The paradigmatic example of a strength of association measure is the *mutual information* (MI) score. While this statistic is very good at identifying closely related pairs, it has the problem that it tends to highlight combinations of very infrequent items. After all, if a word only appears once in a corpus, its occurrence will be entirely exclusive to the words that happen to be found around it in that instance. It is, therefore, likely to be credited with some very strong collocations. In the BAWE corpus, for example, the strongest collocates of *language* according to the MI measure are *Luganda* (a Bantu language spoken in Uganda), *Lenneberg* (a linguist), and *FORMULAEthe* (a transcription error).

The simplest solution to this issue is to combine use of MI with a minimum frequency criterion. We might, for example, decide only to calculate MI measures for combinations that appear at least ten times. Applying this rule to the collocates of *language* in the BAWE corpus, we get the top 20 shown in Table 7.5.

Some researchers have further proposed dealing with MI's low-frequency bias by altering its formula slightly. A group of measures known as *MIk*, for example, adjust the MI formula to give more weight to the overall frequency of collocations, so giving more prominence to high-frequency pairings (Evert, 2008).

The final set of association measures we will discuss here is *directional measures*. These are designed to address the fact that many collocational relationships are

TABLE 7.5 Co-occurrences of *language* with highest MI in the BAWE corpus

Rank	Word	MI	Rank	Word	MI
1	figurative	9.66	11	impairment	7.69
2	taboo	9.09	12	teaching	7.63
3	spoken	8.96	13	deficits	7.62
4	acquisition	8.92	14	gendered	7.51
5	programming	8.87	15	learners	7.51
6	powerless	8.45	16	hemisphere	7.28
7	varieties	8.09	17	abilities	7.18
8	dialect	8.05	18	sign	7.15
9	acquiring	7.93	19	cinema	7.15
10	acquire	7.89	20	comprehension	7.04

relatively one-sided. This can be seen in pairings like *upside down* and *for instance*. *Upside* is closely associated with *down* in the sense that, when we encounter *upside*, there is a good chance that *down* will follow. Similarly, *instance* is closely associated with *for* in the sense that, when we encounter *instance*, there is a good chance that it will be preceded by *for*. However, these relationships do not hold in the opposite direction; *down* and *for* are both used in such a wide range of contexts that encountering one of these does not make the presence of their collocational partner particularly likely. This distinction is captured by the delta-P measure (Gries & Ellis, 2015), which provides two separate numbers: one for the extent to which the first word in a collocation predicts the presence of the second and another for the extent to which the second word in a collocation predicts the first.

Most recent research studying development in learner writing through the lens of collocations has used corpus-external, rather than corpus-internal, frequencies (Durrant et al., 2021). One approach has been to identify each word pair (or each word pair of a particular type, e.g., adjective–noun pairs) in the learner corpus, to retrieve association measures for each pair from a suitable reference corpus, and then to calculate overall average association measures for each learner text. The research conducted to date suggests that MI is the measure most strongly associated with development. In studies of L2 English, MI has consistently been found to increase with increasing proficiency (Bestgen, 2017; Bestgen & Granger, 2014; Garner et al., 2018, 2019; Kim et al., 2018; Paquot, 2018, 2019). Interestingly, the only study I am aware of to look at development in children's L1 English writing found that mean MI did not increase across year groups (Durrant & Brenchley, 2021). It may be, therefore, that this is an L2-specific aspect of development.

A second, so far less widely used, approach to studying learner collocations is to identify word pairs that meet a specified frequency-based definition of collocation and then try to understand the qualitative nature of those collocations. This is seen, for example, in Durrant and Brenchley (2021), which identified verb–noun, noun–verb, and adjective–noun combinations in a corpus of child L1 English writing that could be classified as *academic collocations*, based on their frequencies and MI scores in the BAWE corpus. That study both showed how the use of academic collocations increased across year groups and classified older children's academic collocations functionally to determine how they are used (this latter analysis is comparable to the functional analyses discussed earlier for lexical bundles).

As with lexical bundles, researchers who wish to use collocation as a way of understanding writing development need to pick their way through a forest of methodological issues. One concerns the most appropriate choice of association measure. As we have already seen, different measures can highlight very different types of collocation, so much thought needs to be given to what exactly we want to target. Previous research has been criticized for restricting itself to a relatively small group of measures, especially t-score and MI (McCallum & Durrant, 2022). While there is much to be said for maintaining consistency across studies, it is also possible that by restricting itself in this way, research is failing to find important developmental patterns that could be tapped by other measures.

A second methodological issue concerns which pairs of words we should count as co-occurring, and so as being in a possible collocational relationship with each other. Consider Sentence 2 from earlier in this chapter:

2. *She made a **strong** and persuasive **argument** for her case.*

This sentence was intended to illustrate a possible collocation between *strong* and *argument*. So, we would want our procedure for identifying possible collocations to notice that these two words have occurred together and add one to our frequency count for *strong argument*. But what about the rest of the sentence? Do we also want the procedure to note, for example, that *argument* has occurred together with *she* and add one to our count for this pairing?

The traditional response to the issue has been to treat all words appearing within a specified window (or *span*) of a central (*node*) word as co-occurrences. Most commonly, this span has been set to four words to the left and right of each node. So, in Sentence 2, the words *a, strong, and,* and *persuasive* would all be recorded as co-occurring with *argument* because they are within a four-word span to the left, and *for, her,* and *case* would all be counted because they are within a four-word span to the right. While not all words appearing within the specific span of a node will be collocates, those that recur with sufficient frequency to attain high association measures are, it is hypothesized, likely to be so.

While this time-honoured approach often does a good job of identifying collocations, it is easy to find examples of sentences where it may be misleading. In Sentence 5, for example (from the BNC), *strong* appears ten words to the right of *argument*, well outside the usual span. So, an example like this would have been missed. Conversely, *strong* does appear within four words of the word *faith*, but it may be misleading to count this as evidence for the collocation *strong faith*.

5. *We begin with the **argument** that the evidence for a Deity might be so **strong** as to undermine **faith**.*

One solution to this has been to use dependency parsers (see Chapter 2, Section 2.6) to identify only word pairs that stand in a specified grammatical relationship to each other. Paquot (2019), for example, uses the Stanford CoreNLP parser to identify word pairs occurring in one of three grammatical relationships: adjectives that premodify a noun; adverbs that modify an adjective; and nouns that are the direct object of a verb. Provided the grammatical parse is accurate, this approach should identify all and only co-occurrences of the sort we are interested in, regardless of the span of words that separate them. As we have seen in other contexts, however, grammatical parsing is rarely completely accurate (see especially Chapter 6). This approach is therefore likely to introduce errors of its own. Whether the errors that arise from this technique are greater or less than those arising from counting co-occurrences in a span remains an open question at the time of writing.

7.5 Conclusion

Formulaic language is a fresh and innovative area of research that promises to offer powerful insights into writing development that are not available to more traditional modes of linguistic analysis. It is, therefore, unsurprising that a systematic review of corpus research into writing development found this to be the most rapidly growing area of interest (Durrant et al., 2021). As methods continue to develop, both to meet the challenges described in this chapter and to create new types of analysis, we can expect work on formulaic language to continue to grow apace and to add substantially to our understanding of writing development. Particular areas for growth might include the extension of formulaic language research into studies of first language writing development (Durrant & Brenchley, 2021) and, consequently, a better understanding of how *phraseological complexity* (Paquot, 2019) differs across contexts. Formulaic language also lends itself well to the integration of corpus methods with methods from adjacent fields of study, such as psycholinguistics (Durrant & Siyanova-Chanturia, 2015; Gilquin, 2020). Integration of this sort has the potential to add much to our understandings in the future.

7.6 Taking it further

Several books provide excellent overall introductions to various issues around formulaic language. Perhaps the most notable recent publication is:

Siyanova-Chanturia, A., & Pellicer-Sánchez, A. (Eds.). (2019). *Understanding formulaic language: A second language acquisition perspective*. Routledge.

This edited volume includes chapters on a wide range of topics related to formulaic language in second language acquisition.

A more narrowly focused set of chapters, describing empirical studies of learners' use of formulaic language in a corpus, can be found in:

Granger, S. (Ed.) (2021). *Perspectives on the L2 phrasicon: The view of learner corpora*. Multilingual-Matters.

To understand some of the foundational ideas in formulaic language, it is well worth looking at earlier pioneering works, which remain highly relevant today. Perhaps foremost amongst these is:

Wray, A. (2002). *Formulaic language and the lexicon*. Cambridge University Press.

Other key works include, for lexical bundles:

Biber, D., Conrad, S., & Cortes, V. (2004, September 1, 2004). If you look at ...: Lexical bundles in university teaching and textbooks. *Applied Linguistics*, *25*(3), 371–405. https://doi.org/10.1093/applin/25.3.371

For collocations:

Hoey, M. (2005). *Lexical priming: A new theory of words and language*. Routledge.

Sinclair, J. M. (2004). *The search for units of meaning*. In J. Sinclair & R. Carter (Eds), *Trust the text: Language, corpus and discourse* (pp. 24–48). Routledge.

And for the role of formulaic language in language teaching and learning:

Lewis, M. (Ed.). (2000). *Teaching collocations: Further developments in the lexical approach*. Thomson.

Nattinger, J. R., & DeCarrico, J. S. (1992). *Lexical phrases and language teaching*. Oxford University Press.

References

Appel, R., & Wood, D. (2016). Recurrent word combinations in EAP test-taker writing: differences between high- and low-proficiency levels. *Language Assessment Quarterly*, *13*(1), 55–71. https://doi.org/10.1080/15434303.2015.1126718

Barfield, A., & Gyllstad, H. (2009). Introduction: Researching L2 collocation knowledge and development. In A. Barfield & H. Gyllstad (Eds.), *Researching collocations in another language* (pp. 1–18). Palgrave Macmillan. https://doi.org/10.1057/9780230245327_1

Barnbrook, G., Mason, O., & Krishnamurthy, R. (2013). *Collocation: Applications and implications*. Palgrave Macmillan. https://doi.org/10.1057/9781137297242

Bestgen, Y. (2017). Beyond single-word measures: L2 writing assessment, lexical richness and formulaic competence. *System*, *69*, 65–78. https://doi.org/10.1016/j.system.2017.08.004

Bestgen, Y., & Granger, S. (2014). Quantifying the development of phraseological competence in L2 English writing: An automated approach. *Journal of Second Language Writing*, *26*, 28–41. https://doi.org/10.1016/j.jslw.2014.09.004

Biber, D. (2006). *University language*. John Benjamins. https://doi.org/10.1075/scl.23

Biber, D., Conrad, S., & Cortes, V. (2004, September 1). If you look at …: Lexical bundles in university teaching and textbooks. *Applied linguistics*, *25*(3), 371–405. https://doi.org/10.1093/applin/25.3.371

Biber, D., & Gray, B. (2013). Discourse characteristics of writing and speaking task types on the TOEFL iBT test: A lexico-grammatical analysis. *TOEFL iBT Research Report*, *19*. https://doi.org/10.1002/j.2333-8504.2013.tb02311.x

Chen, Y. H., & Baker, P. (2016). Investigating criterial discourse features across second language development: Lexical bundles in rated learner essays, CEFR B1, B2 and C1. *Applied Linguistics*, *37*(6), 849–80.

Cowie, A. P. (1998). Introduction. In A. P. Cowie (Ed.), *Phraseology: Theory, analysis, and applications* (pp. 1–20). Oxford University Press.

Durrant, P. (2017). Lexical bundles and disciplinary variation in university students' writing: Mapping the territories. *Applied Linguistics*, *38*(2), 165–93. https://doi.org/10.1093/applin/amv011

Durrant, P., & Brenchley, M. (2021). The development of academic collocations in children's writing. In P. Szudarski & S. Barclay (Eds.), *Vocabulary theory, patterning and teaching* (pp. 99–120). Multilingual-Matters.

Durrant, P., Brenchley, M., & McCallum, L. (2021). *Understanding development and proficiency in writing: Quantitative corpus linguistic approaches*. Cambridge University Press. https://doi.org/10.1017/9781108770101

Durrant, P., & Siyanova-Chanturia, A. (2015). Learner corpora and psycholinguistics. In S. Granger, G. Gilquin, & F. Meunier (Eds.), *The Cambridge handbook of learner corpus research* (pp. 57–78). Cambridge University Press. https://doi.org/10.1017/CBO9781139649414.004

Durrant, P., Siyanova-Chanturia, A., Kremmel, B., & Sonbul, S. (2022). *Research methods in vocabulary studies*. John Benjamins.

Evert, S. (2008). Corpora and collocations. In A. Lüdeling & M. Kytö (Eds.), *Corpus linguistics. an international andbook* (pp. 1212–48). Mouton de Gruyter.

Firth, J. R. (1968). A synopsis of linguistic theory, 1930–55. In F. R. Palmer (Ed.), *Selected papers of J.R. Firth 1952–1959* (Studies in linguistic analysis (special volume of the Philological Society, Oxford, 1957, 1–31; pp. 168–205). Longman.

Gablasova, D., Brezina, V., & McEnery, T. (2017). Collocations in corpus-based language learning research: Identifying, comparing, and interpreting the evidence. *Language Learning*. https://doi.org/10.1111/lang.12225

Garner, J., Crossley, S. A., & Kyle, K. (2018). Beginning and intermediate L2 writers' use of N-grams: An association measures study. *International Review of Applied Linguistics*. https://doi.org/10.1515/iral-2017-0089

Garner, J., Crossley, S. A., & Kyle, K. (2019). N-gram measures and L2 writing proficiency. *System, 80*, 176–87. https://doi.org/10.1016/j.system.2018.12.001

Gilquin, G. (2020). Combining learner corpora and experimental methods. In N. Tracy-Ventura & M. Paquot (Eds.), *The Routledge handbook of second language acquisition and corpora* (pp. 133–44). Routledge. https://doi.org/10.4324/9781351137904-12

Gries, S. T., & Durrant, P. (2021). Analyzing co-occurrence data. In M. Paquot & S. T. Gries (Eds.), *Practical handbook of corpus linguistics*. Springer.

Gries, S. T., & Ellis, N. C. (2015). Statistical measures for usage-based linguistics. *Language Learning, 65*(S1), 228–55. https://doi.org/10.1111/lang.12119

Hyland, K. (2008). As can be seen: Lexical bundles and disciplinary variation. *English for Specific Purposes, 27*(1), 4–21. https://doi.org/10.1016/j.esp.2007.06.001

Jones, S., & Sinclair, J. M. (1974). English lexical collocations. A study in computational linguistics. *Cahiers de lexicologie, 24*, 15–61.

Kim, M., Crossley, S. A., & Kyle, K. (2018). Lexical sophistication as a multidimensional phenomenon: Relations to second language lexical proficiency, development, and writing quality. *The Modern Language Journal, 102*(1), 120–41. https://doi.org/10.1111/modl.12447

Kyle, K., & Crossley, S. A. (2016). The relationship between lexical sophistication and independent and source-based writing. *Journal of Second Language Writing, 34*, 12–24. https://doi.org/10.1016/j.jslw.2016.10.003

Lu, X., Kisselev, O., Yoon, J., & Amory, M. D. (2018). Investigating effects of criterial consistency, the diversity dimension, and threshold variation in formulaic language research. Extending the methodological considerations of O'Donnell et al. (2013). *International Journal of Corpus Linguistics, 23*(2), 158–82. https://doi.org/10.1075/ijcl.16086.lu

McCallum, L., & Durrant, P. (2022). *Collocation and writing quality: Measuring effects*. Cambridge University Press.

Nesselhauf, N. (2004). What are collocations? In D. J. Allerton, N. Nesselhauf, & P. Skandera (Eds.), *Phraseological units: Basic concepts and their application* (pp. 1–21). Schwabe.

Pan, R., Reppen, R., & Biber, D. (2020). Methodological issues in contrastive lexical bundle research. The influence of corpus design on bundle identification. *International Journal of Corpus Linguistics, 25*(2), 215–29. https://doi.org/10.1075/ijcl.19063.pan

Paquot, M. (2018). Phraseological competence: A missing component in university entrance language tests? Insights from a study of EFL learners' use of statistical collocations. *Language Assessment Quarterly, 15*(1), 29–43. https://doi.org/10.1080/15434303.2017.1405421

Paquot, M. (2019). The phraseological dimension in interlanguage complexity research. *Second Language Research, 35*(1), 121–45. https://doi.org/10.1177/0267658317694221

Pawley, A., & Syder, F. H. (1983). Two puzzles for linguistic theory: Nativelike selection and nativelike fluency. In J. C. Richards & R. W. Schmidt (Eds.), *Language and communication* (pp. 191–226). Longman.

Ruan, Z. (2017). Lexical bundles in Chinese undergraduate academic writing at an English medium university. *RELC Journal, 48*(3), 327–40. https://doi.org/10.1177/0033688216631218

Simpson-Vlach, R. A. (2010, January 12, 2010). An academic formulas list: New methods in phraseology research. *Applied Linguistics, 31*(4), 487–512. https://doi.org/10.1093/applin/amp058

Sinclair, J. M. (1966). Beginning the study of lexis. In C. E. Bazell, J. C. Catford, M. A. K. Halliday, & R. H. Robins (Eds.), *In memory of J.R. Firth* (pp. 410–30). Longman.

Siyanova-Chanturia, A. (2015). On the 'holistic' nature of formulaic language. *Corpus linguistics and linguistic theory, 11*(2), 285–301. https://doi.org/10.1515/cllt-2014-0016

Siyanova-Chanturia, A., & Pellicer-Sánchez, A. (2019). Formulaic language: Setting the scene. In A. Siyanova-Chanturia & A. Pellicer-Sánchez (Eds.), *Understanding formulaic language* (pp. 1–15). Routledge. https://doi.org/10.4324/9781315206615-1

Staples, S., Egbert, J., Biber, D., & McClair, A. (2013). Formulaic sequences and EAP writing development: Lexical bundles in the TOEFL iBT writing section. *Journal of English for Academic Purposes, 12*, 214–25. https://doi.org/10.1016/j.jeap.2013.05.002

Tomasello, M. (2003). *Constructing a language: A usage-based theory of language acquisition.* Harvard University Press.

Vidakovic, I., & Barker, F. (2010). Use of words and multi-word units in Skills for Life Writing examinations. *University of Cambridge ESOL Examinations Research Notes, 41*, 7–14.

Wray, A. (2019). Concluding question: Why don't second language learners more proactively target formulaic sequences? In A. Siyanova-Chanturia & A. Pellicer-Sánchez (Eds.), *Understanding formulaic language* (pp. 248–69). Routledge. https://doi.org/10.4324/9781315206615-14

Wulff, S. (2019). Acquisition of formulaic language from a usage-based perspective. In A. Siyanova-Chanturia & A. Pellicer-Sánchez (Eds.), *Understanding formulaic language: A second language acquisition perspective* (pp. 19–37). Routledge. https://doi.org/10.4324/9781315206615-2

8

FORMULAIC LANGUAGE RESEARCH IN PRACTICE

Academic collocations

8.1 Introduction

In this chapter, we will quantify the use of academic collocations in a corpus of learner writing. This is similar to the analysis of academic vocabulary that we carried out in Chapter 4. Again, we will take a list of academic vocabulary (this time collocations, rather than individual words) and determine how frequently they are used by writers at different levels in our learner corpus. Much of the material here will, therefore, mirror what we did in that chapter. The key difference is that we will need to create our own list of academic collocations, rather than using an existing list as we did in Chapter 4. This will be the task of Sections 8.2.1–8.3.2, and they are perhaps the most challenging sections in this entire book, so hold on tight! In these sections, we will determine which verb + noun combinations meet some specified frequency thresholds in the BAWE corpus and so might be considered academic collocations. In Section 8.3.3, we will then calculate the extent to which these collocations are used by writers in different year groups in our corpus. Although, for the sake of simplicity, I have focused only verb + noun collocations, a similar analysis could be extended to other types of combinations by adapting the scripts used here.

8.2 Identifying collocations in a reference corpus

8.2.1 Editing the parsed corpus

For this analysis, I will use a version of the BAWE corpus that has been parsed using the Stanford Core NLP parser (see Chapter 2, Section 2.5, for details of how to download this corpus). In Chapter 4, we made a few adjustments to the files that the Stanford parser produces to make them easier to work with. Specifically, we added meaningful column names, simplified the POS codes, and saved the texts

DOI: 10.4324/9781003152682-12

as .csv, rather than .conll files. We will do the same again here, but we will also make one additional change that will be important in our collocation analysis: we will add sentence numbers to the texts. The new version of the corpus will be saved to a folder called 'BAWE_revised'. You will need to create this as a new, empty, folder, within the main 'Corpora' folder before executing the script.

The first stages in this task are the same as those we used in Chapter 4 (Script 4.3.2) and are reproduced in this chapter as Points a–e of Script 8.2.1. You should review Chapter 4 now if you need a reminder of how this section works. The one difference between this and the earlier version is the way we access filenames. Rather than retrieving these from metadata, filenames are read directly from the folder in which the corpus is stored using the *dir()* function (Point a).

SCRIPT 8.2.1.a–e   PREPARE THE PARSED CORPUS FOR ANALYSIS

```
# a) set the working directory. Get file names for the parsed corpus
setwd('~/CLWD')
files <- dir('corpora/BAWE_conll/')
# b) start a loop to go through all files in the corpus
for (i in files){
  # c) read the corpus file
  text <- read.delim(paste('corpora/BAWE_conll/', i, sep=''), sep='\t', header=F)
  # d) add column names
  colnames(text) <-c ('word_number', 'word', 'lemma', 'pos', 'ner', 'dep_on', 'dep')
  # e) simplify part of speech codes
  text$pos <- gsub('^J.*', 'j', text$pos)
  text$pos <- gsub('^N.*', 'n', text$pos)
  text$pos <- gsub('^RB.*', 'r', text$pos)
  text$pos <- gsub('^V.*', 'v', text$pos)
```

As I noted earlier, we need to make an additional change to the files which we did not make in Chapter 4. That is, we need to add sentence numbers (if you look ahead to Figure 8.2, you can get a preview of what we are trying to achieve). Although the parser output does not itself provide sentence numbers, it does very helpfully number the words in each sentence, with the numbering restarting at the beginning of each sentence. This gives us a good start in our task. To identify sentences, we simply need to tell R to look for places where word numbers have been reset to 1 and note that these mark the start of a new sentence.

In Script 8.2.1.f, therefore, we start by creating an empty vector (*sentence_number*) that we will use to store sentence numbers (Point f). In this vector, we will eventually record one sentence number for each word in the text. So, the first entry in *sentence_number* will be the sentence number of the first word in the text, the second entry will be the sentence number of the second word, etc. (again, you can see what this looks like in Figure 8.2). We also create a variable called *current_sentence*,

SCRIPT 8.2.1.f   ADD SENTENCE NUMBERS

```
# f) add sentence numbers
sentence_number <- vector()
current_sentence <- 0
for(j in 1:length(text$word_number)){
  if(text$word_number[j] == 1){
    current_sentence <- current_sentence+1}
  sentence_number[j] <- current_sentence
}
text<-cbind(sentence_number, text)
```

which will keep track of which sentence we have reached in the text. This is initially set to 0.

The next part of 8.2.1.f then starts a loop that will go through the text word by word and, at each word, will do two things:

a)   Check to see if it is the start of a new sentence (i.e., if the *word_number* is 1). If it is, we will increase *current_sentence* by 1. For the text in Figure 8.1, for example (which comes from the BAWE corpus), when R looks at the first word (*Qualitative*) and notes that it has a *word_number* of 1, it will increase the *current_sentence* number from 0 to 1. Later, when it reaches *It* and again finds a *word_number* of 1, it will increment the *current_sentence* number to 2, etc.

b)   Record the *current_sentence* number for that word to the appropriate place in the *sentence_number* vector. Thus, the first position in *sentence_number* should be

word_number	word	lemma	pos	ner	dep_on	dep
1	Qualitative	qualitative	j	O		2 amod
2	research	research	n	O		4 nsubjpass
3	is	be	v	O		4 auxpass
4	associated	associate	v	O		0 ROOT
5	with	with	IN	O		6 case
6	meanings	meaning	n	O		4 nmod
7	and	and	CC	O		6 cc
8	interpretation	interpretation	n	O		6 conj
9	.	.	.	O		4 punct
1	It	it	PRP	O		2 nsubj
2	is	be	v	O		0 ROOT
3	not	not	r	O		2 neg
4	reliant	reliant	j	O		2 xcomp
5	upon	upon	IN	O		7 case
6	numerical	numerical	j	O		7 amod
7	data	datum	n	O		4 nmod

FIGURE 8.1   Word numbers indicating sentence breaks

assigned a value of 1. The next eight rows then get the same value. When we get to *It* (in the tenth row) and the *current_sentence* number is increased to 2, this value is recorded to the tenth position in *sentence_number*.

To achieve this, we first initiate a for-loop that will go through each word in the text and check whether it has the word_number 1 – that is, whether it is the start of a new sentence. There are two important points to note here. First, you will recall that in the previous snippet of script (specifically, Script 8.2.1.b), we already initiated a for-loop so that our procedures are carried out separately for each text. This means that we are now opening *a for-loop within a for-loop!* This time, the loop is iterating through each word in the text.

Up to now, we have used 'i' as the value marker in for-loops – thus, Point b was *for(i in files)*. However, now that we are opening a second loop within our first for-loop, we cannot do this: *i* is already being used to keep track of the filename of the text we are working on, so it can't be used also to keep track of which word within the text we are looking at. We, therefore, need to pick another letter to use here. I have chosen the letter *j* (which is the conventional choice for loops-within-loops. Should things get really complicated and we wanted to open another loop within this one, it would conventionally use the value *k*, and further loop within that would be *l*, and so on).

Within our new for-loop, we then bring in our *if()* function. This has a very similar structure to the *for()* function. That is:

```
if(condition){
      procedure
      }
```

It tells R to carry out the procedure within curly brackets only if the condition within round brackets is met. In the current case, the condition is that the current word that we have reached in our for-loop has a word_number of 1. In other words, the procedure in curly brackets will be executed if *text$word_number[j] == 1*. In this case, the procedure is that of increasing the value of *current_sentence* by 1. So, the overall effect of the *if()* function is that, whenever R reaches a word that has the word_number 1, it will indicate that a new sentence has started by adding 1 to the sentence number.

Exiting the *if()* function, the script then records the *current_sentence* number to position j in the *sentence_number* vector and returns to the start of the loop, moving on to the next word in the text and repeating the process of checking whether *word_number* is 1. Once sentence numbers have been assigned to every word in the file, the *cbind()* function is used to attach this new vector as a column in our *text* file.

Finally, at Point g, this new-look file is saved as a .csv file to the 'BAWE_revised' folder that we created earlier and moves on to the next text. Note that the file names retrieved from the folder in which the original folder was stored had the extension '.txt.conll', which is not appropriate for a .csv file. I have used *gsub()* to replace the extension with '.csv'.

SCRIPT 8.2.1.g–h   SAVE THE REVISED CORPUS FILE

```
# g) save the revised corpus file in a new folder
write.csv(text, file=paste('corpora/BAWE_revised/', gsub('txt.conll', 'csv', i),
                   sep=''), row.names=F)
# h) close the loop
}
```

Figure 8.2 shows what the text excerpted in Figure 8.1 would look like at the end of this process. Note that, because Script 8.2.1 asks R to perform quite a large job, you will need to wait quite some time for the process to complete. This may be an appropriate point to make a cup of tea!

8.2.2 Identifying lemmas and verb + noun combinations

With our amended version of the corpus prepared, we can now proceed to find collocations. For this exercise, we will be defining collocations as any verb + noun combination that appears in the BAWE corpus more than five times per million words and with an MI score of at least four (see Chapter 7, Section 7.3.3 if you need to refresh your knowledge of MI scores). It is important to bear in mind that there is no sharp frequency cut-off between collocations and non-collocations, so these thresholds are fairly arbitrary; I have chosen them on the basis that they provide a substantial but manageable number of intuitively satisfying collocations. As we will see in Section 8.2.3, changing the frequency thresholds to be more or less inclusive is quite easy, so it is possible to experiment with different cut-off values. Before we

sentence_number	word_number	word	lemma	pos	ner	dep_on	dep
1	1	Qualitative	qualitative	j	O	2	amod
1	2	research	research	n	O	4	nsubjpass
1	3	is	be	v	O	4	auxpass
1	4	associated	associate	v	O	0	ROOT
1	5	with	with	IN	O	6	case
1	6	meanings	meaning	n	O	4	nmod
1	7	and	and	CC	O	6	cc
1	8	interpretation	interpretation	n	O	6	conj
1	9	.	.	.	O	4	punct
2	1	It	it	PRP	O	2	nsubj
2	2	is	be	v	O	0	ROOT
2	3	not	not	r	O	2	neg
2	4	reliant	reliant	j	O	2	xcomp
2	5	upon	upon	IN	O	7	case
2	6	numerical	numerical	j	O	7	amod
2	7	data	datum	n	O	4	nmod

FIGURE 8.2 Text with sentence numbers

sentence_number	word_number	word	lemma	pos	ner	dep_on	dep
1	1	Racism	racism	n	MISC		2 nsubj
1	2	is	be	v	O		0 ROOT
1	3	still	still	r	O		2 advmod
1	4	a	a	DT	O		5 det
1	5	problem	problem	n	O		2 xcomp
1	6	within	within	IN	O		8 case
1	7	our	we	PRP$	O		8 nmod:poss
1	8	society	society	n	O		5 nmod
1	9	today	today	n	DATE		2 nmod:tmod
1	10	,	,	,	O		2 punct
1	11	and	and	CC	O		2 cc
1	12	many	many	j	O		14 amod
1	13	ethnic	ethnic	j	O		14 amod
1	14	minorities	minority	n	O		15 nsubj
1	15	face	face	v	O		2 conj
1	16	inequalities	inequality	n	O		15 dobj
1	17	in	in	IN	O		19 case
1	18	many	many	j	O		19 amod
1	19	areas	area	n	O		16 nmod

FIGURE 8.3   A parsed text from the BAWE corpus

can assign frequencies and MI scores to combinations though, we need first to find all cases of verb + noun combinations in the corpus so that we can count them.

We are interested specifically in cases where a verb takes a noun as either its direct or indirect object. An example of such a combination can be seen in rows 15 and 16 of Figure 8.3, where the noun *inequalities* is marked as the direct object of the verb *face*. We know this because *inequalities* (row 16) has a *dep_on* value of 15 (that is, it is dependent on *face*, which is in row 15) and a *dep* value of *dobj* (showing that *inequalities* is a direct object).

To find combinations like this, we need to identify all nouns that are dependent on verbs with either a direct object (*dobj*) or indirect object (*iobj*) dependency marked in the *dep* column. To calculate MI scores, we will also need to know the individual frequencies of the words that make up each combination. We, therefore, also need a list of the lemmas in the corpus.

As in Script 8.2.1, we start (Point a) by using the *dir()* function to get a list of the files in the corpus (this time using the 'revised' version that we created earlier). We then (Point b) generate two empty vectors: one to store all the lemma tokens in the corpus (this will be used to make a word frequency list) and another to store all the verb + noun combination tokens.

In Script 8.2.2c–g, we initiate a loop so that the remaining functions are applied individually to each file in the corpus (Point c). Within the loop, we first read the corpus file, using the *read.csv()* function (Point d). Points e–g are then devoted to identifying the lemmas in the files. As in Chapter 4 (Script 4.3.1), we can create labels for lemmas by pasting together the lemma column and the POS column (Point e). Applying this to the file in Figure 8.3 would create a new vector (*text_lemmas*) including the items *racism_n, be_v, still_r*, etc.

SCRIPT 8.2.2.a–b   (A) GET CORPUS FILE NAMES; (B) GENERATE VECTORS TO STORE OUTPUTS

```
# a) get file names for the parsed corpus
files<-dir('corpora/BAWE_revised')
# b) create empty vectors to store all lemmas in the corpus and
# all cases of verb+noun combinations
lemma <- vector()
verb_noun_lem <- vector()
```

While this is a step in the right direction, it is still not quite a list of lemmas because, as we can see from the comma in row 10 in Figure 8.3, not all rows include words. Fortunately, punctuation marks are easily spotted in a corpus tagged by Stanford CoreNLP because the corresponding tag in the *dep* column is always *punct*. At Point f, we use subsetting to remove from our vector of lemmas any items matching this description. Note that we have used the 'not equal to' (!=) operator to indicate that we want to include only items that are not 'punct'. This gives us our final list of lemmas for the text. Point g then uses the *c()* function to add these lemmas to the master vector for the corpus as a whole.

SCRIPT 8.2.2.c–g   IDENTIFY AND RECORD LEMMAS FROM EACH TEXT

```
# c) start a loop to go through all files in the corpus
for (i in 1:length(files)){
  # d) read the corpus file
  text <- read.csv(paste('corpora/BAWE_revised', files[i], sep='/'),
                   header=T, stringsAsFactors = F)
  # e) identify all of the lemmas in the file
  text_lemmas <- paste(text$lemma, text$pos, sep='_')
  # f) identify which rows in the file contain words
  text_lemmas <- text_lemmas[which(text$dep != 'punct')]
  # g) add the text lemmas to the master list of all lemmas in the corpus
  lemma<-c(lemma, text_lemmas)
```

The most complex task facing us in this step is to identify verb + noun combinations. As noted previously, we need to find all cases where a noun has a *dobj* (direct object) or *iobj* (indirect object) dependency on a verb. Returning to Figure 8.3, we can see that the noun *inequalities* in row 16 is dependent on the verb *face* in row 15 thanks to the match between the *dep_on* and *word_number* columns. That is, the *dep*_on value for *inequalities* is the same as the *word_number* value for *face*. Moreover, we can see from the dep column for row 16 that this dependency has been marked as *dobj*. This is the information we will use to find verb + noun combinations in our script.

One slight complication is that, to a computer, the information in the *word_number* and *dep_on* columns is ambiguous. It knows that *inequalities* is dependent on word number 15, but in the corpus file from which Figure 8.3 is taken, there are 46 different words with a word number of 15 (because there are 46 sentences in the text containing 15 words or more). To find which of these words *inequalities* depends on, we need to be more explicit. That is, we need to show that the 15 in the *dep_on* column refers specifically to the 15th word of sentence 1. For this reason, it would be helpful if both the *word_number* and *dep_on* columns included entries of the form *1_15*, where the first number refers to the sentence we are dealing with and the second number to the word.

This is easy to achieve using the *paste()* function. Script 8.2.2.h uses *paste()* to combine the information in the *sentence_number* column with that in the *word_number* and *dep_on* columns to produce two new vectors: *refs*, which combines *sentence_number* and *word number*, and *deps*, which combines sentence number and *dep_on* number. These two vectors will be used in place of the *word_number* and *dep_on* columns to determine which nouns are dependent on which verbs.

SCRIPT 8.2.2.h   CREATING UNIQUE REFERENCES FOR ROWS IN THE CORPUS FILE

```
refs<-paste(text$sentence_number, text$word_number, sep='_')
deps<-paste(text$sentence_number, text$dep_on, sep='_')
```

To find nouns that are dependent on verbs, we first need to find the unique references (*refs*) for all verbs in the text. This is done in Script 8.2.2.i using subsetting and the *which()* function to identify the *refs* of all words that have *v* in their pos

---

SCRIPT 8.2.2.i   IDENTIFY NOUNS THAT ARE DEPENDENT ON VERBS

```
# i) find nouns that are objects of verbs
# i.1) find unique references for verbs
verb_refs <- refs[which(text$pos == 'v')]
# i.2) find all words that are dependent on verbs
verb_deps <- which(deps %in% verb_refs)
# i.3) find all nouns
nouns <- which(text$pos == 'n')
# i.4) find which verb_deps are nouns
verb_nouns <- intersect(verb_deps, nouns)
# i.5) find all object (dobj or iobj) dependencies
objects <- grep('obj', text$dep)
# i.6) find which verb_nouns have an 'object' (dobj or iobj) dependency
noun_rows <- intersect(verb_nouns, objects)
```

column. Because this section requires a lengthy explanation, you may want to enter the script before reading its explanation.

In this part of the script, first, the *refs* of all verbs are recorded in the vector *verb_refs* (Point i.1). Next, we again use the *which()* function to find which rows contain words that are dependent on a verb. Specifically, we use the *%in%* operator to find which of the *deps* entries created at Point h match one of the entries in verb_refs (i.2). This gives us the *verb_deps* vector, which stores the positions of all words that are dependent on verbs.

Now that we know which words are dependent on verbs, we next need to find out which of these words are nouns. To achieve this, we first use *which()* to create a vector identifying all nouns in the text (i.3). So, we now have one vector of words that are dependent on verbs (*verb_debs*) and a second vector of all nouns (*nouns*). What we really want to know is how these two overlap. In other words, which words both are dependent on verbs and are nouns. We can do this using the *intersect()* function, which shows which items in one vector are also present in a second vector. In this case, we want to find out which words in *verb_deps* are also in *nouns*. The resulting vector of nouns dependent on verbs is stored as *verb_nouns* (Point i.4).

Finally, we want to know which of the nouns that we have found to be dependent on verbs have the *dep* relationship of either *dobj* or *obj*. The technique for this is similar to that in i.3-4. That is, we first identify all rows with the required dependency (i.5) and then use *intersect()* to see how this overlaps with our vector of verb + noun combinations (Point i.6). You will notice that, unlike the lines that identified nouns and verbs, Point i.5 does not use the *which()* function. Although *which()* could have been used here, I have decided to use a slightly different function: *grep()*. Like *which()*, this identifies the elements in a vector that meet a particular criterion. For our purposes, the key difference is that, whereas *which()* needs us to specify an exact value that we are trying to match (that is the pos must be 'n' or 'v'), *grep()* allows us to search for regular expressions. This is helpful here because we want to count an item as a match if either of two values is present – that is, *dobj* or *iobj*. Using *grep()*, we can specify the value *obj*, which will match both of these values, since the string *obj* appears in both. A similar effect could have been achieved using *which()* and the OR ('|') operator (*which(text$pos == 'dobj' | text$pos == 'iobj')*). However, *grep()* both enables a briefer command and has allowed me to introduce a key function that we haven't met elsewhere.

This, at last, gives us what we were looking for: the positions of nouns that have a *dobj* or *iobj* dependency on a verb. These are recorded with the vector name *noun_rows*.

Before going any further in identifying verb + noun combinations, an important initial point is that we only want the rest of the process to be executed if we have actually found some verb + object noun combinations. If there are no such combinations (i.e., if the *noun_rows* vector is empty), we can skip the rest of the script for this file. This is partly a matter of not wasting computer resources, but more importantly, some parts of the script that follow will only work if relevant nouns have been identified (if they haven't, we will get an error message). For this reason, Script 8.2.2.j initiates an *if()* function to check whether nouns have been found. As we saw earlier, the *if()* function tells R to execute a procedure (in curly brackets) only in a particular condition (in round brackets) is met. In the current case, we want the remainder of the script to be executed only if the *noun_rows* vector is not empty – that is, if it has a length greater than 0. If this condition isn't met, R will skip over the section in curly brackets and move directly to checking the next text in the for-loop.

SCRIPT 8.2.2.j   INITIATE AN *IF()* FUNCTION

```
# j) conduct the following only if relevant nouns have been found
if (length(noun_rows) > 0) {
```

So far, we have created a vector (*noun_rows*) showing the positions in the file of all nouns that are objects of verbs. To compile our list of potential collocations, however, we also need to know what the corresponding verbs are in these combinations. To do this, we can again use the *refs* and *deps* vectors that we created in Script 8.2.2.h. It will be recalled that *refs* contains unique referents for each word in the text, based on their sentence number and word number (e.g., for Figure 8.3, *Racism* is *1_1*, *is 1_2, still* is *1_3*), while *defs* shows the *refs* value of the word that a given word is dependent on (so *Racism* is *1_2, is 1_0, still* is *1_2*, etc.). Thus, if we look at the *deps* value for each of the nouns we identified in Script 8.2.2.i, this will tell us the unique reference (the *refs* value) for the corresponding verb. Returning to Figure 8.3, the *deps* value for the noun *inequalities* is *1_15*, which is also the *refs* value for the verb *face*. Script 8.2.2.k uses this fact to identify the row numbers of the relevant verbs.

First, k.1 uses subsetting to find the *deps* values of the nouns we have identified. These are stored as the vector *verb_refs*. K.2 then uses the *match()* function to find the row numbers of verbs whose *refs* values match those in *verb_refs*. These are stored as the vector *verb_rows*.

SCRIPT 8.2.2.k   IDENTIFY THE VERBS IN VERB + OBJECT NOUN COMBINATIONS

```
# k) if appropriate nouns have been found, find their corresponding verbs
# k.1) find refs of corresponding verbs
verb_refs <- deps[noun_rows]
# k.2) find row numbers for these verbs
verb_rows <- match(verb_refs, refs)
```

Now that we have the row numbers of both the verbs and nouns in each verb + noun combination, it is relatively straightforward to retrieve and record those items (Script 8.2.2.l). For both verbs and nouns, we use the *paste()* function and subsetting to combine the *lemma* and *pos* value for each row where these items are found. The use of paste to combine columns is the same as we used to create a list of lemmas in Script 8.2.2.e and produces vectors of the same format (e.g., *face_v*). Once we have our vectors of verbs and nouns, we can then combine these into a vector of verb + noun combinations, again using the *paste()* function. Note that this time I have used a different separation marker (_:_). This is to avoid confusion by making the marker separating the two parts of the combination different from the marker separating lemma form from pos information. The format of items in this vector will thus be *face_v_:_inequality_n*.

SCRIPT 8.2.2.l   CREATE VECTORS OF ALL RELEVANT NOUNS, VERBS, AND VERB + NOUN PAIRS

```
# 1) create vectors of identified nouns, verbs, and verb+noun pairs
nouns <- paste(text$lemma[noun_rows], text$pos[noun_rows], sep = '_')
verbs <- paste(text$lemma[verb_rows], text$pos[verb_rows], sep = '_')
pair <- paste(verbs, nouns, sep = '_:_')
```

The *pair* vector now contains all verb + noun combinations for the file we are looking at. All that remains is to add these to the master vector that we created to store all combinations for the corpus. This is done at Script 8.2.2.m, again using the *c()* function to add the new vector to the master vector. This is followed by two sets of curly brackets: the first (Point n) to close the *if()* function that we opened in Script 8.8.2j, and the second (Point o) to close the loop that we opened in Script 8.2.2.c. The latter shows R that it can now close the file it's been working on and move to the next file in the corpus (if there is one).

SCRIPT 8.2.2.m–o   ADD PAIRS TO MASTER LIST

```
    # m) add verb+noun pairs to the master list
    #    of combinations in the corpus
    verb_noun_lem <- c(verb_noun_lem, pair)
  # n) close the if() condition
  }
# o) close the for-loop
}
```

Once this process has been completed for all files in the corpus (which will probably take a minute or two), we are left with completed versions of the two vectors we created way back in Script 8.2.2.b: *lemma* and *verb_noun_lem*. The former records all the lemma tokens found in the corpus. The latter records all the verb + noun combination tokens. For the BAWE corpus I have been using, the first few entries in these vectors are shown in Figures 8.4 and 8.5, respectively. These will be the basis of the list of academic collocations that we will create in Script 8.2.3.

```
> lemma[1:10]
 [1] "racism_n"   "be_v"     "still_r"    "a_DT"     "problem_n" "within_IN" "we_PRP$"
 [8] "society_n"  "today_n"  "and_CC"
```

FIGURE 8.4 First items in *lemma*

```
> verb_noun_lem[1:10]
 [1] "face_v_:_inequality_n"    "ask_v_:_sample_n"        "enrich_v_:_quality_n"
 [4] "cover_v_:_area_n"         "explore_v_:_explanation_n" "use_v_:_feature_n"
 [7] "subordinate_v_:_group_n"  "maintain_v_:_control_n"   "take_v_:_place_n"
[10] "play_v_:_part_n"
```

FIGURE 8.5 First items in *verb_noun_lem*

8.2.3 Identifying collocations

Our ultimate aim in this part of the chapter is to create a list of academic collocations. We have said that these will be defined as verb + noun combinations that have a frequency greater than five per million words and a MI score greater than four in the BAWE corpus. Now that we have a complete list of the verb + noun combinations in the corpus, our next step is to get frequency and MI scores for each combination.

Making a frequency list is very straightforward in R. The *table()* function will go through our vector of combinations (*verb_noun_lem*) and create a table showing each combination type and the number of times it occurs. In Script 8.2.3.a, we execute this function and record the resulting table as *pair_freq*.

SCRIPT 8.2.3.a   GET FREQUENCY LIST OF VERB + NOUN COMBINATIONS

```
pair_freq <- table(verb_noun_lem)
```

To get a sense of what this table looks like, we can use the *sort()* function to show the most frequent items identified. Figure 8.6 displays the top ten pairs. We can see that *have + effect* occurred in the corpus 982 times, *take + place* appeared 810 times, and so on.

In order to calculate MI scores (or any other association measure), we need not only the frequencies of word combinations but also the frequencies of their

```
> sort(pair_freq, decreasing = T)[1:10]
verb_noun_lem
   have_v_:_effect_n      take_v_:_place_n      play_v_:_role_n   have_v_:_impact_n
              982                    810                  693                 494
make_v_:_decision_n      use_v_:_method_n     have_v_:_power_n   have_v_:_value_n
              322                    296                  258                 224
    make_v_:_use_n solve_v_:_problem_n
              223                    217
```

FIGURE 8.6 Most frequent verb + noun combinations

component words. To enable this, we can again use the *table()* function to create a frequency list of lemmas in the corpus, based on the *lemma* vector. This is saved as the table *lemma_freq* in Script 8.2.3.b.

SCRIPT 8.2.3.b GET FREQUENCY LIST OF LEMMAS

```
# b) get frequency list of lemmas
lemma_freq <- table(lemma)
```

This results in a table like that shown in Figure 8.7.

```
> sort(lemma_freq, decreasing = T)[1:10]
lemma
  the_DT     be_v    of_IN    to_TO   and_CC     a_DT    in_IN    as_IN  have_v  that_IN
  452014   281633   238249   182440   177914   152349   135563    61060   56351    54961
```

FIGURE 8.7 Most frequent lemmas

We can now use this table of lemmas to assign word frequencies to each of the component words in the *pair_freq* table, as shown in Script 8.2.3.c. Point c.1 splits the combinations in the *pair_freq* table into their component words. This is done using the *gsub()* function and a wildcard search. It will be recalled that the component words in each pair are separated by the marker _:_ (see Script 8.2.2.1 and Figure 8.5). We can use this to create a search term that will remove this marker and everything that follows it ('_:_.*'), so leaving us with just verbs, and a second search term to remove this marker and everything that precedes it ('.*_:_'), so leaving us with just nouns. The verbs are then saved to the vector *verb* and the nouns to the vector *noun*.

Point c.2 uses the *match()* function to identify which items in the lemma frequency table (*lemma_freq*) correspond to these verbs/nouns (note that the regular expressions in the two lines here are different – make sure you check these carefully when entering!). The word names (as opposed to the frequency values) are stored in a part of the table called *rownames*. We, therefore, need to match our vectors of verbs and nouns with the rownames of *lemma_freq*. This returns vectors showing the position in the table of each of the words we are looking for, which we record as *verb_matches* and *noun_matches*. Point c.3 then uses these vectors and subsetting to get the frequencies of each word and record them in the vectors *verb_freq* and *noun_freq*.

SCRIPT 8.2.3.c GET FREQUENCIES OF VERB + NOUN COMPONENTS

```
# c) get frequencies of verb + noun components
# c.1) split combinations into their component words
verb <- gsub('_:_.*', '', rownames(pair_freq))
noun <- gsub('.*_:_', '', rownames(pair_freq))
# c.2) find corresponding entry in the lemma frequency table
verb_matches <- match(verb, rownames(lemma_freq))
noun_matches <- match(noun, rownames(lemma_freq))
# c.3) get frequencies for each component
verb_freq <- lemma_freq[verb_matches]
noun_freq <- lemma_freq[noun_matches]
```

For each verb + noun combination identified in Section 8.2.2, we now have both an overall frequency (stored in the *pair_freq* table) and separate frequencies for each component word (stored in the *verb_freq* and *noun_freq* vectors). We also have a complete frequency list for all lemmas in the corpus (stored in the *lemma_freq* table). This gives us everything we need to calculate MI scores.

In common with other association measures, MI is calculated based on the *observed frequency* of a combination (i.e., the number of times it actually appears. This is the information we've already recorded in the *pair_freq* table) and its *expected frequency*. Expected frequency is based on the idea that high-frequency words are expected – other things being equal – to combine more often than low-frequency words. As we discussed briefly in Chapter 7 (Section 7.3.3), this expectation can be expressed in terms of the probability that any randomly selected word or word pair is the word/word pair we are interested in. The probability that a randomly selected word will be the item we have in mind can be calculated as:

$$P = \frac{word\ frequency}{corpus\ size}$$

For example, we saw in Figure 8.4, that the verb *have* appears in the BAWE corpus 56,351 times. Because there are 6,305,272 words in the corpus in total (as we will see, we can get this number using *sum(lemma_freq)* to add up the frequencies of all lemmas in the lemma list), the probability of a randomly selected word being *have* is, therefore:

$$\frac{56,351}{6,305,272} = .00894$$

That is, there is about a 0.9% chance (i.e., less than 1 in 100) that our randomly selected word is *have*. In comparison, the probability that our randomly selected word is the much less frequent noun *effect*, which occurs 4,649 times, is more than ten times lower than this (i.e., less than 1 in 1,000):

$$\frac{4,649}{6,305,272} = .000734$$

So much for the chances of encountering individual words. What about word pairs? We know from basic probability theory that the probability of two independent events both occurring can be found by multiplying the probabilities of each. This means that the probability of encountering a given word pair can be found by multiplying the probability of encountering each word individually. Thus, the probability of a randomly selected pair being *have effect* would be:

$$.00894 * .000734 = .0000066$$

This is obviously a very small number. However, because the corpus is rather large, we would still expect it to occur a few times across the length of the corpus. Specifically, the *expected frequency* is calculated by multiplying this probability by the total number of words in the corpus. Thus, we would expect *have* to combine with *effect* approximately 40 times:

$$.0000066 * 6,305,272 = 41.61$$

Note that, stringing together the previous steps, to calculate expected frequency, we have done the following calculation:

$$expected\ frequency = \frac{verb\ frequency}{corpus\ size} * \frac{noun\ frequency}{corpus\ size} * corpus\ size$$

Fortunately, this monster can be simplified to the synonymous form:

$$expected\ frequency = \frac{verb\ frequency * noun\ frequency}{corpus\ size}$$

MI uses *expected frequency* in conjunction with the word pair's actual frequency to quantify the strength of collocation between two words. Specifically, it uses the formula:

$$MI = \log_2 \frac{observed\ frequency}{expected\ frequency}$$

Continuing with our previous example, we know from Figure 8.4 that *have + effect* actually appears 982 times, so the MI for this word pairing would be calculated as:

$$MI = \log_2 \frac{982}{41.61} = 4.56$$

By most standards, this indicates that *have + effect* should be counted as a moderately strong collocation.

Script 8.2.3d calculates MI scores for the verb + noun combinations we have identified by, first, calculating the expected frequency of each word pair. As we saw earlier, this is the product of the verb and noun frequencies, divided by the total corpus size. This calculation can cause a technical problem in R because the product of verb and noun frequencies can (depending on the size of your corpus) be a very high number which not all versions of R are able to calculate. To work around this problem, I have used the formula:

$$expected \ frequency = \frac{verb \ frequency}{corpus \ size} * noun \ frequency$$

This gives us the same result but avoids creating very large numbers during the calculation.

We then use the previous equation to calculate a vector of MI scores for each combination, as shown in Script 8.2.3d.

SCRIPT 8.2.3.d   CALCULATE ASSOCIATION MEASURES

```
expected_freq <- verb_freq/sum(lemma_freq)*noun_freq
MI <- log(pair_freq/expected_freq,2)
```

As noted previously, we have decided to define academic collocations as combinations with frequencies greater than five per million words and MI scores of greater than 4. The code for this is shown in Script 8.2.3.e. To identify collocations, we first combine the frequency and MI data into a single data frame using the *cbind()* function. We then exclude non-collocations in two steps using subsetting. First, we restrict collocations to those that meet the frequency criterion, and then we restrict the remaining combinations to those that meet the MI criterion. The resulting data frame (*output*) is then saved to the output folder in the usual way. Note that, if we wanted to use different thresholds for counting pairs as collocations (e.g., frequency > 10/million; MI > 5), we would simply need to change the numbers in the corresponding lines.

SCRIPT 8.2.3.e   IDENTIFY COLLOCATIONS

```
output <- data.frame(cbind(pair_freq, MI))
output <- output[output$pair_freq > 5*sum(lemma_freq)/1000000,]
output <- output[output$MI > 4,]
write.csv(output, 'output/BAWE_verb_nouns.csv')
```

	A	B	C	D
1		pair_freq	MI	
2	achieve_v_:_goal_n	99	8.08482091	
3	achieve_v_:_level_n	42	4.26456627	
4	achieve_v_:_objective_n	48	6.97317655	
5	acquire_v_:_language_n	42	6.86123749	
6	add_v_:_value_n	44	4.30782515	
7	address_v_:_issue_n	67	7.25526084	
8	address_v_:_problem_n	34	5.58751092	
9	adopt_v_:_approach_n	85	7.41781087	
10	adopt_v_:_strategy_n	32	6.38002621	
11	affect_v_:_performance_n	60	5.95882037	

FIGURE 8.8   Listing of academic collocations

The outcome of this is a .csv file of combinations that meet our definition for academic collocations, in alphabetical order, as shown in Figure 8.8.

8.3 Quantifying the use of academic collocations across learner groups

In Chapter 4 (Section 4.3), we saw how to integrate information from a reference source into an analysis. Specifically, we analyzed the extent to which learners writing at different levels used words appearing on the AVL (Gardner & Davies, 2014). There, we started by preparing the list of academic vocabulary. We then created a loop that opened each text in the learner corpus and created a list of lexical words in the same format as our academic vocabulary list. Finally, we determined how many items in the list of lexical words for the learner text were also found in the academic vocabulary list.

Here, we will follow a similar logic. We have already created our list of academic collocations, which now looks like Figure 8.8. What remains is to (1) put our learner corpus into the same format used for the reference corpus, (2) write a loop that will create a list of verb + noun combinations for each learner text, and (3) determine the overlaps between these lists and our list of academic collocations.

8.3.1 Preparing the learner corpus

We can prepare the corpus using an R script similar to that described in Script 8.2.1. The only things that need to change are the names of the folder where the original parsed corpus can be found and the folder to which the revised corpus should be written. Specifically, I have changed 'BAWE_conll' and 'BAWE_revised' to 'GiG_conll' and 'GiG_revised'. Remember that you will need to create the empty 'GiG_revised' folder within your 'Corpora' folder before running the script.

SCRIPT 8.3.1   PREPARE THE LEARNER CORPUS

```
# a) get file names for the parsed corpus
files <- dir('corpora/GiG_conll/')
# b) start a loop to go through all files in the corpus
for (i in files){
  # c) read the corpus file
  text <- read.delim(paste('corpora/GiG_conll/', i, sep=''), sep='\t', header=F)
  # d) add column names
  colnames(text) <-c ('word_number', 'word', 'lemma', 'pos', 'ner', 'dep_on', 'dep')
  # e) simplify part of speech codes
  text$pos <- gsub('^J.*', 'j', text$pos)
  text$pos <- gsub('^N.*', 'n', text$pos)
  text$pos <- gsub('^RB.*', 'r', text$pos)
  text$pos <- gsub('^V.*', 'v', text$pos)
  # f) add sentence numbers
  sentence_number <- vector()
  current_sentence <- 0
  for(j in 1:length(text$word_number)){
    if(text$word_number[j] == 1){
      current_sentence <- current_sentence+1}
    sentence_number[j] <- current_sentence
  }
  text<-cbind(sentence_number, text)
  # g) save the revised corpus file in a new folder
  write.csv(text, file=paste('corpora/GiG_revised/', gsub('txt.conll', 'csv', i),
                  sep=''), row.names=F)
# h) close the loop
}
```

8.3.2 Identifying academic collocations in the learner corpus

Once the study corpus is ready, we next get the corpus file names and create two output vectors (Script 8.3.2a–b). One vector (*ac_coll_count*) will store the number of academic collocations found in each text. Because texts with more verb + noun combinations overall will have more opportunities to use academic collocations, a second vector (*ac_coll_percent*) is used to store a normalized version of this, i.e., the percentage of verb + noun combinations that are academic collocations. To enable qualitative follow-up of our findings, it will also be useful to record which collocations were found in each text. For this, we create the list *ac_colls*.

SCRIPT 8.3.2.a–b GET FILE NAMES AND CREATE OUTPUT VECTORS/LIST

```
# a) get file names
metadata <- read.csv('corpora/metadata_gig.csv')
filenames <- metadata$file_id
# b) create empty output vectors and list to store results
ac_coll_count <- vector()
ac_coll_percent <- vector()
ac_colls <- list()
```

Script 8.3.2.c–i replicates what we have already done for the reference corpus in Script 8.2 (Points c–d and h–l), so it will not be discussed in detail again here. Briefly, a loop is opened, unique references and dependencies are created for each text, which are then used to identify nouns and verbs with an appropriate dependency relationship. These verb + noun combinations are then stored in the vector 'pair'.

SCRIPT 8.3.2.c–i IDENTIFY VERB + OBJECT NOUN COMBINATIONS IN THE LEARNER CORPUS

```
# c) start loop
for (i in 1:length(filenames)){
  # d) read the corpus file
  text <- read.csv(paste('corpora/GiG_revised/', filenames[i], '.csv', sep = ''))
  # e) set up unique references for each row in the file
  refs <- paste(text$sentence_number, text$word_number, sep = '_')
  deps <- paste(text$sentence_number, text$dep_on, sep = '_')
  # f) find nouns that are objects of verbs
  # f.1) find unique references for verbs
  verb_refs <- refs[which(text$pos == 'v')]
  # f.2) find words dependent on verbs
  verb_deps <- which(deps %in% verb_refs)
  # f.3) find all nouns
  nouns <- which(text$pos == 'n')
  # f.4) find which verb_deps are nouns
  verb_nouns <- intersect(verb_deps, nouns)
  # f.5) find all object (dobj or iobj) dependencies
  objects <- grep('obj', text$dep)
  # f.6) find which verb_nouns have an object dependency
  noun_rows <- intersect(verb_nouns, objects)
  # g) conduct the following only if relevant nouns have been found
  if (length(noun_rows) > 0) {
    # h) if appropriate nouns have been found, find their corresponding verbs
    # h.1) find refs of corresponding verbs
    verb_refs <- deps[noun_rows]
    # h.2) find row numbers for these verbs
    verb_rows <- match(verb_refs, refs)
    # i) create vectors of identified nouns, verbs, and verb+noun pairs
    nouns <- paste(text$lemma[noun_rows], text$pos[noun_rows], sep = '_')
    verbs <- paste(text$lemma[verb_rows], text$pos[verb_rows], sep = '_')
    pair <- paste(verbs, nouns, sep = '_:_')
```

Now that we have a vector of the verb + noun combinations in the open text (stored as *pair*), we can use subsetting and the *which()* function to identify which of these is also in (*%in%*) the vector of academic collocations generated in Section 2. This is done in Script 8.3.2.j–k. Academic collocations form the row names of the *output* data frame, so can be accessed using the *rownames()* function. Combinations from the text that are found amongst the academic collocations are stored at the appropriate slot in the *ac_colls* list.

In the second and third lines, we then refer to this slot to determine how many such collocations there are in the text (stored at the appropriate point in *ac_coll_count*) and what percentage of all combinations this constitutes (stored in *ac_coll_per-cent*). Finally, the *if* sequence that we started at Script 8.3.2.g is closed (Point k).

You will recall that in Script 8.2, when no nouns were found as the objects of verbs, the script simply moved on to the next file. In the present case, however, this

---

SCRIPT 8.3.2.j–k   RECORD AND QUANTIFY ACADEMIC COLLOCATIONS

```
# j) record collocations and their numbers and percentages
ac_colls[[i]] <- pair[which(pair %in% rownames(output))]
ac_coll_count[i] <- length(ac_colls[[i]])
ac_coll_percent[i] <- 100*length(ac_colls[[i]])/length(pair)
# k) close the if condition
}
```

---

is not sufficient. If there are no appropriate combinations, we want to record that no academic collocations have been found. For this reason, the *if()* function is followed by an alternative (*else*) instruction, as shown in Script 8.3.2.l–m. This part of the script will only be executed if there are no verb + noun combinations (i.e., if

---

SCRIPT 8.3.2.l–m   RECORD ZEROS WHERE NO COMBINATIONS ARE FOUND

```
# l) if no combinations are found, record zeros
else {
  ac_colls[[i]] <- 0
  ac_coll_count[i] <- 0
  ac_coll_percent[i] <- 0
}
# m) close the loop
}
```

the length of the *noun_rows* vector is zero, so the condition in the *if* clause is *not* met). Thanks to the *else{}* instruction, whenever R encounters a text with no verb + noun combinations, it will write a value of 0 to the appropriate places in the *ac_coll_count* and *ac_coll_percent* vectors. Once this has been completed, the loop that we started at Point c is closed so that the process can move on to the next file (Point m).

In Script 8.3.2.n, the quantitative results are combined along with the corpus data into a data frame using the same *cbind()* function we have seen previously. As usual, the results are then written to the *output* folder using *write.csv*.

SCRIPT 8.3.2.n   COMBINE RESULTS WITH METADATA

```
results <- cbind(metadata, ac_coll_count, ac_coll_percent)
write.csv(results, file = 'output/academic_collocations.csv', row.names = F)
```

8.3.3 Understanding the use of academic collocations across levels

These quantitative results can be analyzed in a similar way to our analysis of academic words in Chapter 4. Thus, for example, we could use the script shown in Script 8.3.3a to produce Figure 8.9 showing the percentage of verb + noun combinations that are 'academic' for each year group (see Chapter 4, Section 4.3, for an explanation of this script[1]).

SCRIPT 8.3.3a   VISUALIZE RESULTS

```
library(ggplot2)
library(Hmisc)
data <- read.csv(file = 'output/academic_collocations.csv')
data$year_group <- factor(data$year_group,
                    levels = c('Year_2', 'Year_6', 'Year_9', 'Year_11'))
ggplot(data, aes(year_group, ac_coll_percent, linetype=genre)) +
  stat_summary(fun='mean', geom='line', aes(group=genre)) +
  stat_summary(fun.data='mean_cl_boot', geom='errorbar', width=.2) +
  labs(y="Academic collocations %")+labs(x="Year Group")
ggsave('output/collocations_line_graph.jpeg')
```

It will be recalled that we have created not only quantitative results but also a list showing which academic collocations were found in each text. By default, the positions in this list (each of which corresponds to a text) have the values *1, 2, 3*, etc. For ease of reference, it will be preferable to give these the names of the files they relate to. This can be achieved using the *names()* function to assign the contents of the *filenames* vector to these positions, as illustrated in Script 8.3.3.b. The first

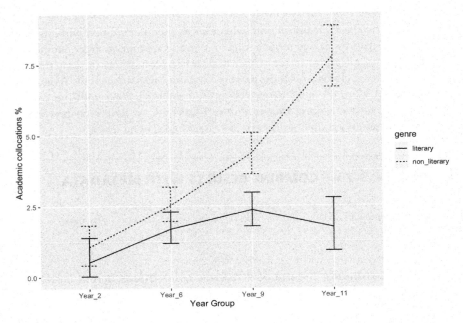

FIGURE 8.9 Academic verb + noun collocations across year groups

---

SCRIPT 8.3.3b   ADD FILENAMES TO THE LIST OF COLLOCATIONS

```
names(ac_colls) <- filenames
```

---

few entries in this list can be seen in Figure 8.10. Note that the entry *character(0)* indicates that no academic collocations were found. This can be used to follow up quantitative analyses by checking which academic collocations were found in particular texts or groups of texts.

As we discussed in Chapter 4, a follow-up analysis might start by asking some questions about the overall quantitative patterns. Looking at Figure 8.9, for example, we might ask what is driving the strong increase in academic collocations seen across year groups for non-literary texts. Is this simply a case of learners gaining control of a more appropriate phrasal vocabulary? Or is the increase a response to functional differences in the types of texts that children are writing? What types of meanings do the collocations convey, and how (if at all) does this vary across year groups? Since collocations can differ across academic disciplines, we might also want to ask whether characteristically different academic collocations are being used in humanities vs. science writing. The collocations recorded in *ac_colls* can give us a

```
> ac_colls[1:5]
[[1]]
[1] "have_v_:_impact_n"

[[2]]
character(0)

[[3]]
[1] "do_v_:_nothing_n"  "have_v_:_effect_n"

[[4]]
character(0)

[[5]]
character(0)
```

FIGURE 8.10 Contents of the *ac_colls* list

start towards answering these more detailed questions by allowing us to access, for example, all examples of collocations used by students at Year 11 (see Figure 8.11), all examples of collocations used in Year 6 Science texts (see Figure 8.12), etc. As with the vocabulary examples discussed in Chapter 4, an initial scanning of the collocations could be followed up with concordance searches of the collocations to see how they are used in context. Examples of this sort of analysis in practice can be found in Durrant and Brenchley (2021) and McCallum and Durrant (2022).

```
> year_11_colls <- ac_colls[data$year_group == 'Year_11']
```

FIGURE 8.11 Accessing Year 11 academic collocations

```
> year_6_sci_colls <- ac_colls[data$year_group =='Year_6' & data$discipline == 'science']
```

FIGURE 8.12 Accessing Year 6 collocations in science writing

8.4 Conclusion

Perhaps fittingly for the final chapter, this has, to my mind, been the most technically challenging of the three hands-on chapters in this book. In particular, the task of identifying collocations has required more complex scripts than those used in those other chapters. However, I think that this is time well spent. As I hope this and the previous chapter have convinced you, collocation can provide an extremely useful window into writing development. Moreover, the programming skills learned in this chapter are essential for any analysis that looks at words (or other linguistic elements) in relation to each other, rather than as independent items. Because such relationships are fundamental to language use, analyses of this type may well play a prominent role in your research of writing development.

The chapter has also introduced several important new functions and techniques. Specifically, we have seen how to

- get the names of files in a folder using *dir()*;
- make performance of commands conditional by using *if()*;
- create for-loops within for-loops;
- identify elements that match a regular expression using *grep()*;
- identify the positions in a vector that share values with another vector using *match()*;
- create a frequency list using *table()*; and
- give meaningful names to the elements in a list using *names()*.

The functions, together with those discussed in Chapters 2, 4, and 6, should provide a useful library, or *phrasebook*, to help you get started in carrying out your own research into writing development.

Note

1 Note that I have made one small change here so that the figure shows literary vs. nonliterary texts, rather than also dividing for discipline. This is to make the figure easier to read.

References

Durrant, P., & Brenchley, M. (2021). The development of academic collocations in children's writing. In P. Szudarski & S. Barclay (Eds.), *Vocabulary theory, patterning and teaching* (pp. 99–120). Multilingual-Matters.

Gardner, D., & Davies, M. (2014). A new academic vocabulary list. *Applied Linguistics, 35*(3), 305–27. https://doi.org/10.1093/applin/amt015

McCallum, L., & Durrant, P. (2022). *Shaping writing grades: Collocation and writing context effects*. Cambridge University Press.

INDEX

INDEX OF R FUNCTIONS
AND CONCEPTS

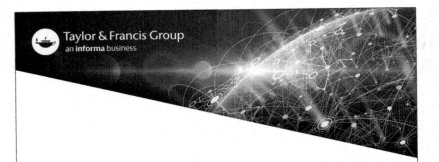